MW00713586

Take Charge of
Your Financial Future

Take Charge of Your Financial Future

STRAIGHT TALK ON MANAGING YOUR MONEY FROM THE FINANCIAL ANALYST WHO DEFIED DONALD TRUMP

Marvin B. Roffman

With

Michael J. Schwager

A Citadel Press Book
Published by Carol Publishing Group

Carol Publishing Group Edition, 1996

A Citadel Press Book
Published by Carol Publishing Group
Citadel Press is a registered trademark of Carol Communications, Inc.

Editorial, sales and distribution, rights and permissions inquiries should
be addressed to Carol Publishing Group, 120 Enterprise Avenue,
Secaucus, N.J. 07094
In Canada: Canadian Manda Group, One Atlantic Avenue, Toronto,
Ontario M6K3E7

The charts on pages 56 and 98 have been used with permission.
© *Stocks, Bonds, Bills, and Inflation 1993 Yearbook*™, Ibbotson Associates,
Chicago (annually updates work by Roger G. Ibbotson and Alex A.
Sinquefield). Used with permission. All rights reserved.

Carol Publishing Group books are available at special discounts
for bulk purchases, sales promotions, fund raising, or
educational purposes. Special editions can also be created to
specifications. For details contact: Special Sales Department,
Carol Publishing Group, 120 Enterprise Ave., Secaucus, N.J. 07094

Manufactured in the United States of America
10 9 8 7 6 5 4 3 2 1

Library of Congress Cataloging-in-Publication Data

Roffman, Marvin B.
Take charge of your financial future : straight talk on managing
your money from the financial analyst who defied Donald Trump /
Marvin B. Roffman with Michael J. Schwager.
  p.   cm
"A Citadel Press book."
ISBN 0-8065-1718-2 (pbk.)
1. Finance, Personal. 2. Portfolio management. I. Schwager,
Michael J. II. Title.
HG179.R56 1996
332.024—dc20
                                                          95-9363
                                                              CIP

To my mother and father, who instilled in me the value of saving, the virtue of patience, and the importance of working at something I truly enjoy.

M.B.R.

To the memory of Darrell Sifford, whose encouragement and support have been a shining light in my career.

M.J.S.

CONTENTS

ACKNOWLEDGMENTS

Many people helped in the preparation of this book.

I'm particularly grateful to my partner, Peter Miller, for the countless hours he spent in roundtable discussions about the text and for his wonderful insights, his humor, and his gift of making complex subjects easy to understand.

In selecting Michael Schwager as my coauthor, I did my homework well. He did a superb job of helping me shape the material.

Jane Dystel, my agent, showed endless belief in the significance of my story and was untiring in finding the book a home.

Bruce Shostak, my editor, had the vision to see the book's potential and shepherded it through publication with cheer and great skill.

Tony Fischer read the chapter on insurance and generously made significant contributions to it.

Scott Miller, my stockbroker, reviewed the draft and shed important light on several topics, especially annuities.

Bill Wartman gave incisive advice on crucial sections of the book.

Raymond J. Fabius, M.D., supplied valuable information on HMOs.

I'm also thankful to my clients and employees for their confidence and trust. And I appreciate the people—too numerous to mention—who helped me over the years with stories, problems, and experiences they shared.

Special thanks to Donald Trump for pressuring Janney Montgomery Scott to fire me and to Edgar Scott Jr. for carrying it out. Their actions opened the way to my becoming an author.

Kudos to all the conscientious, hardworking brokers in the investment community who, despite sometimes enormous pressures, remain dedicated to preserving the wealth and financial security of their clients.

INTRODUCTION

Twenty years ago, I never thought I'd someday write a book called *Take Charge of Your Financial Future*. I did not feel compelled then to warn investors of the obstacles that the financial industry strews in their path or the need to guide investors safely past those obstacles. Having already worked in the industry for more than ten years, I had faith in my employers and the system they were part of. Only later would I discover, to my grief, that the system has built-in, serious conflicts.

From the experience I'll soon relate, I know now that far too many brokerage firms are more concerned with their own well-being than with that of their clients—investors like you. I know that investors must act as watchdogs over their money. Since I've confronted this system, which victimizes investors by the thousands, my eyes have been opened. I want to open yours.

I've dealt with hundreds and hundreds of stockbrokers during my thirty-five years in the industry. I have the distinct feeling that some could just as soon sell a pair of shoes or a television set as a stock. Traditionally, common stocks have been the cornerstone of investment success. Investors need help in picking the right stocks and holding them for the proper length of time. But many brokers are unconcerned with that. They're transaction-oriented and sell investment innovations that bring them hefty commissions but fail to serve their clients' interests.

In *Take Charge of Your Financial Future*, you'll find information on how brokers operate, how to invest your assets, how to spot good companies to invest in, how to plan for your future.

The events that led me to write this book began in March 1990. Heading down the Atlantic City Expressway from Philadelphia, I was on the verge of a revelation. Just for me, Donald Trump had arranged a tour of his soon-to-be-opened Taj Mahal, the casino-hotel that his organization was touting as the "Eighth Wonder of the World."

I was motoring toward the building not as a tourist or a high roller. I was approaching it as a stock analyst covering the gaming and food industries for Janney Montgomery Scott, an old-line Philadelphia brokerage house. The tour was Trump's way of trying to change my mind about his "Eighth Wonder." Several times, I had predicted that the Taj would bring him—and others—financial disaster. In reports for Janney, in newspaper interviews, as a guest on television programs, I was conveying the same message: Trump had borrowed so much money to finish building the $1 billion Taj that it would need well more than a million dollars a day in revenue just to cover the debt service. And those who had invested in Taj Mahal bonds were at risk of losing their money.

In June 1989, I had written a report entitled "Casino Gaming in Atlantic City: A Crisis Ahead?" Of the Taj, I said: "Because this is a single-use structure, holders of its $675 million in first mortgage bonds have little to fall back on should the Taj not work. Certainly, it can't be made into a 'K Mart.'"

The original Taj Mahal, in India, is a lavish, opulent tomb. The namesake, I believed, might bury Donald Trump.

My mother, not long before she died, gave me a piece of advice: "You'd better stop criticizing this Donald Trump, because you're going to get fired."

For all his high-powered, media-grabbing dealings with world-class tycoons such as Adnan Khashoggi, for all his public preening, for all the boasting in his books, Trump bruised easily. My comments on the Taj rankled him. A few times a year, Trump would phone with a suggestion or a question. In 1988, soon after purchasing the unfinished Taj from Merv Griffin for $273 million, he had called me and asked what I thought of the deal.

"You got a great deal, Donald," I said, "but I think you made a mistake. How are you going to differentiate the Taj from your other casinos? Why own three in Atlantic City?"

"Marvin," he said, "you have no vision. The Taj is going to be a monster."

A monster could be a two-headed dragon that eats itself piece by piece. But I doubted that it was the image Trump had in mind.

"I know you're down on the Taj Mahal," he told me in March 1990. "But I think you're going to be so taken by the property, I want you to see it." Trump arranged for his brother Robert to take me on a tour of the Taj. Robert managed the Trump casino empire. I was to meet him at about noon on Tuesday, March 20.

That very day, an article that would soon change my life appeared in the *Wall Street Journal*. Reporter Neil Barsky quoted me on Trump and the Taj Mahal: "When this property opens, he will have had so much free publicity he will break every record in the books in April, June, and July. But once the cold winds blow from October to February, it won't make it. The market just isn't there."

"Atlantic City," I said in the article, "is an ugly and dreary kind of place. Even its hard-core customers aren't coming down as much."

As the car sped toward the Jersey shore, I had no idea that the *Journal* had published the article that day. I had spoken to Barsky on March 10, ten days earlier. Barsky wrote a regular column on Trump. Several times, he told me, The Donald had tried to have him fired. That my quotations came out a few hours before I was scheduled to tour the Taj was one of life's little coincidences.

Nearing the Taj, I gazed at Trump's 1,250-room "monster." So this is what a billion dollars can buy, I thought. Four and a half million square feet, including the hotel rooms, a 120,000-square-foot casino, 175,000 square feet of meeting space, and a parking garage for more than 5,000 cars. To say that it struck me as extravagant would be an understatement.

When Robert Trump arrived, I offered my hand. He didn't offer his. "I'm here to greet you," he said, "and to tell you, Get the hell off the property."

"I think I ought to see it," I said of the Taj. But Trump was livid. I tried to calm him, but he was spewing four-letter words. "Get the f—— off the property," he shouted. "Goodbye!"

Crossing the street to Resorts International, I phoned Janney. Michelle, my secretary, said the director of research, Jim Meyer, wanted me back in Philadelphia immediately. "It's absolutely urgent. Drop everything you're doing and get back to the office."

I was in a state of shock. Understand, Donald Trump was the top player in the Atlantic City casino industry. Much of my livelihood came from covering that industry. The *Journal* article presented nothing new, nothing I hadn't said before. Yet Trump was enraged. Who knew what problems his reaction might rouse?

Before I left, I stopped at the Sands to tell my old friend Bill Weidner what had just happened. Weidner was president of the Pratt Hotel Corporation, which owns the Sands. I was shaking.

From Weidner's office, I again phoned the office. Trump had faxed a letter to Norman Wilde, Janney's CEO. Michelle faxed it to me at Weidner's office. Here's how it went, complete with mistakes:

Dear Mr. Wilde,

A number of months ago we spoke about Mr. Roffman's problem with Steve Wynn [I had angered Wynn with a comment on the Golden Nugget, of which Wynn was chairman]. I came to Mr. Roffman's defense even knowing that he is considered by those in the industry to be a hair-trigger and, in my opinion, somewhat unstable in his tone and manner of criticism.

Today, Mr. Roffman states in THE WALL STREET JOURNAL that "Atlantic City is an ugly and dreary kind of place. Even its hard-core customers aren't coming down as much. When this property (The Taj Mahal) opens, he will have had so much free publicity he will break every record in the books in April, June, and July, but once the cold winds blow from October to February, *it won't make it*. The market just isn't there."

For Mr. Roffman to make these statements with such definity [*sic*] is an outrage. I am now planning to institue [*sic*] a major lawsuit against your firm unless Mr. Roffman makes a major public apology or is dismissed. For a long while I have thought of Mr. Roffman as an unguided missle [*sic*]. His statements about the Mirage have proven false and, his statements about the Taj will also prove false.

You will be hearing shortly from my lawyers unless Mr. Roffman is immediately dismissed or apologizes.

Sincerely,
Donald J. Trump

cc: Marvin Roffman

I showed the fax to Weidner. As it happened, his in-house counsel was in house. The lawyer, Roberto Rivera-Soto, said to me, "Marvin, I wouldn't worry about a thing."

Rivera-Soto's words couldn't console me. I was a nervous wreck— finally realizing that honesty might not be the best policy when speaking about Trump, and doubting that Janney would back me in a battle with the most powerful man in Atlantic City. "They're going to fire me."

Hinting at what he must have envisioned as a surefire victory in a lawsuit, Rivera-Soto said: "I wish *I* would receive a letter like that. If I were you, I would think about sipping margaritas on the beach at St. Martin for the rest of my life."

But I couldn't think about St. Martin. I couldn't think about the rest of my life. I was having trouble thinking at all. Even the beach at Atlantic City seemed remote, and it was only a hundred yards away. I couldn't think past the reception I was likely to get at Janney.

Back at the office about 4:30, I walked through a gauntlet of stares rivaling the ones that fell on Charlie Sheen in *Wall Street*. In the movie, federal agents had nailed Sheen in an inside-trading scam and were waiting to handcuff him when he stepped into his cubicle. That only happens in the movies, I thought. So I didn't figure on a run-in with federal agents.

And I was right. Jim Meyer told me, "Edgar wants to see you." Edgar Scott Jr. was Janney's co-chairman of the board.

"The Executive Committee had a meeting today about the Trump letter," Meyer said to me. "Actions have been taken that you're not going to like. I can tell you, under no circumstances question anything. Don't open your mouth. Edgar is furious."

Rarely did a sentence contain both *Edgar* and *furious*. Edgar had grown up on Philadelphia's ritzy Main Line. His Social Register upbringing, amid the nannies and the servants, the boarding school masters and the cricket coaches, had frowned on plebeian displays such as public outbursts. Sometimes, when he was angry, he snarled and gritted his teeth. Those were his signs of displeasure. But they were infrequent. And I had never seen him furious.

After Trump demanded a public apology, Edgar had told him, "Mr. Trump, Janney Montgomery Scott has been in business since 1832, and to my knowledge, we have never publicly apologized to anyone." Clearly, Edgar wanted me to back down.

Meyer had portrayed Edgar's mood exactly. The *Journal* article had ratcheted his temper up several notches. "I should fire you on the spot," he said. "Your comments on Atlantic City were reprehensible. We have an office there."

For the first time, I realized that this wasn't just about Donald Trump. I could see that Edgar was more concerned with Janney's interests than with those of its clients. The office he referred to was not in Atlantic City but in Linwood, ten miles inland. Confusing Linwood with Atlantic City was like comparing Bryn Mawr to downtown Philadelphia.

Saying nothing about my comments on the Taj itself, Edgar went on: "The Executive Committee met this afternoon. We have outlined three new conditions for your employment.

"One, you can no longer speak to the media. Two, no bonus over your base salary. Three, we're putting you on probation. At the end of the year, we'll decide if we're going to keep you. I want your decision now. Either agree to the conditions or resign."

Sixteen years with a company, I thought, and this is what I get. All three conditions were untenable. The first—*you can never speak to the media again*—particularly galled me. An analyst who never speaks to the media is a novice, has nothing to say, or is wrong too often. I was none of the three.

Silence had no place in my modus operandi. The media called me constantly. Sometimes I got requests for five or six interviews a day from reporters all over the world. It was almost unusual if I didn't get at least one call daily. If a company I was following made headlines, got taken over, or ceased dividend payments, ten calls might come my way.

Awaiting my answer, Edgar glared at me as if I were a disobedient filly. "Ed," I said, "I need to think about it."

"Go ahead. Give me your answer by ten A.M. tomorrow."

I walked out of Edgar's office with Meyer. "Jim, this thing stinks. I want to discuss it with counsel. I don't think I can have an answer by ten tomorrow morning. I need more time."

He ran down a flight (apparently to Edgar's office), came back, and delivered a reprieve. "You have," he said, "till two."

That night, I spoke with my father. "Do everything you can to work this thing out," he said. As I mulled over his words, I felt like an investor who has blind faith in his brokers. I had always had confidence in my employers. If I cooperate, I figured, I can salvage this mess. So I decided to go along.

Trump had said he wanted an apology, but he really wanted an endorsement of the property. "Write me a letter stating that the Taj is going to be one of the greatest successes ever," he said to me when I spoke with him the next day, "and I'm going to have it published."

Rather than having me write the letter, Janney drafted one for me to sign. Edgar came to my office and asked, "Can you live with this?" Reluctantly, I signed it. The next day, Trump demanded more changes, which would have made the letter even more complimentary. I refused and went to my attorney. He helped me compose a new letter to Trump, a letter retracting the endorsement letter I had signed. I knew the step could cost me dearly, but I was certain it was the right thing to do. The heck with my career, my conscience said. More important matters—people and principles—are at stake.

The day after I sent the retraction, Edgar showed up at the office. "Why did you write that letter of retraction?" he asked. I started to tell him, but he said, "No, I don't want to *hear* why you wrote that letter. I want you to put it in writing. And now I want your files on Campbell Soup, the Golden Nugget, and the Taj Mahal." It didn't take a genius to see that he was undercutting my position as a Janney employee.

I visited my attorney and then Edgar again. He was hospitable. "Let me take your coat," he said. When Jim Meyer came in, Edgar said to me, "I personally like you very much, but you left me no alternative. I have to terminate you immediately. I want all your personal effects removed by five. All of your files are the property of this firm."

Escorting me to the front door, Meyer said, "Let me give you a little friendly advice, Marvin. Keep your mouth shut, or you'll never work in this business again."

The story of my firing galvanized the financial community and the public. After the *Philadelphia Inquirer* published a piece, the wire services picked it up. At the office, I must have had a hundred telephone calls. At home, I got hundreds and hundreds. CBS called, and the Canadian Broadcasting System. A week after the firing, *Barron's* did a cover story. Articles appeared in *Fortune*, *Business Week*, *Time*, *Newsweek*, and *Vanity Fair*. I was invited to appear on the *Today* show, *Good Morning, America*, and *Wall Street Week with Louis Rukeyser*. At my lawyers' insistence, I turned them down.

Even though I remained silent, Meyer's warning about not working in the industry proved true. I had become something of a folk hero, but I couldn't find a job. Part of the problem was consolidation in the industry. When I started, Philadelphia had about two dozen brokerage firms. Janney is now the only Philadelphia-based regional firm left. All the others have been swallowed up. The same trend happened nationally. Drexel disappeared. Bache was taken over by Prudential, and it became Prudential Bache, and now the Bache name has gone. Who listens to E. F. Hutton?

I had interviews with ten firms in New York, Philadelphia, and Baltimore. They all wanted to hear my story but offered no job. Brokerage firms thought: "This guy turned on a member firm. How do we know he won't turn on us?" One headhunter in New York said, "Marvin, you're too hot."

Attempting to redress some grievances, I began proceedings. I sued Trump. But because of New York Stock Exchange rules, I couldn't sue Janney; I had to go to arbitration. Anyone who wants to pursue a dispute with a brokerage—including doctors, executives, and investors like you—has to go to arbitration. Immediately, I saw that the deck was stacked. The chairman of my arbitration panel had a son who was a senior partner in Morgan Lewis Bockius, the law firm representing Janney. We petitioned the New York Stock Exchange to replace him, but the exchange considered it no conflict. When the hearings started, my attorneys made an impassioned plea for that arbitrator to withdraw (to *recuse* himself, in legal parlance). A second member of the panel added, "For the record, let me state that Norman Wilde [Janney's CEO] and I have been friends, but I haven't seen him in several years." The three arbitrators stepped out and returned fifteen minutes later. The chairman of the panel said, "Let's get the show on the road."

Normally, arbitration takes a couple of hours. My hearings took place in seven sessions over ten weeks. Ultimately, I prevailed. The arbitrators awarded me $750,000. Ordinarily, I might have won about $10,000, but the case had attained high visibility. Although the award covered my attorneys' fees, I was on the hook for out-of-pocket legal expenses. Travel, photocopying, and the like cost me more than $100,000. Had I lacked that money, I could never have brought the case.

In the suit against Trump, depositions went on for seven or eight hours a day over six weeks. When we deposed Edgar Scott, he rarely looked anyone in the eye. Eighty percent of the time, he looked down at the floor. Edgar sat at a long conference table. He said, "Gentlemen, if you don't mind, I'd like to sit at the other side of the table because there's this draft blowing on my neck." I said to him, "Ed, it must be those cold October winds."

Trump's lawyers subpoenaed everyone whose name I mentioned, and at every turn they tried to destroy my credibility.

They asked me what type of car I drove. "A 1974 BMW."

"Where do you live?" I gave them my address, in downtown Philadelphia.

"Why is the car registered in Northeast Philadelphia?" they asked, implying I had given the insurance company a phony address to save on premiums.

"Because it's my father's car."

The police knocked on my door one day and said, "Somebody's going through your trash." Trump had constructed a billion-dollar empire—precarious but still immense—and he felt the need to fire a shotgun at me in the hope that some pellets would hit.

We never did go to trial. As soon as I won the arbitration against Janney, Trump settled.

Yet I was out of work, and employers were shunning me. I turned to Peter Miller, a former colleague I held in particularly high regard. Unlike many brokers, Peter avoided products that didn't make sense. He held investments for the long term. In many ways, he operated like a money manager.

Years earlier, I had gone to lunch with him and told him, "If I weren't in this business, you would be my broker." After he read the newspaper story about my being fired, he called me. "Marvin, I read all about your situation. Does this mean I have your account?" Yes.

Peter then proposed that we start a money management firm. But I was too distracted to think about that. Some larger questions troubled me. Why didn't the Securities and Exchange Commission discipline Janney for its actions toward me? How could the New Jersey Casino Control Commission let Trump do what he did?

In addition, I had always worked for someone else. I couldn't imagine being self-employed. But the more I spoke with Peter and the more I pondered the outrageous conduct by captains of the financial industry, the more convinced I became that this would be the right move. And I could see how vital it is to give investors guidance and to help them ward off the financial predators poised to swoop down on them. Launching my own firm would give me the opportunity.

In the spring of 1991, we opened Roffman Miller Associates. Roffman Miller is not a broker-dealer, and we don't sell tax shelters, partnerships, insurance, or any other products. We don't participate in any commissions. We're bringing a philosophy and a discipline to investors. The firm, with a growing list of clients, lets me put into practice the countless insights that I've gained and that I'm passing along in this book.

Events proved my Taj prediction to be accurate. Trump's empire was on the verge of crumbling when he turned his situation around through refinancing deals with his bondholders and bankers that saved him hundreds of millions of dollars. I'm happy to say that although my willingness to speak out cost me my job, it saved millions for the Trump bondholders who listened.

But I don't gloat. My story underscores the crying need for honesty in the financial industry. The numbers I used to back up my words held together. Trump's numbers didn't. My emphasis on fundamentals—investment basics such as making sure that bonds have strong companies behind them—enabled me to recognize before anyone else the shaky state of Trump's casinos.

Because I want to reach far more people than I can in my company, I've written this book. In recent years, I've spoken out against unscrupulous brokers while counseling clients and making them money. Here I speak out further, and I aim to help make investing more profitable for you.

Take Charge of Your Financial Future shows you how to set financial goals and how to reach them. It is not a book on how to get rich quick. It's not a book on how to get rich. It's a book about making money work for you, while you work for your money.

If you want to get rich quick, rob a bank (not recommended). Or be a stockbroker during spectacular bull markets ($1 million annually is within reach), play major league baseball, or run a giant corporation and receive an annual salary in the millions even as you slice shareholders' dividends and lay off employees by the tens of thousands.

The love of money may be the root of all evil, but the understanding of money is crucial to a good life. I aim this book at both small investors and large: those with $5,000 to invest and those with millions, those who define financial success as being able to afford a new Rolls-Royce every year and those for whom it means simply being debt-free. The book is primarily for people with little experience in investing, but seasoned investors and professionals will also find much material that's useful and informative.

The way I define the term, an investor is anyone who makes, spends, or saves money. To make the most of what you have, and to make more of it in the future, however, you have to be active on your own behalf.

If you like paying others for their services, you'll find tips on how to select a professional money manager and how to scrutinize the manager's activities. If you're the roll-up-your-sleeves type and prefer doing things yourself, you'll find time-tested, step-by-step advice to put into practice.

The book lays out principles that help you spot important trends, be disciplined, avoid moves based on emotion, and make sound financial decisions—no matter what obstacles and problems confront you. As you navigate a financial sea fraught with sharks cruising for prey, this book teaches you how to fish.

The information I present here has proved its value throughout my career. It's not an academic theory whose real-life worth is unknown. I have diligently followed the principles I present. In doing so, I've earned clients millions of dollars and ensured my own financial independence.

Money management and investing are complex and confusing subjects. The book is intended to make them much clearer. Anecdotes from my years on Wall Street and my more recent work with money management clients vividly depict many of the points I want to convey. I've lived through almost every investment environment: the bowling stock craze of the late 1950s; the run-ups of Xerox and Polaroid; the disastrous market correction of 1974, when many stocks lost 70 percent of their value; the crash of 1987. I have seen people lose fortunes—and make them.

Because of my success in the stock market, and because common stocks are such an effective vehicle for most investors, I devote a significant part of the book to stocks. You'll find information on how to research companies, when to buy and sell, what advantages you'll find in mutual funds and discount brokers, and how to avoid mistakes.

A key ingredient of success is knowing which stocks to select. That means investigating companies before you invest. Interspersed through the book are stories of my investigations. Some produced buys that turned small investments into large sums of money. Others showed me, "These are companies to avoid." I present the stories as examples of what to look for as you pursue companies to invest in.

Please note that the examples—of companies, mutual funds, and the like—are not recommendations of what to buy or sell. They're illustrations of what can happen to investors and the companies they own.

This is a personal book on personal finance. For more than thirty years, I've been paid to identify facts and offer my opinions. I've met both with success and with some notable opposition. If you want neutral information that pulls punches and has no commentary, check other sources. If you want no-nonsense, hard-hitting, honest information, you've come to the right place.

The need to invest wisely is greater than ever. The stakes are enormous. Negative economic news (it comes often) can stir near-panics. Improved medical care introduces two vexing challenges. People are living longer than ever, and the sky-high costs of health care can bankrupt the most prudent investor. The problem is not about dying, but living.

Choices are baffling, and people are at a loss what to do. Many rightly don't trust brokers, and others find themselves in deep financial and consequent emotional trouble. If the Trump episode could happen to me— a professional analyst with decades in the business—imagine the disasters that can befall *you*.

On the phone was a widow in her sixties. She was near tears. "I just heard from my accountant," she said. "I've lost eighteen thousand dollars." That was a sizable part of her life savings.

The broker had invested her retirement money in Executive Life, an insurance company that issued junk bonds. Despite two years of signs that the company was failing and despite ample opportunity to move her funds to a safer harbor, the broker kept her money ensconced at Executive Life.

Why? He was looking out for himself, not her. Executive Life plied brokers with unusually high commissions. It offered what industry insiders call "yield to the broker." The client came last.

Her tale is all too typical. I'm sick and tired of seeing people's life savings devastated and investors being taken advantage of by aggressive brokers whose eyes light up at the lure of high commissions, or by financial planners and money managers who have conflicts of interest and products to sell.

The United States has eighteen thousand "money managers." Only four to five hundred of them conduct their research in-house. The others read someone else's work. Many have products to sell. Many are insurance salesmen disguised as financial planners. Why does the public put up with all this? After you read this book, I hope *you* won't.

Firing a broker is a consideration for investors whose brokers are more concerned with earning money for their firms and themselves than for their clients. The brokers who put themselves first are the ones I caution against. Some brokers, I know, are honest and do have their clients' best interests at heart. With those brokers, I have no quarrel.

One broker I've worked with is a big producer at a major brokerage firm. I have an account with him. He has maybe $200 million in assets under management. He's been successful for twenty years. When I asked him how, he said, "I've always conducted myself to do what's best for the client, and I've never stressed high-margin products that the firm was pushing." Like all the best brokers, he treats his clients the same way independent money managers do. He looks for investments well suited to his clients' needs. He doesn't push products that make no sense. He doesn't create activity for the sake of increasing his commissions. He puts his clients first.

Before Trump thrust me into Andy Warhol's fifteen-minute pantheon of fame, I was well respected in the financial community, but the public knew nothing about me. Since the lawsuit was settled, I've gained some attention. Radio stations across the country ask me to retell my tale and to recount my thoughts about money. Ted Koppel has interviewed me on ABC's *Night Line*. I was a featured guest on *Wall Street Week with Louis Rukeyser*.

One comment that makes me especially proud appeared in the *Wall Street Journal*. In January 1991, its "Heard on the Street" column said: "Mr. Roffman predicted ahead of others that Atlantic City in general and Donald Trump's casinos in particular would fall on hard times. He was right, and he was fired."

Donald Trump called me an unguided missile. Steve Wynn, chairman of the Golden Nugget (now called Mirage), said, "Who do you think you are, you little s——?" Actually, I'm not reckless at all. I just tell the truth.

I hope the truth serves you in your financial quest. I hope you gain all you dream of—and more—from the pages that follow.

PART I

PLANNING

1

THE TWELVE WORST
INVESTMENT MISTAKES
PEOPLE MAKE

In the midst of the January 1992 bull market, a client voiced a complaint. She was unhappy with the performance of my money management firm, Roffman Miller Associates, in handling her portfolio.

"You made only seven percent for me last quarter," she said. "I've read about money managers who made ten and twelve percent. What are you doing wrong?"

We weren't doing anything wrong. She was. She had succumbed to one of the most common, and worst, mistakes investors make. The downfall of most investors is greed.

Please don't misunderstand me. Money is vitally important—I know that. It affects your choice of job, how you spend your leisure time, where you live, even how long you live. It has consequences for your children's lives, your grandchildren's lives, the lives of your descendants a century from now.

Ensuring that you have the money you need is one of the main aims of this book. Investment mistakes interfere with that aim. In this first chapter, I'll talk about the worst investment mistakes you can make. In later chapters, I'll show how you can overcome them and reach your financial goals.

1. FORGETTING ABOUT RISK

Risk lurks behind almost every investment. Everyone recognizes that the stock your cousin touted last month could drop 50 percent in one day if news breaks that the CEO bought a $400,000 Ferrari with company funds and drove off into the Mexican sunset.

United States government bonds would seem much safer. If you buy a thirty-year government bond and hold it for the full thirty years, you will get back your principal, as well as interest paid every six months. The federal government *will* be around in thirty years.

But suppose something happens eight years from now and you need money. Maybe an accident causes you to lose time from work, or it's time to pay the bill for your daughter's college tuition. And suppose, meanwhile, that inflation has returned to double digits. The value of the bond could tumble: instead of being $1,000, it might have dropped to $900. If you need to sell before the bond's term, you could take a hit—10 percent of your money in this example—depending on the direction that interest rates have taken. The longer the term of the bond, the more volatile the price changes during the term. Yes, even U.S. government bonds have risk.

2. GREED

Here's a story I know well, because I was the subject. In early 1974, when I was thirty-four years old, I became a doggedly aggressive investor. I was the Donald Trump of Northeast Philadelphia. I borrowed money to buy into the stock market. I borrowed well into six figures.

I was buying bonds—which had a 6.25 percent return and could be converted into stock. On the money I had borrowed, I was paying 6 percent interest. So I had an immediate positive cash flow of .25 percent. The more money I put up, the more I'd make.

"How can I go wrong?" I was thinking. "I love the company. Everything looks great."

Six months went by, and suddenly the stock that the bond was convertible into had dropped from $64 a share to $9. And the interest I was paying on the borrowed money had risen from 6 percent to 13.25. My broker called in the loan.

If my father hadn't come to my rescue, I would have been bankrupt. I learned a lesson that I've never forgotten: Don't be greedy.

3. ACTING ON EMOTION

For many years I followed the casino industry for Janney Montgomery Scott in Philadelphia. When one of my wealthy friends told me he was heading to Atlantic City, I'd say, "Be careful."

"Oh," he'd reply, "I set a limit. As soon as I lose a hundred dollars, I'm out."

But he didn't set a limit on the upside. He should have said, "As soon as I *win* a hundred dollars [or two hundred or whatever], I'm walking away."

If every gambler did that, casinos wouldn't thrive as they do. Length of play is the decisive factor. Bet long enough at the casino, and you'll lose.

With investing, the length of investment is also crucial. The result, though, is the opposite. Keep your money in stocks long enough, and you'll probably win.

If you sell too soon, you may very well lose. Brokers disregard that and play on fears of a downturn. As soon as a stock rises 10, 15, or 20 percent, they're on the phone. "Let's nail down that profit," they say. You forget that they're motivated by an impending commission.

You shouldn't buy and sell, buy and sell, buy and sell. Don't let a broker prevent your investments from reaching maturity.

The problem is, it's easy to act on emotion. Discipline can easily vanish when you let yourself react rashly to a stock's volatility.

Your neighbor made a quick profit on XYZ Yo-yos. You want to do the same. But do you have the discipline to get in and out at the right time? Most people buy when a company is generating excitement and its stock price is rising. They usually panic and sell at the wrong time.

Others walk around with the *Wall Street Journal* in their back pockets and call their brokers five times a day. They have no discipline. The best investments, as I'll show you, are made over time.

4. FINDING REASONS NOT TO INVEST

"The market is heading downward."

"My job is uncertain."

"I have bills to pay."

You can always find reasons not to invest. But what happens to your money?

In 1929, my Uncle Sam had invested heavily in stocks. He was about thirty-two, a smart fellow who ran the family's uniform business. He sensed the overheating of the economy and the rampant speculation in the stock market that were taking place. He was astute enough to sell all his stocks just before the crash. He made a lot of money—more than a million dollars, I believe, when a million dollars was a lot of money.

The market crashed, and the depressed prices that followed lured my uncle back in. In 1931, the market fell even more precipitously than it had in 1929. He got clobbered—lost almost everything.

Although my uncle had tremendous wisdom, he never returned to stocks. Instead, he put his money in bonds. Bonds aren't a bad investment. But over time, stocks have proved to be much better. In the sixty-five years from 1926 to 1991, stocks performed twenty-two times better than bonds.

It's easy to make the mistake my uncle did and refrain from buying stocks, especially if you've been burned or if you're wary of the economy or your employment situation. But if you shun stocks, you'll miss some of the best investment opportunities you'll ever have.

5. "CASH IS TRASH"

The flip side of finding reasons not to invest is looking askance at an unglamorous facet of investing: cash.

In 1992, the Federal Reserve Board's efforts to combat a tenacious recession plunged interest rates to their lowest levels in two decades. Certificates of deposit (CDs) were paying less than 4 percent.

"Cash is trash," many were saying. The abysmal interest rates caused people to seek alternatives.

Some investors pushed large amounts of money into a new mutual fund consisting of medical and health stocks. Within six months, the fund had dropped 27 percent. So while some people were dismissing cash as trash, those who had invested in six-month CDs at 4 percent got back $102 for every $100 they had invested—versus the $73 their $100 would have become in the medical mutual fund.

The lesson? Cash is not trash. Markets are unpredictable.

6. FAILING TO DIVERSIFY

Later in this book, I'll explain why I believe strongly that common stocks should be the cornerstone of most portfolios. In general (or at least in theory), you should buy when a stock's price is low, of course, and sell when it's high. Yet no matter how low the prices of stocks may be, you should never sink 100 percent of your money into stocks.

Failing to diversify exposes you to several hazards:

- If the overall stock market plummets, your stocks may sink with it and you could lose money. You're also in a weak position to buy stocks later, at friendlier prices.
- If, on the other hand, you eschew stocks and put all your money in low-paying fixed-income investments (such as CDs or money market mutual funds), you might lag well behind inflation.
- If you favor CDs, you lock up your money and could miss attractive opportunities for other investments.
- And if you've put all your money in bonds, and interest rates rise, your bonds could lose value.

The solution? A balanced portfolio of stocks, bonds, and some cash in the form of CDs or money market funds. You adjust the mix of ingredients (in the industry, the mix is called *asset allocation*) according to economic conditions and your own situation. We'll talk much more about this later.

7. PUTTING ALL YOUR TRUST IN YOUR BROKER

A man who consulted me for financial advice told me what his broker had done with his $250,000 portfolio. The broker had invested a hefty portion of it in a bond mutual fund. In this case, that's almost criminal.

Bond mutual funds, specifically no-load funds (those that charge no commission), may be suitable for small investors—people with, say, $1,000 to $5,000 to invest. By lending money to scores or even hundreds of corporate or government borrowers, such funds avoid the risk inherent in a single bond. For small investors, that benefit may outweigh the 1 or 1.5 percent annual management fee the fund charges—especially for investors who don't want to go to the trouble of buying bonds directly. But someone with hundreds of thousands to invest can save hundreds, even thousands, of dollars a year in sales and management fees by buying individual bond issues. That broker had no business putting the money in a bond fund. And the man didn't know enough to question it. He mistakenly trusted the broker.

8. NOT UNDERSTANDING WHAT YOU'RE INVESTING IN

A letter arrived recently. "Dear Marvin, is there anything anyone can do about this, or do I just forget it? I'd appreciate it if you could look over this annual report. P.S. It was purchased in 1983 for $25,000. All I have received is $300."

It was a limited partnership that had invested in Texas real estate. The report was an audited financial statement of its demise. "We sincerely regret this outcome to your investment in Krupp commercial properties," it said. "The partnership's goals were inhibited by the economic difficulties in the Texas region and the near real estate depression and more recently the economic recession."

In other words, her investment was worthless. She'd lost all $25,000 except for the $300 in dividends she'd received.

Hold one of these bad investments, and it can cancel the proceeds from all your good ones for years. And remember, if she had invested that $25,000 in a savings account, she would have received interest for almost ten years. So it wasn't merely that she lost the $25,000. She also lost the interest on $25,000 for almost ten years, which in itself is many thousands of dollars. Why did all this happen? She didn't know what she was getting into.

"Read the prospectus before you invest," you're warned. But the prospectus was never designed to be read. Prospectuses are written to intimidate, and people tend not to read them. Those who do read them rarely understand them. That's the idea. If you knew what you were getting into, many investments would never attract you.

The thicker the prospectus, the more wary you should be.

9. IF IT SOUNDS TOO GOOD TO BE TRUE, IT PROBABLY IS

Don't be attracted to a stock just because it has a high yield. If something sounds too good to be true, it usually is.

When I worked at Janney Montgomery Scott, one of my clients liked Bally Manufacturing. He had bought Bally when it was selling in the high 20s because it was the undisputed leader in the slot machine market. The company was building a huge casino in Atlantic City. Then Bally decided to buy two huge casino-hotels in Nevada. To many people, it seemed that everything was dandy. But Bally grossly overpaid for the Nevada properties and was leveraged to the hilt. And it forgot about innovation.

The stock started to tumble. It went from the upper 20s to the lower 20s, then to the teens. The client called me and said, "Listen, the stock is down fifty percent. Let's buy it." I said, "No. I don't think much of the management."

Just because a stock is down 50 percent doesn't mean it's time to buy it. Ultimately, Bally stock fell to 1⁷/₈.

At one point in the 1970s, many investors who bought new issues lost money. The new-issue market got so hot that many companies brought their shares to the market to capitalize on the booming stock prices. But the window of opportunity slammed shut after many of these highly speculative issues failed. Then it became difficult to market new issues— even the attractive ones. I said, "The same thing will happen all over again."

In the early 1970s, the new-issue market was so hot that one client said, "Marvin, no matter what stock it is, I want you to buy me a hundred shares of every new issue you can get your mitts on."

Why does this happen? Enormous demand and great expectations. The market heats up. One stock comes out and goes up 30 percent, and another goes up 50 percent or more. Investors clamor for new issues.

My client? Almost all his new issues were wiped out. He got caught up in the craze and lost thousands of dollars.

In the 1980s, new issues in medical and biotech companies were especially popular. Of course, many did not deliver, and many promising underwritings failed. Now they're called not new issues, but IPOs. Be careful of start-up companies and hopping on bandwagons that may be slowing down. Read the prospectus. It takes the gloss off investments that brokers can be overly enthusiastic about.

10. FAILING TO PLAN

A companion to this lack of discipline is lack of planning. Too many people have not assessed where they are and where they want to be. Are they putting enough money into savings for emergencies? What are they doing about their children's education? What about preparing for retirement? The sooner you start, the better. The horror is that many people first think about all this decades after they should.

One retired couple who came to me were living off the income from their certificates of deposit. Their CDs totaled about $100,000.

When CDs were yielding 7 or 8 percent, they were earning about $7,000 or $8,000 a year plus Social Security. Now that CD yields have dropped in half, they're in trouble. Their income is insufficient. To increase it, they'd have to increase their risk. They can't afford to take risk. They can't afford the possibility of a loss. Unfortunately, they came to me too late.

11. WORSHIPING GURUS

Don't believe everything you hear. People don't talk about their failures. During the late 1970s and early 1980s, Joe Granville had a reputation as one of the best stock pickers and market timers ever. Granville is a technician, using charts and graphs to predict changes in the market. So strong was his reputation that he could move the market single-handedly. He caused major market movements simply by putting out buy or sell signals. Sometimes when he pulled the plug and said, "Sell everything," the market tumbled.

A projection he made in January 1981 was harshly negative. The market had one of its largest single-day declines in years—on Granville's word. Granville fled stocks soon after, and many of his investors sat on the sidelines during one of the biggest bull markets in history.

He was out of the market for a significant part of the giant run-up of the eighties. Then, before the market crash of 1987, he became bullish. He grew bearish again in the early 1990s. What was the effect of his gyrations? He was often bearish when the market was bullish and vice-versa.

Henry Kauffman was the interest rate guru. When he spoke, Wall Street listened. He had a long string of correct calls. Then he began making mistakes.

You know why? Because nobody knows with any consistency where interest rates are heading or where the stock market is going. And the gurus who guess right today could be way off the mark tomorrow. There is no formula.

It reminds me of the predictor who sends out a thousand letters. Half say the stock market will rise in its next big move, and half say it will drop. After that prediction, whichever way the market went, he sends letters to the five hundred who received the correct prediction. Two hundred fifty get the letter saying the market will go up; the other two hundred fifty, that it will go down. And so on. By the sixth letter, fifty people think he's a genius. But in the end, he will fail. Because nobody knows the future. The best guru today may be out to pasture tomorrow.

12. MISMANAGING DEBT

"Neither a borrower nor a lender be," Shakespeare's Polonius warns. Sensible advice—but hard to follow. At times—when buying an expensive item such as a house or a car, for example—you may have little choice but to borrow. An unforeseen illness can also force your hand.

But problems can arise when you use credit cards or lines of credit to finance purchases you can't afford. It's an easy trap to fall into. Charging seems so painless. The bills take a while to arrive. You can pay a minimum amount each month.

Unfortunately, the interest rates on credit cards are usually astronomical; in years past, they would have been considered usurious. The interest and miscellaneous charges on your card could easily total 20 percent.

Your debt piles up rapidly, far faster than your income. You fall deeper and deeper into trouble. In the worst case, you might have to declare bankruptcy.

Or consider the following scenario:

From your brother-in-law at Consolidated Feather, you get a tip that the company is about to roll out an innovative product, Newfuzz, that will render feather dusters obsolete tomorrow. The stock is selling at $3^1/8$, and you want to buy ten thousand shares.

You have a margin account with your broker, which lets you put down only 50 percent of the cost of a stock. So instead of having to plunk down $31,250 for Feather, your outlay is just $15,625. Then Newfuzz comes out, and the public goes wild. Kids, teenage girls, even men in their late fifties can't get enough Newfuzz. Articles about Consolidated Feather appear in the daily papers, the financial magazines; there's even a spot on *60 Minutes*. In two weeks, the stock has soared to 14. You cash in, receive $140,000 minus commission, and repay the difference between the $31,250 that you owed and the $15,625 you already paid. You've secured a neat profit of $108,750, minus commission.

You like that? Well, how often do you think it happens? Much more often, the Newfuzzes of the world appear briefly in stores (if they're lucky enough to get shelf space) and then fizzle. Consolidated Feather drops from 14 to $1^7/8$. You have to put up more collateral. Then your margin call comes in, and you have no more collateral to cover it. You're sold out.

That's exactly what happened in 1929, when New York City sidewalks became landing pads for ruined investors. Despite safeguards enacted afterward, a similar situation occurred in October 1987. Stocks were falling so precipitously that investors had to liquidate accounts. People lost a fortune.

It doesn't matter if Consolidated Feather stock rises to 65 tomorrow. You have to sell. The stock is no longer yours.

The people who prosper during stock market crashes are the ones who buy, not the ones who sell. But margin accounts can take the choice out of your hands. When you go into debt, you lose control—just as companies do when they leverage. So absolutely, positively, never buy stock on margin.

Investors make many more mistakes than the ones I've discussed here. But we'll have plenty of opportunity to cover them in later chapters. Let's look now at your own situation so we can begin suggesting a smart financial course for you.

The Twelve Worst Investment Mistakes People Make

1. Forgetting about risk
2. Greed
3. Acting on emotion
4. Finding reasons not to invest
5. "Cash is trash"
6. Failing to diversify
7. Putting all your trust in your broker
8. Not understanding what you're investing in
9. If it sounds too good to be true, it probably is
10. Failing to plan
11. Worshiping gurus
12. Mismanaging debt

2

A FINANCIAL CHECKUP

Stick out your bank statement and say, "Aah." In this chapter, I'll act as your financial doctor, just as I do with clients in my office. We'll do a checkup of your fiscal health. With the information secure in your file, we can proceed to build a plan for your financial future, a plan that matches your pocketbook and temperament.

Our purpose here is to discover what assets you have and where you are in your career and your life. (In the next chapter, we'll explore where you want to be.) Your investment posture varies depending on your stage of life. If you're on the eve of retirement, the time remaining to accumulate assets and let them grow is much less than if you're a recent college graduate. If you have forty years ahead of you before you retire, you should focus on investments that grow over time. On the other hand, a forty-two-year-old with three children on the verge of college has to have money for their education. Her investment needs differ from those of a single woman just starting a career.

To give you one example, I recently opened a $200,000 account for a twenty-two-year-old fellow who's in graduate school. (He got that big chunk of money from an insurance company in an out-of-court settlement for an automobile accident.) Because he supports himself, he needs money every month for his apartment, car, meals, and so on. I'm putting most of his money—70 percent—in investments that produce income. But at his age, I told him, it's important to look for growth vehicles, even though he still has to meet those big monthly expenses. He agreed that we would dedicate 30 percent of his portfolio to growth.

His needs, however, will change in about two years. When he graduates and gets a job, he'll be earning the money for his car, housing, and other expenses as he goes. Then he'll focus less on income investments and more on growth.

The form below is a *profile sheet*. Answering all the questions will give you a picture of your financial situation that will serve you throughout the book.

If you're married or living with someone, make sure you fill it out jointly. Life partners should both have a say in evaluating your financial situation and (in the next chapter) your goals.

Be open and honest. Painting a rosier-than-true picture only hurts you.

PROFILE SHEET

1. How old are you? ____

2. Do you have any children? ____ How many? ____

3. What do you do for a living? _____

4. Annual salary $_____

5. Do you own a house or apartment ____ or rent ____

6. Value of your house or apartment (if you own) _____

7. Monthly mortgage payment (including maintenance or common charges for apartments) _____ or rent _____

8. Type of car _____ cost _____ age ____

9. Financial assets (total for each category):

> Bank accounts ____
> Certificates of deposit (CDs) ____
> Money market accounts ____
> Stocks (including mutual funds) ____
> Bonds (including mutual funds) ____

Stocks	Number of Shares	Current Share Price	Current Value	Share Price when Purchased	Total Cost
_____	_____	_____	_____	_____	_____
_____	_____	_____	_____	_____	_____
_____	_____	_____	_____	_____	_____
_____	_____	_____	_____	_____	_____
_____	_____	_____	_____	_____	_____
Total			_____		_____

Bonds (list sequentially by maturity date)	Principal Amount	Current Price	Current Value	Cost per Bond	Total Cost
_____	_____	_____	_____	_____	_____
_____	_____	_____	_____	_____	_____
_____	_____	_____	_____	_____	_____
_____	_____	_____	_____	_____	_____
_____	_____	_____	_____	_____	_____
Total			_____		_____

10. Yearly income from:

Bank accounts _____
CDs _____
Stocks _____
Money market accounts _____
Bonds _____

11. Yearly changes in income and expenses of 10 percent or more:

Item	One year ago	Today
_____	_____	_____
_____	_____	_____
_____	_____	_____
_____	_____	_____
_____	_____	_____

12. Other valuable assets and their worth:

Rental properties _____
Jewelry _____
Furs _____
Business property _____
Collections, such as stamps or coins _____

13. Outstanding debts:

	Principal	Monthly payment	Interest rate
Mortgage	_____	_____	_____
Car	_____	_____	_____
Credit cards	_____	_____	_____
Lines of credit	_____	_____	_____
Education loans	_____	_____	_____
Other loans (such as debt owed to relatives)	_____	_____	_____

14. Annual tax payments:
    Federal income _____
    State income _____
    Other income _____
    Real estate _____
    School _____
    Personal property _____

15. Annual insurance premiums:

    Life _____
    Health _____
    Disability income _____
    Auto _____
    Homeowner's _____
    Other _____

16. Miscellaneous expenses:

    Educational _____
    Other _____

17. Medical conditions or problems:

18. Major life changes on the horizon (e.g., retirement, change in careers, going back to school, expected inheritance):

    _____

Some items on the sheet deserve comment.

Your *salary* may change year to year depending on whether you're on a payroll or independent. For example, if you're a self-employed artist or a salesman working on commission, your income can vary markedly. If it does, do you know how much you'll make this year? If it does not vary much, you can use an average of the past three or four years' income.

What is your *house or apartment* worth? Are you sure? The value may have changed dramatically since you bought it. If you bought in the 1970s or before, your house could be worth five times the amount you paid. Conversely, if you bought in the late 1980s, you might be in for a painful surprise. Since 1988 or so, many houses have lost thousands of dollars in value, and others have hardly appreciated. The enormous run-ups of the eighties will almost certainly not repeat themselves in the next dozen years.

What kind of *car* do you drive? Is it a $10,000 car or a $50,000 car? What shape is it in? Will you replace it soon?

In compiling the list of your financial *assets*, remember to include all accounts: CDs, bank accounts, money market accounts, stock and bond holdings, mutual funds. If you don't know the amounts and can't put your hands on the latest statements, check with whoever has your account. You need to have complete, up-to-date information.

Also under assets, don't forget the jewelry or other keepsakes you've tucked away in a safe deposit box. Or maybe you have another investment, say in an apartment or a building. Be sure to account for all your important assets.

If you have stocks or bonds (including stock or bond mutual funds), list each—along with the information requested. In the stock section, the Current Value equals the Number of Shares multiplied by the Current Share Price. The Total Cost equals the Share Price when Purchased multiplied by the Number of Shares. In the bond section, the Current Value equals the Principal Amount multiplied by the Current Price. The Total Cost equals the Cost per Bond (when you purchased it) multiplied by the Number of Units. It's vital to know what stocks or bonds are in your portfolio, how much they're worth, and whether they've increased or decreased in value.

The profile sheet might show that you have an inordinately high percentage of your total allocated to one stock. I recommend putting no more than 10 percent of your total assets in one stock. A figure of 10 percent or more poses the risk of significant losses if the value of that one stock plummets. We'll talk more about this in later chapters, and we'll also find out whether you have a special loyalty to any companies in your portfolio.

Major *changes in your income and expenses* can arise because of a job promotion, a move, and many other factors. We've included them—when they change by 10 percent or more in a year—because they could induce you to make changes in how you invest. In this chapter, you write them down. In later chapters, you'll see how to manage them.

The *debts* category shows how much total debt you have and breaks it down by type of loan. The column for interest rates is important: if any percentages are beyond today's low rates, you should consider reducing expenses by refinancing your mortgage or consolidating other debts.

Insurance is on the form because you must know how much you have (if any) and whether it's enough. How much you need varies depending on whether you're married and have dependents and on what stage of life you're in. Disability income insurance is important because it permits you to continue your present lifestyle in the event of serious accident or illness.

Under *miscellaneous other expenses*, list educational expenses, such as college or private school tuition. College tuition and room and board, as you know, can cost $20,000 or more a year.

You'll see the category *major life changes on the horizon*. These are known or predictable events or conditions that will soon affect your income, expenses, and other important facets of your life. For example, will you soon retire? Your income will most likely drop. Do you have a life-threatening illness? Does it sap your funds or prevent you from working full time? Will you soon receive an award from an insurance case or lawsuit?

Are you coming into an inheritance? If you are, you may find yourself wanting to buy a new house or car or to pay off an old one. One of my new clients is a woman whose husband recently died. She had previously bought a car and was paying 17.99 percent interest on a four-year loan. "I can't stand this interest," she said. Fortunately, she had more than enough money to pay it off. In today's economic climate, it's unlikely that I can earn 18 percent on her money. "For satisfaction and peace of mind," I said, "pay it off."

With all this information at your fingertips, you should have a solid handle on your financial situation—better, perhaps, than ever before. You'll be in a strong position to follow and consider the suggestions I make throughout the book.

Your next step is to determine what you want from your money and how comfortable you are about taking risks.

3

SETTING YOUR SIGHTS

What do you want from your money? Do you want to buy a house? Do you want enough cushion to survive for a year if you lose your job? Do you want a new car? Have you ever dreamed of starting your own business?

Do you want a quarter-million-dollar nest egg for retirement? Are you longing to escape from debt? Do you want to fund your child's way to an Ivy League diploma?

To manage money well, you have to know what you want. In this chapter, I'll talk mostly about significant life changes: what having money (or financial security) can enable you to do in the way of career, education, travel, family. I'll also touch on your tolerance for risk.

Don't look for me to tell you what you want. My purpose here is to show you important considerations for the future so that *you* can then decide which of them (or any others that occur to you) apply and appeal to you.

Chapter 2 covered where you are; this chapter covers where you're going. You have to know the constraints on building a portfolio. Do you primarily need income? Are you looking for your money to grow?

Age makes a big difference. When you're sixty-five years old, you're looking for dependable income, not risk. When you're twenty-five, you have to set sights forty years ahead. When you're forty or fifty, your children's education may be paramount.

19

A college student who isn't working needs income. That will change when he finds a job, because he has forty years before retiring. Who knows what the cost of a telephone call will be forty years from now? Or a loaf of bread?

A retired couple who aren't working also need income, but their prospects are different. They don't have forty years of work before retiring; they're there. They need to provide for themselves both now and for the future.

ESTABLISHING GOALS

When I entered the financial industry nearly thirty-five years ago at age eighteen, I earned forty dollars a week. By living with my parents, I saved most of the salary I took home. I put money aside to buy stocks. I would save until I could buy a hundred shares of this stock and a hundred shares of that. And now I'm independent.

My thinking was to save when I was young so that when I retired, I would have a good income—I wouldn't have to work. It wasn't that I intended to retire at a certain age. I just thought, When I retire, I want enough money to live on without worry. I never tried to figure out exactly how much money that would be. If I could have an extra $200 a week income in retirement, I felt, I would be happy. Now, of course, adjust the $200 to inflation, and it comes to a lot of money, perhaps $800 or $1,000.

A friend who's a writer has a situation typical of the self-employed. He endures cold periods and hot periods. From year to year, his income can fluctuate unpredictably—and dramatically. He can go months with no paychecks. His main goal is to have enough savings and investments so that if his income shrinks or he has a drought—say six months with no revenue—he can continue his writing career rather than forsake it for a full-time job. What he needs is the discipline to put aside money every week until he has accumulated enough to let him live income-free for six months, a year, or more. He should read this book.

One former associate of mine made $100,000 a year but was $160,000 in debt. He owned high-priced cars, furniture, artwork, and a house. I thought it was inexcusable for someone with a six-figure income to be mired in the debt he had. He didn't even have $10,000 in savings. I told him to force himself to save money every month until he had a positive cash flow, so that he could escape that debt.

What follows are prime examples of goals or life changes you must plan for.

Owning a Home

I've always been a strong believer in owning a home—whether it be a house, an apartment, a condominium, or a cooperative. I prefer owning to renting. I like to be in control, rather than at the mercy of a landlord. Landlords have a disturbing tendency to let properties deteriorate and to raise the rent. That's not for me. Owning a home gives you independence. It's the American dream.

After a real estate boom in the 1980s, the recession of the early 1990s caused a drop in the value of many houses. That worsened the recession, because it made people feel poorer and they spent less.

Still, I think you should look at housing as a lifestyle issue, not a financial one. The demographic trends that caused real estate to skyrocket in most of America throughout the 1980s have subsided. Housing prices are likely to remain close to stagnant into the foreseeable future—possibly for decades.

The issue is your comfort level in owning versus renting. Some people sleep better knowing that a small piece of land is theirs. Others don't want a lawn to mow and landscaping to sculpt. They don't want to be responsible for repairing a faucet.

Home ownership isn't for everyone, even those who can afford the down payment. Owning a house is a big responsibility. A house needs maintenance, which many people—particularly as they get older—just won't or can't stay on top of.

I don't like seeing older people move away from their houses, but they can reach a point where it makes sense to leave a big house. When the children move away, for example, or when your strength fails, you don't need a big house anymore. If your mobility is poor, climbing steps can become a hardship or even a hazard, and a two-story house is a liability. Your kitchen is likely to be on the first floor, and the bathroom and bedroom on the second.

When I was young I lived in downtown Philadelphia, where I had a four-story house. The kitchen was on the ground floor. The living room was a flight up from that. The bedrooms were upstairs. The layout was crazy. It was okay for me, but if you're sixty-five years old, do you want that?

Your housing needs change as you age, just as your investments do. When you get older, an apartment with an elevator may serve you better—and you won't have to deal with overgrown grass or leaky gutters or dying trees. I just noticed that a spruce tree is dying in front of my house. Homeowners always have problems.

My twenty-two-year-old client who's soon finishing graduate school and expects to enter the job market in two years intends to buy a house then. I've talked to him about how much house he can afford in the location he wants, and how much down payment he'll need. Let's say the down payment is $20,000. He and I will discuss how the investments we make today will earn him $20,000 in three, four, or five years.

Getting Married or Moving in With Someone

At one time (and even now in some parts of the world), marriage was a financial arrangement. The bride's dowry, the merging of families—these were two reasons people got married. In this country, the practice has changed to accommodate notions of romance. But marriage still has financial repercussions that can last a lifetime—and beyond.

Similarly, moving in with a "significant other" affects your income and outflow. Although two can't live as cheaply as one, a life partnership entails financial benefits and liabilities. Don't undertake such a significant step without considering the monetary impact.

Having Children

In come the patter of little feet; out go big bucks. When America had a farm economy, kids were a financial plus. They helped you do the house chores, plant and harvest the crops, tend the animals. Today, in our urban and suburban society, children are a monetary liability; having them is much like buying a new Cadillac every few years. Have you priced kids' shoes? Seen the cost of higher education?

I'm not suggesting that you opt for childless bliss. But recognize that you'll bear major expenses from the moment you commit to becoming a parent. If you doubt me, check with an obstetrician.

Too many people have children without being prepared for the fiscal consequences. (I'll leave the emotional consequences to Dr. Spock.) Make sure you understand the drain on your bank account that you'll unleash. Then enjoy your contribution to the future of the world.

Divorce

The statistics on the dollar effects of divorce vary widely. For men, divorce often brings a net gain; for women, it's usually a terrible minus. Few people should stay in a harmful relationship to stave off poverty. But again, know the impending fiscal repercussions, and plan for them. Take stock of your skills, if you've been out of the job market, to see what you might offer employers. Go back to school if you want or need to. Remember, major life changes bring both challenges and opportunities.

Changing Careers

The job market of the early 1990s was the worst I've seen in decades. Millions of people couldn't find work, and the prospects of a quick improvement in the financial environment were low.

In investing, I want to know whether you're generating what I call *free cash flow*. That is, are you generating enough money to live in the style to which you're accustomed and still save some money? Or are you using it up? People's circumstances change.

Imagine if you lost your job or took a new job in a lower-paying field. Suddenly, you'd need to redirect your priorities. Instead of being aggressive in your investments, you should move into fixed-income instruments, until you find another job or get a high enough income from the new job. When circumstances change, you have to change with them.

Starting Your Own Business

Another major change is starting a business. Few people have that goal, because it's so daunting. Consider the obstacles to opening a pharmacy. Years ago, you went to the corner pharmacy and bought toothpaste. Now there's a good chance that you go to a chain, such as Rite Aid or Drug Emporium. Rite Aid sales are more than $4 billion a year.

Remember Chadwick? Autocar? Packard? Ortlieb's? Seventy-five years ago, the United States was home to dozens of car manufacturers. There were a thousand brewers. Now you can count the car makers on one hand and the brewers on both. We're in a mature country that's phasing down manufacturing and moving toward service. Go into business yourself, and you compete with the big boys. The mom-and-pop corner grocery store is almost extinct. Hardly anyone delivers milk to houses anymore.

Starting a business today is iffy. I'm not saying the entrepreneurial spirit has vanished, but it's tough to compete. Some businesses offer a more likely chance of succeeding than others, but I urge you to think long and hard before taking the plunge.

I told you about my friend the writer. He's chosen that career not so much to make money but because he likes it. That's a very important point with me, and it may be with you too. When I took my first job at a brokerage firm, making only forty dollars a week, I enjoyed my work and felt I had a future there. I figured that I could work my way up, that I wouldn't be making forty dollars a week forever. I always tell people, "If you can, pursue a career you enjoy." I consider myself privileged because I love what I do.

A couple I know started their own business. For years they worked for somebody else and made $200 a week. When their boss decided to sell the business, they asked me whether I thought they should buy it. I said yes. They bought it. They're not making much more than $200 a week, and they have a lot of worries. But they like what they do.

I've been on both sides—working for someone else and being self-employed. For me, being your own boss is the best. If you feel that way too, recognize the obstacles. If the obstacles don't give you pause, go to it. You have my good wishes.

Planning for Retirement

Retirement differs utterly from a life of paid work. Once you're retired, you don't have the benefit of receiving inflation-adjusted salary increases. I hope you have a pension tied to a cost-of-living increase. Social Security continues to be adjusted for inflation—so far.

If you're forty, you have about twenty-five years of work left until you retire. You have to plan so that you can live a comfortable life during those intervening years and once retirement arrives.

In the next chapter, I give examples of how inflation clobbers your purchasing power. Here's a preview. By now, you should know what you need to live on. Let's say it's $40,000. And let's say that inflation over the next two and a half decades will average 5 percent a year. In twenty-five years, then, that $40,000 figure will inflate to a staggering $135,454. That's how much money you will need to maintain your present comfort level. You won't get that money from Social Security.

The key is to consider your monthly costs, how much you pay in taxes, what your savings and investments are, how much they generate each year, and what your pension and Social Security are likely to pay. You can't figure on preserving all your capital and living only off pension, Social Security, and interest. If you're sixty-five, the life tables show that you could easily live another fifteen or twenty years.

Every situation is different. Some people have enough savings, investments, pension, and Social Security to produce all the money they need. For others, the numbers don't add up. Unless they take a lot of risk, their assets will not produce enough income. And people that age should not take a lot of risk.

Look at my cousin Darlene. She's sixty-two, single, and fiercely independent, and she recently lost her job. She has $100,000 in the bank. A few years ago, she was enjoying 8 percent return on her money. Now she's earning less than half that. She's desperate—she doesn't want to use up her capital.

"How much is it going to take for you to live the way you like to live?" I
asked her. With rent and other expenses, she said, "it's more than $12,000
year." I said, "It'll be tough." If she bought CDs, she'd make less than
·3,000 a year.

She should have talked to me years ago. But she didn't. With her, the
numbers didn't add up, and I couldn't expose her to the risk of common
stocks. I sought out other investments. I put a small amount of money in
convertible preferred stock, where she could get capital appreciation and
high yields with low risk. Other than the convertible preferred stock, I
can't do much to increase her wealth without taking too much risk. I just
have to make sure she can live without drastically diminishing her
lifestyle.

What About Nursing Homes?

One of my clients, affectionately known as Aunt Myrtle, lives in a nursing
home that costs $26,000 a year. She's ninety-three years old and has about
$200,000 capital to sustain her. I want to preserve the capital, because
she'd like to leave money to her nieces.

Going into a nursing home—or having a loved one in a nursing home—
is a definite possibility that you should factor into your decision making.
The problem isn't dying; the problem is living. People are living longer
than ever before. Those in their sixties, seventies, even early eighties can
be vibrant and vital. But when you reach eighty-five or ninety, you may
need nursing care. Who knows? By the time you reach what you think of
as advanced years, strides in medicine may extend your life for decades
more.

One woman who talked to me about becoming a client has an elderly
mother who lives at home. "I'm concerned she might have to go into a
nursing home," the woman said. "*I* will have to pay for it. I'll try to keep
her at home as long as possible, but if I can't, all of a sudden I'll have a
huge financial burden."

Middle-aged children often want to share the cost of nursing care. But
these children are in a bind themselves, having to make their own living
and support children of their own. No, you can't rely on children or anyone
else; you have to be independent. You have to plan. In chapter 4, I show just
how important that planning is.

HOW MUCH RISK CAN YOU STAND?

Before coming to me, my very first client owned one million dollars in
tax-free bonds. He held no stocks, because, as he put it, "I don't trust the

stock market." But he opened an account with me for $100,000 to test how I would do at managing his money. I spoke with him and convinced him that the best choice would be stocks. At all times, I invest all the money he's entrusted to me in the stock market.

After one year, his account had risen to $112,000, and he's adding to it every quarter. The other day, he sent a check for another $25,000. By now, he has $175,000 invested with me, plus the increases I've earned him. He likes me, he trusts me, and he sees he's doing well. His goals haven't changed, but he's more comfortable at taking risks than he was before turning part of his money over to me. Even a hardened cash-lover can change his tolerance level.

Right now I have about seventy clients. Each differs from the next. Some have 100 percent of their money invested in stocks, some have 20 percent. Some have almost no stocks.

Your choices have to make financial sense, and they have to make you comfortable. If worrying about the market's direction will keep you awake at night, stay away from risk.

REMEMBER INSURANCE

I urge you to have enough insurance to protect yourself, your spouse (if you're married), and any dependents. Types of insurance you may need include life, health, disability, homeowner's, and automobile.

I devote all of chapter 22 to the important, misunderstood, and easily overlooked subject of insurance.

A WORD ON SOCIAL SECURITY

Most American workers and their employers pay into the Social Security system. When they retire or become disabled, Social Security will send them a monthly check. The amount will depend on several factors, primarily how long they worked and how much money they and their employers contributed to the Social Security fund.

Many people think that Social Security is the answer to the financial needs of old age. They're mistaken. Social Security will not cover your retirement needs. Even the top monthly payment is too low to do that. Social Security was never meant to be your only source of retirement money. It was meant to supplement other sources of income.

And who knows whether it will even be able to do that? Who knows how the government will mangle Social Security in future years?

Some politicians—Ross Perot, for one, during his 1992 presidential campaign—have said that the government should no longer index Social

Security payments to the cost of living. The elimination of indexing would save the government money over the years but would have a deleterious effect on recipients: if you're on Social Security, it would be tantamount to reducing your income—to the tune of 3 to 5 percent a year. If inflation goes up (as I think it will) and your income stays constant, you'll be falling behind.

Moreover, with "baby boomers" now in middle age and approaching retirement, the demographics paint a dim picture for Social Security's future. When the system could count three workers for every retiree, it had plenty of money for the monthly payments it was issuing to retirees. But soon, with many fewer workers to support many more retirees, the money will not go around.

Unless the government makes changes, Social Security recipients ten, twenty, thirty years from now can expect to see checks far lower than those their parents received, and that's in absolute dollars. Taking inflation into account, their Social Security checks will be lower still—if the Social Security trust fund has anything left.

4

WILL IT BE ENOUGH?

A fifty-five-year-old client who earned more than $100,000 a year recently stopped in to see me. He had just lost his job as a fund-raiser.

"I can't get another job for anything like that," he lamented. He has no idea how long he'll be out of work. It could be months. Suddenly, his whole future—and his whole financial outlook—has changed.

Is your job secure? Is anyone's? As the world economy becomes more competitive and as the U.S. economy shifts from manufacturing into service, a hard fact of the job market becomes plain: No one's job is secure. Guaranteed jobs don't exist anywhere.

If the point needed emphasizing, millions of workers heard it full blast during the recession of the early 1990s. It made them realize that lifetime security is an illusion. Loyalty from employer to employee has disappeared. I found that out at Janney Montgomery Scott. Millions of others have discovered it, as the pink slips roll out of employers' payroll departments far faster than new jobs arise.

Even career politicians in Washington are being unceremoniously voted out of office after decades in Congress. I know many physicians who have said, "Thank goodness I've had my good times in medicine. They're gone."

House painters are having difficulties. Painters used to think, How could they make painting obsolete? But then someone came up with vinyl siding. Vinyl windows. New technologies in painting. Better rollers. Paint sprayers. Homeowners can do it themselves and save. No job is certain.

Investors used to think that public utility companies were safe bets. After all, you have to have electricity, right? You have to buy from Philadelphia Electric. But you don't. Now cogeneration of electricity is having an impact. Even public water supply companies are subject to droughts, pollution, and chemical spills.

So you have to be ready for a world turning topsy-turvy. No matter how aware you are of the possibility, losing your job is unsettling. That's why you have to save. You have to recognize that rainy days *will* come—not that they *might* come. You need to cultivate a discipline, which we'll talk about in chapter 5.

Do you want to finance a college education ten or twenty years from now? You'd better have a ton of money. Even today, a four-year stint at the most expensive schools can cost $100,000. Ten or fifteen years from now, it will cost far more. It could be more than a quarter million.

What will the dollar be worth in ten years? Nobody knows, but I can say with certainty: less than it is today.

Recently, a seventy-one-year-old client spoke with me about giving his grandchildren money for college. His five children have given him three grandchildren, who are just a few years old. He believes they should have $200,000 each for their education.

"How much would I have to put aside in zero-coupon bonds each year," he asked me, "to accumulate that much money in fifteen years?"

"I can't tell you," I said, "because I don't know how high interest rates will be. Tell me that, and I'll give you an answer."

Well, neither of us could say what interest rates will be. My client was looking at a young child and already projecting fifteen years into the future. The figure he arrived at was $200,000. If you look at the inflation in education, it's not an unrealistic number. It may even be optimistic.

He is wise to plan. In front of me I have an article that appeared in the *Philadelphia Inquirer* on October 14, 1992. Written by John Marcus of the Associated Press and headlined "College Costs Rise Yet Again," it tells a grim story of rising college tuition: "The cost of attending public colleges and universities has increased at a rate triple that of inflation for the second straight year, the College Board reported yesterday." The 10 percent rise in 1992 followed a 13 percent rise in 1991, the article said. The most expensive college was Sarah Lawrence: a year of tuition and room and board there cost $24,380.

The reasons higher education costs are rising far faster than the general rate of inflation are too complicated to go into here. But they underscore two basic points of this chapter:

- Inflation is still with us and can wreak havoc no matter how much money you have.
- It's a factor you must consider when planning and investing.

You can long for halcyon days, if you insist. You can cast a wistful glance toward the penny postcard, or point out that a first-class letter cost two cents to mail in 1900 and three cents in 1950. That was a different world. In 1993, a first-class stamp was twenty-nine cents.

When I was a teenager in the 1950s, I dreamed of making enough money to buy a nice car. The price was modest compared with today's. You could buy a really nice car—such as a Plymouth Belvedere or Chevrolet Bel Aire—for two to three thousand dollars.

In 1968, a friend bought a Cadillac Fleetwood for $10,000. That was about the top price you could pay for an American production car. Nowadays it's much less than the cost of an *average* car. Today's average car costs $17,000, and you have to add another thousand or so in sales tax.

Serious inflation invaded the U.S. economy with the Vietnam War in the 1960s. It has persisted in greater or lesser degree ever since. I see no reason to think we've seen the end of it. Inflation is built into the world economy. All over the world, governments believe that the way to finance their operations—especially in lean times—is to create deficits by borrowing. They'll pay back the debt with cheaper money in the future.

When you're a government, you don't have to balance your checkbook the way an individual does. If you as an individual acted the way many governments do, the banks would close you down. As long as citizens tolerate government deficits, they're almost guaranteeing inflation.

Another factor contributing to inflation in the United States is cost-of-living adjustments (COLA) in salaries and Social Security. Designed to protect people from inflation, they're also a cause of it. The COLA in Social Security alone adds billions of dollars to the government's annual tab.

Staggering population increases around the world are another ominous indicator for inflation. The earth has no more land than ever, but the number of people on the land keeps soaring. And jobs aren't keeping pace.

Japan, even with the declining economy that began in 1991, needs workers. Japanese companies have lifetime employment; they don't let people go. Also, government policy in Japan encourages saving and discourages consumption. The Japanese levy high income taxes, value-added taxes, and other taxes on goods sold. Encouraging saving stimulates the formation of capital and builds industries. It helps governments curb inflation.

But Japan's policies are atypical. The policy of the U.S. government is to spend. Even Republican presidents spend. (You have to admit that both they and the Democrats are good at it.)

Why is the job market in the United States so weak? For decades, we've been moving to a service economy. We've been scaling back industrial production. We're no longer the world leader in technology. And we will not return to an industrial economy. (One exception may be high-definition television, which an article in the *Wall Street Journal* says has the potential to be a multibillion-dollar U.S. industry.)

Other than anomalies like that, the U.S. industrial economy is history. I even wonder whether the dollar should be the world currency. You need a couple of standards, I think, like the yen and the Deutschmark.

That brings me to an example of how American manufacturers contributed to inflation and harmed the American economy. Earlier in the chapter, I mentioned my youthful dream of making enough money to buy a car. In those days, all you thought of buying were American cars. Then came the foreign onslaught.

For two decades beginning in the early 1970s, U.S. auto makers saw their share of the domestic automobile market tumble. The market share held by Japanese manufacturers, such as Toyota, Honda, and Nissan, rose sharply—from 0 in the 1950s to 30 percent in 1992. In the late 1980s, the Japanese companies escalated prices—one reason being the rise in the value of the yen against the dollar. Did American manufacturers take advantage of the opportunity to reclaim some of that lost market share? Did they keep their prices stable and thus more competitive? Not at all. They raised their prices too.

The two worst instances of inflation run amok, however, are higher education and health care. The rise in education costs, which I talked about earlier in this chapter, is a horror. Academia has been unchecked. It lacks accountability. For institutions relying on government and private grants, the flow of money is slowing. That's how we get yearly bills— tuition and room and board—of $15,000, $20,000, $25,000. Students and parents are picking up more of the tab.

Similarly, health care costs have skyrocketed. According to the Health Insurance Association of America, a day's stay in a semiprivate hospital room averaged less than $45 in 1964. By 1989, it had shot up to $637. As the cost of living during that period was increasing fourfold, hospital stays rose more than fourteenfold.

Recognizing that you could lose your job, and recognizing the ever-increasing nature of costs because of inflation, what can you do to make sure you can afford things in the future? You have to invest. And you have to ensure that your money grows faster than inflation.

You'd better count on 5 percent inflation yearly. For the past twenty-five years, that's the way it's been. It could go higher. If you disagree and don't plan for such an increase, you'll find the outcome unacceptable. You don't want to deny yourself food, health care, a good place to live. So it's better to be cautious and err on the high side.

Another reason to be cautious is that you have no control over tax rates. Federal taxes in 1992 were about as low as they'd been in modern times. But I can tell you, they can't stay that way. They'll go higher. And the government is likely to raise the tax on Social Security income. Err on the side of caution. Save more, prepare more. You don't want to fall behind.

A 5 percent yearly rate of inflation may not sound like much to you. But look how it affects prices:

ITEM	TODAY'S PRICE	IN 10 YEARS	IN 20 YEARS
Basket of groceries	$100	$163	$265
Month's rent	$600	$977	$1,592
Automobile	$17,000	$27,691	$45,106
College tuition	$20,000	$32,578	$53,066

In this chapter, I've emphasized two points:

• You must realize that your job is less secure than you think.
• You must guard against the ravages of inflation.

The next chapter tells you when to start preparing. Later chapters tell you how.

5

WHEN TO START—NOW

Portfolios should start at birth.

From decades of advising clients and observing friends and relatives, I know that most people put off making hard decisions. They'll get around to it "tomorrow." Then tomorrow creeps in its petty pace from day to day, and time makes their decisions for them. Don't let that happen. Start managing your money today.

The ideal way to begin investing is to learn it from your parents. A few of my clients are buying stock for their one- and two-year-olds' college educations. Those babies are receiving a head start on sound investment habits.

When my friend Steve had his bar mitzvah years ago, his parents bought him one share of stock. Today a gift like that makes little sense, because brokers' commissions are so high. Many firms have a minimum commission of $75. So the days of giving somebody a single share of AT&T have passed, along with the old AT&T itself.

You don't want your children to have bad teeth or clogged arteries, so you watch what you feed them—not much bubble gum, not many hamburgers at McDonald's. Similarly, parental supervision can develop good investment habits. Along with your physical health, your financial health takes on great importance in your life. You can have a satisfying, well-paying job. You can meet the right person, buy a house, and raise a family. But a shaky financial picture can ruin everything. It can destroy your marriage. It can make you miserable. It can be a constant source of tension and dispute.

Conversely, a strong financial situation lets you do things you might otherwise be unable to: start your own business, travel, retire early, collect rare coins or masterpieces on canvas.

From an early age, I was frugal, a habit I inherited from my parents and my grandparents. They were always savers. Always. By the time I was fifty, I had accumulated enough capital to weather two turbulent storms— neither of which I could have foreseen. The first erupted after my longtime employer, Janney Montgomery Scott, fired me in 1990 under pressure from Donald Trump. I sued both Janney and Trump. I couldn't have afforded to take on the lawsuits without substantial capital. As soon as I hired the attorney, I had to sign a form that put me on the hook to cover the attorney's out-of-pocket expenses, which in major litigation cases can easily top six figures. How many people could do that? Even though I won the arbitration against Janney and settled with Trump, I was responsible for a considerable sum of money. I never could have won my legal victories without having money to fuel the lawsuits.

The second storm was related to the first. After I lost my job, no one in the financial industry would hire me. I had crossed a member firm of the New York Stock Exchange; the industry regarded me as a loose cannon. Who knew what I might do next? Fortunately, with money I had saved over the years, I started my own firm.

As it turned out, then, I had set the course of my life when I was young. For the tendency and discipline to save money for a rainy day, I can thank my ancestors. By instilling good investment practices at your birth, your parents ingrain habits that endure. Before I was ten, I would sit on my grandmother's lap and she would go over the *Wall Street Journal* with me. She explained what she read, and we talked about money.

As a child, you can read annual reports and cash your dividend checks—checks that are your money, even if they go into a college fund. If your parents want you to have financial discipline, they should give you an allowance and let you balance your own budget. When they hand you a dollar, you shouldn't immediately buy something with it. Learn to save.

When I was in elementary school, my parents gave me a couple of dollars a week. At nine, I got my first job; I earned about $6 a week delivering Philadelphia's *Evening and Sunday Bulletin*. For two years I did that, and then I got a job delivering something else—prescription medicines for a drugstore. So I always earned money, and I saved it.

At the Rudolph S. Walton School in North Philadelphia, I enrolled in the Philadelphia Saving Fund Society's banking-for-students program. PSFS, founded in 1816, was America's first savings institution. Its headquarters at Twelfth and Market Streets, built in 1930, stood as the city's second highest skyscraper (after City Hall) and the tallest private building in Philadelphia. I still remember my PSFS account number—S24606—and I still have my original passbook. It has the smiling face of Benjamin Franklin and the words "A penny saved is a penny earned." You'd bring your passbook to school, and you'd make a deposit.

PSFS instituted the program because they wanted children to bank there when they grew up. They advertised, as I recall, "Never a penny lost in 100 years." That was true when I was a kid: they had never lost a penny. In the late 1980s and early 1990s, alas, they lost millions of dollars thanks to imprudent investments. Their stock collapsed, federal banking regulators took them over, and a 175-year-old Philadelphia tradition folded.

Also at school, you could buy savings stamps, which you pasted in a booklet like the ones for S & H Green Stamps. Some saving stamps were red; some green; some red, white, and blue. They all had a Minuteman on them. Save up $18.75 in stamps, and trade your booklet for a U.S. savings bond. Ten years later, the bond would be worth $25.

Student banking programs such as the one at PSFS and the U.S. government's saving stamps were aimed at building a nation of savers. The idea was that children would grow up and save more than 4 or 5 percent of their after-tax income. Unfortunately, the idea failed.

Savings serve as the cornerstone of both individual and national success. That's conventional wisdom, but far too many people disregard it. Wisdom comes hard. When I was in my early teens, I enjoyed lolling in the sun. I used to love to get suntans, though I have fair skin. People warned me, but I didn't listen, and now I have severely sun-damaged skin. When you're young, you don't think things out. Learning from experience—that's wisdom. You don't gain it without going through difficult times.

But I made a conscious judgment when I was fourteen or fifteen: I would save enough money so that if something should interrupt my income, I could take care of myself. That's why I was working when I was nine. I always leaned toward saving money. Although I didn't know it then, I was atypical.

In its November 2, 1992, issue, the *Wall Street Journal* reported that over the past ten years, Americans had saved only 4 to 5.5 percent of their income: "For eight years, in fact, it has been stuck around a measly 4 to 5 percent after-tax personal income. After bouncing up to 5.5 percent in

April, it was 4.6 percent in September. And at that rate, it's far below the double-digit savings rate in Germany and Japan." In Japan, 15, 16, or 1 percent of after-tax income goes into savings. The average Japanese famil has more than $100,000 in savings. Government policy in Japan encou ages saving and discourages borrowing and consumption. Governmer policy in America encourages borrowing while penalizing saving an investment. Americans can't force themselves to save.

So what should you do if you didn't learn to save as a child and you hav barely five dollars in a savings account? How do you break the logjam an become a saver?

You have to make a conscious decision to start saving. First, make sur you've completed the questions in chapter 2 to see how much money yo take in. Now fill in the form below to see how much you have left ove after paying each month's bills.

The form includes the expenses that most people regularly pay. If som of your expenses fall into categories not included on the form, by all mean add them.

And if you don't know some figures (likely to be items you buy wit cash, such as groceries), estimate them for the moment. But to be mor accurate, carry a small notebook with you at all times. For at least two o three months, keep a log of all the cash you spend. Then classify the item: according to the expense form. Revise any of your estimates that proved to be inaccurate.

If you spend more money than you take in, cut back on your expenses I'll show you how in the section "Cutting Expenses" after the chart.

EXPENSE SHEET

(monthly unless otherwise noted)
1. Mortgage payment _____ or rent _____
2. Car payment _____
3. Other loan payments (see profile sheet in chapter 2) _____
4. Utility bills: electricity, gas, oil _____
5. Telephone bill _____
6. Insurance premiums (prorate per month if you pay quarterly or semiannually) _____
7. Taxes (see profile sheet in chapter 2) _____
8. Gasoline _____
9. Groceries _____
10. Clothing _____
11. Medical bills, including drugs _____

12. Parking and other travel expenses _____
13. Car repairs and maintenance _____
14. House repairs and maintenance _____
15. House furnishings _____
16. Jewelry _____
17. Eating out _____
18. Entertainment and recreation (including books, newspapers, magazines) _____
19. Vacation _____
20. Contributions to charity _____
21. Miscellaneous other expenses (such as bank charges) _____

CUTTING EXPENSES

The list above has three parts. Items 1 through 7 are expenses you're obligated to pay. Items 8 through 14 are expenses that are difficult to avoid. The rest are discretionary. You have some leeway in the second group, and considerable leeway in the third. Items in the third group are the first candidates for paring if you must cut your expenses. Items in the middle group come next.

Start with things you can manage without. Stop buying them. I realize that a new ring or watch may make you happy, but must you have it? Will the emotional satisfaction it gives you outweigh the grief that could come later if you have to borrow money for an unavoidable expense when you can least afford it? Will today's pleasure compensate for the hardship that inadequate funds at retirement bring?

I say no. You can learn to go without the "luxuries." These include high-priced clothing and jewelry, costly vacations, eating out, concerts, and magazine subscriptions. I'm not advocating that you deprive yourself of all enjoyment. What I am recommending is that you make saving and investing a higher priority than you make some discretionary items. Perhaps you can cut back, rather than cut out. Shop around for less expensive but high-quality substitutes for luxury items. Don't run the heat or air-conditioning when you're not home. Sound silly or miserly? The dollars add up. Put them all together, and they can make a difference. The experience will also help you start forming prudent habits.

If, despite all your efforts, you somehow cannot reduce your expenses below your net income, you have two choices. (1) Find a higher-paying job—or change careers, if you can. (2) Seek professional help, either from a therapist or a qualified money manager.

I'll talk more about spending wisely in the next chapter.

HOW TO SAVE

Let's say the form shows that you have $100 a month left over after paying all your bills. Or if you've had to cut expenses as I have just outlined, let's say you've reached the point where you now have at least some money left over. Before splurging on an expensive dinner at a fancy restaurant or on a new suit or dress, exert a stern discipline. Every paycheck, set aside $100 and deposit it in a bank or money market mutual fund. When your account totals $1,000, move it to a stock or bond mutual fund ($1,000 is the usual minimum). I'll talk a lot about where to invest it in later chapters. Here we're talking about learning to save now. *Pay yourself first.*

To attract small investors, a few mutual funds let you open an account with a minimum of much less than $1,000. Beyond that, they usually require you to invest a specified sum every month, as little as $25 or $40. Usually the monthly investment must be automatically deducted from your bank account. One such fund is Twentieth Century, 800/345–2021.

Although I find it easy to set money aside for saving, many people just can't do it. One fellow I know earns more than $100,000 a year. He's $300,000 in debt. He can spend money, but he sure can't save it.

YOU HAVE TO PLAN

I admit that life often calls for short-term decisions that run counter to those that affect you over the long term. Whether you're a doctor, a lawyer, or a bank clerk, you have to "pay your dues." But if you have vision and scope your life out over time, rather than just for next week or next month or next year, you can overcome the short-term thinking that plagues most people, who limp from paycheck to paycheck.

When as a teenager in the late 1950s I was interviewed for my first job in the brokerage business, for forty dollars a week, the guy said to me, "You can be a truck driver and make $500 a week. Ten years from now, you'll still be making $500 a week." The point is that you have to plan. You have to think long term.

But your long-term thinking has to begin now. If you've never got into the habit of saving, learn it. If you haven't already done the exercises I outlined in chapter 2 and earlier in this chapter, do them. And then declare: "Okay, I'm going to put $50 or $100 a week into a saving program."

One place for that saving program is an individual retirement arrangement (IRA, often called individual retirement account). If you earn any money at all, you're eligible for an IRA. The contribution to the IRA (up to $2,000 a year) is deductible as long as you (or your spouse, if you're married) have no pension plan at work. The money may not be deductible if either of you has a pension plan and makes more than a certain amount of money each year. I would not recommend using nondeductible IRAs. A good alternative is tax-free bonds or EE bonds, which I will describe later. The earnings compound themselves over the years, tax-deferred.

What sort of saving and investment program should you have? I'm a strong believer in owning common stock. Over time, it's proved to be a powerful hedge against inflation. But when you have limited resources, you shouldn't buy a single stock. A lone stock exposes you to too many risks. For people with very limited amounts of money to invest, I favor mutual funds—but they're difficult to pick. I will discuss mutual funds later. Put your fifty or a hundred dollars a week into a savings account until you have a thousand. Then exert that discipline, using what is called *dollar-cost averaging*.

DOLLAR-COST AVERAGING

With dollar-cost averaging, you invest equal amounts of money in the same investment vehicle at regular intervals—regardless of what happens to the price. For example, the X Mutual Fund is selling at $12.50 a share. Following advice you'll read later in the book, you've investigated and found that the fund is well managed, has performed superbly over at least several years, meets your goals, and has a minimum investment of $1,000 (some funds have higher minimums). With the $1,000 you've saved, you buy 80 shares. Twenty weeks later—by then, at $50 a week, you've saved another thousand—the fund is selling at $11.80. You buy additional shares despite the drop in price. In fact, you can buy more shares than you could before. At $11.80 a share, your $1,000 now buys you 84.746 shares. Another twenty weeks pass, and the fund's share price has risen to $13.05. You send in your thousand and acquire 76.628 shares.

In sixty weeks, little more than a year, you've invested $3,000 and own 241.374 shares. The total value of those shares—at $13.05 each—is $3,149.931. You're already ahead by $149.

THE MIRACLE OF COMPOUND INTEREST

If you think you can't afford to save, you're wrong. You can't afford *not* to save. With inflation and the likelihood that you will face more frequent and higher medical expenses as you get older, you absolutely need money set aside. So set money aside. Realize, too, that starting to save now builds

money more effectively than if you wait even three or five years. Why?
The eighth wonder of the world: compound interest.

Look at what will happen to $1,000 invested in January 1994 at 5
percent and 10 percent annual interest:

	Jan. 1994	Jan. 1996	Jan. 1999	Jan. 2019
at 5%	$1,000	$1,103	$1,276	$3,386
at 10%	$1,000	$1,210	$1,611	$10,835

Now see how much less you would have if you waited two years before
investing:

	Jan. 1996	Jan. 1999	Jan. 2019
at 5%	$1,000	$1,158	$3,072
at 10%	$1,000	$1,331	$8,954

By starting now and investing at 5 percent, you wind up in the year 2019
with about $314 more than if you wait two years before you make your first
investment. (The $314 is 31 percent of your initial investment.) Invest at 10
percent, and the difference amounts to $1,881. That's almost double your
initial investment.

When to start saving? Now!

PART II

PRINCIPLES

6

SAVING VS. SPENDING
VS. BORROWING

Last October, a thirty-one-year-old friend who cuts hair came to me. "Could you lend me fifteen hundred dollars?" he asked. One of his teeth was infected. He had to have the tooth removed and a bridge put in. The matter was pressing. He had to do it, but he didn't have the money. He didn't have $1,500 in the bank.

Some people who earn decent money can't save a penny. They have to have the latest in fashions. Every article of clothing has to bear a designer label. I lent him the money. Someday I'll get it back, I think, but he has to change his habits. I just talked to him and said, "You've got to have discipline. You must start saving."

"Neither a borrower nor a lender be." The familiar advice may be oversimplified, but in principle it hits the mark. In the 1980s, America went on an unprecedented borrowing binge, building an economy on a mountain of debt. Americans wanted to buy, but they didn't have the money. So like Uncle Sam himself, many consumers overextended themselves terribly. Both the nation and its citizens will take years to recover fully.

In chapter 5, I talked about when to begin saving and investing. Here I broaden the discussion to include when to borrow, when to spend—and when to do none of the above. You'll also find material on spending wisely using credit cards sensibly, and shopping for bargains.

BUYING A HOUSE: A TIME FOR DEBT

Never go into debt? That's not what I advise. In some situations, going into debt is okay: for instance, buying a house. How can you acquire real estate without borrowing? Because of the hefty cost, it's not surprising that 99 percent of the people who buy a house must mortgage.

The purchase of a house, though, is not an expense in the usual sense. A house is an asset, one that may or may not increase constantly in value. In 1980, I bought a house in downtown Philadelphia for $115,000. In 1989, its value had risen to $225,000. But I sold it in 1991, unfortunately after its price had dropped—to $170,000.

A CAR CAN COST YOU

Another purchase that can push you into debt is a car. In owning a house, you may have an appreciating asset. With a car, you have an asset that depreciates. Don't go overboard in buying a car because you're enamored of its style or prestige. In this age of TV and advertising, we're constantly pressured to buy, buy, buy.

I'm not saying to avoid buying a new car when you need one. One idea is to buy a one- or two-year-old car from a leading rental company, which constantly maintains and then updates its fleet. These are guaranteed bumper to bumper, giving you a reliable late-model car at a considerably lower price.

My father used to buy a new car every two or three years. But cars today are made better than ever. They can last decades—if you take care of them. It's like maintenance on a house. Keep the roof in good shape, and it will serve you well. Defer maintenance, don't repair that roof, and eventually you'll have beam problems. One way to pamper your car is to change the oil every 3,000 miles. You'll lengthen the engine life and avoid make-your-head-shake repair bills later.

Car care is particularly important given the rise in car prices. My car cost $6,500 new in 1974. Now a new edition of the same car costs $30,000. In the fifties, my father could buy a new Plymouth for $2,500. Today that buys you an accessory package.

When cars cost $2,500 and interest rates hovered around 4 percent, a three-year car loan was affordable. But when cars cost $20,000 and borrowing costs are closer to 10 percent, car buyers often overextend themselves. To keep their monthly costs down, some take out five-year loans. That's too long a term. If you need a five-year loan to make the monthly payment, you've stretched your car budget too far.

My house is about fifteen miles from my office. I take public transportation to work every day. I could drive. But the train ride costs much less than gas, parking, and tolls and is much more peaceful. Sometimes when I see heavy city traffic, I ask myself, Are these people crazy? They're so conditioned to drive. An alternative is available and may even be more pleasant. Still, some people regard driving as a sign of independence. I don't worry about what people will think. If I drive a car that cost $6,500 and my neighbor has a car that cost $25,000, I don't care, as long as my car works reliably and takes me where I want to go.

Remember, the purpose of a car is transportation. If you can't afford an expensive car, don't borrow excessively to be able to make a statement or keep up with the Joneses in the TV sitcom. Be happy with a Honda rather than a Lexus. Eventually, if you start to save and make wise investments, you'll be able to afford the Lexus.

PAYING FOR COLLEGE

A college education is so expensive today that many students have no choice other than borrowing. I've pointed out that 1992 tuition with room and board at Sarah Lawrence was $24,000. That's money paid out *after* you pay income taxes. You have to gross about $40,000 to net the $24,000—and that doesn't cover books and miscellaneous expenses.

Many people benefit from higher education, but you shouldn't view it as any guarantee for your future. After you've spent thousands educating yourself, you may not find a satisfying, well-paying job. Also, not everyone needs a college education. You don't need one to become an auto mechanic, a house painter, or a carpenter. I won't discourage you from getting the best or costliest education, but don't do so just because you think you must.

DO YOU NEED THE LATEST AND GREATEST?

Last week I discovered that one of the broilers in my oven didn't work. It's a Thermador oven and has two broilers, an upper and a lower. I called a repair place, which sent a guy over. He had never worked on a Thermador oven. To pry the oven out from its wooden cabinet, he used a screwdriver. He dented the oven door and made some marks on the cabinet, which is made of cherry. I called the repair place.

"This has to be fixed," I said. "It has to be perfect." It was perfect before the man worked on it.

"Don't worry," they told me. "We're insured." They sent over an adjuster. I had no idea how much the oven was worth, because it was there when I bought the house earlier in the year. The insurance company sent me a check for $4,500.

I told this story to a friend of mine. He said, "You ought to get a Sub-Zero refrigerator with that money. Consider it found money."

"There's nothing wrong with the refrigerator I have," I said. "I'm not going to do that."

My friend's attitude—consume whatever you can—is what I'm cautioning you against. My refrigerator works fine. Why buy a new one just because I received some unexpected money? You have to be prudent. Resist the temptation to live beyond your means.

SHOPPING FOR BARGAINS

My message isn't "Don't buy anything." It's "Spend according to your means." Shop for bargains; many consumers do. A *Wall Street Journal* article in November 1992 reported that many people now go to K Mart to buy their clothes. Another article, about Christmas shopping, quoted a woman who had shopped at Wal-Mart. "Last year I bought these $25 cotton robes that look like $200 robes. I just bought them as gifts for all my friends."

People are shying away from department stores and moving toward discounters. The department store business has taken a tailspin. People are looking for bargains. The mentality seems to be: I won't buy anything unless it's on sale.

I commend that approach. People should think about every penny they spend and not throw money away frivolously, whether in the supermarket, the auto showroom, wherever.

Here's another example. I just got the renewal notice for my home-owner's insurance policy. They had raised the premium. I called three other companies to see what their prices were. After one phone call, I found I could get the same policy and save $70 a year. I'm changing insurance companies.

Some people I know have plenty of money and don't live beyond their means in the sense of buying more than they can afford. But they often pay way too much, either because they enjoy spending money or because they don't care how much they spend. Even if you're like them, and even if I can't convince you to save prudently for the future, don't overpay. You'll have more money left to buy other things you want.

AID TO SMART BUYING

One of the best investments I've made is a subscription to *Consumer Reports*. I read it religiously. It's unbiased, takes no advertising, and does its homework. As a longtime researcher, I find that appealing. Even when I bought the furniture in my office, I did my homework. What do I know from buying office furniture? So I researched products, suppliers, and prices.

Consumer Reports can save you scads of money. Often the highest-priced item is not the best. They'll test, and point you in the right direction. The November 1992 issue, for instance, had a comparison of breakfast cereals. It rated cereals by taste. The best-tasting raisin bran, it found, was none of the national brands. Rather, it was one Consumers Union made up adding raisins to store-bought bran. With packaged cereals, the raisins mixed with grains in the box quickly dry out and become hard. You save money and get a better-tasting cereal in the bargain.

Brand X: Often Just as Good

For decades, Coke and Pepsi have dominated the cola business. But now some store brands taste as good as Coke and Pepsi, or even better, thanks to a dramatic improvement in the product. Yet the store brands cost much less, because their manufacturers don't have the advertising costs that the national titans bear.

Even with orange juice, store brands have made strides. Much of the orange juice sold in this country is made from concentrate. Tropicana Pure Premium and a few other brands are not. Many people, I among them, prefer the not-from-concentrate. Stores have gotten around that too. They now sell premium orange juice at about 50 cents less than Tropicana. You buy Tropicana when it goes on sale or you have a coupon. In the eastern United States, Tropicana, Breyer's ice cream, and Tide detergent are big loss leaders—that is, from time to time, stores drastically cut prices on those products to lure you in.

Of course, if you go to the store to buy something, you rarely walk out with just that item. Once you're in the store, they hope, you'll purchase other items. Every major supermarket, moreover, is laid out to generate the most business. Milk and dairy products, which perish quickly and which you have to replenish frequently, lie at the farthest corner from the entrance.

Also, stores count on and encourage impulse buying. In a change in marketing from years past, the ends of aisles have specials. The super-markets charge some manufacturers for shelf space when the manufacturers want to move huge quantities at a discount. To move items, they'll put them on the ends of aisles.

Coupons attract shoppers. Manufacturers rely on them to gain brand loyalty, introduce customers to new items, and create a sense of bargain. In addition, many supermarkets offer double the face value for manufacturers' coupons.

Unless you hate the time it takes or don't consider the savings to be worth your time, you should devote a few minutes a week to organizing the coupons you receive in the mail and clip from the newspaper. Manufacturers often factor the cost of coupons into their food prices. Unless you use the coupon, you're paying too much. This is especially true of ready-to-eat cereals, where at least half the purchases are made with coupons.

Why Pay Extra for a Little Convenience?

With more and more people working and seemingly having less spare time, a new type of store has cropped up in the last thirty years. This is the "convenience" store, such as Cumberland Farms, 7-Eleven, and, in my part of the country, Wawa. They're like the mom-and-pop grocery stores of the past, except that they're larger, they're usually chains or franchises, and they cater to modern tastes. Most significantly, they charge a considerable premium. I resent that practice and avoid convenience stores except when I need something in an emergency.

GETTING OUT OF DEBT

Joe, a self-employed artist who's forty-four years old, makes too little money to save. In fact, he makes too little money to live comfortably. But he's committed to his career and is willing to limp along with credit card purchases, cash advances, loans from family and friends, and the occasional welcome sale of his work. For the past fifteen years, he's been in debt: $5,000, $10,000, $15,000.

Without a change of tactics, Joe is doomed to perpetuate this pattern. But what will happen when he's too old or sick to work and doesn't have money set aside? Can he afford to write that future for himself?

Beware the Credit Card Peril

A huge culprit in problems like Joe's is that fatal piece of plastic, the credit card. People easily sound the cry of "Charge!" Buy one item on mail order, and you'll be inundated with catalogs. About two months ago, I made a mail order purchase for the first time in my life. Already I'm on a list of a dozen mail order catalogs. A dozen. I got two yesterday.

Do you know how easy it is to buy from these catalogs or to pay by credit card in stores? The bill won't come till weeks later. You grow accustomed to having these goodies; before you know it, you're forty or fifty years old and you don't have any money saved. (God forbid you lose your job.) The habit starts innocently enough. Then it snowballs, and you become mired deeper and deeper.

The 13 percent, 15 percent, 19 percent interest you may be paying on the card is devastating. Surmounting it becomes harder and harder. Like an alcoholic, once you start buying, you can't put the card down.

The best step to take if your debt goes haywire is to cut your credit cards in half and throw them away—the sooner the better. Never go back. For years, people managed without them. I never knew what a credit card was until I was an adult. Today, kids can have ten cards. They're setting themselves up for the trouble Joe got himself in.

Credit card companies make it easy for people to tumble into disaster. I enjoy going to flea markets, and I sometimes see a stand promoting J. C. Penney credit cards. They'll give you a free umbrella, a free packet of candy, or a free set of glassware if you sign up for a Penney's credit card. People sign up because they want the candy. Then all they have to do is use the card once and they fall into bad habits. They don't treat credit cards like money. The darn card is plastic. It doesn't seem like money out of your pocket—until you get the bill.

Then, too, credit card companies abet the hapless consumer in plunging into even further trouble. They let you pay a minimum amount, maybe ten dollars a month, and carry the rest of the balance over—at immense interest rates. As if that weren't enough, they also sock you with administrative or miscellaneous charges.

Although most credit cards offer a grace period—pay for an item within twenty-five days of receiving your statement, and there's no interest charge—you have no interest-free ride if you already had a balance. In other words, if you have a zero balance in February, you can buy $1,000 worth of goods in March, pay the $1,000 statement on time, and you'll incur no interest charge. But if you carry over a mere $25 balance from February and buy $1,000 worth of goods in March, the credit card company will charge you interest on the $1,000 *from the date you made the purchase*. With an outstanding balance greater than zero, you have no opportunity to buy the goods without the high interest charge.

One cause of high interest rates on credit cards is the people who don't pay their credit card bills. Years ago, credit card companies used more selectivity in extending credit. They avoided bad risks. But in the last fifteen years or so, demand has ascended so high that they've accommodated it by lowering their standards. They're making cards available to people with poor credit histories, who never would have qualified before.

The only sensible way to use a credit card is for convenience or emergencies. Use it only when you can pay off the balance immediately. I use a credit card that way; I even buy my monthly transportation pass on it. But I pay credit card bills a week before they're due (my card offers a twenty-five-day grace period), which in effect gives me an interest-free loan. I never carry a balance. Sadly, I'm in the minority. Most people have balances—about $2,000 on average.

Home Equity Loans: Too Much of a Risk

In the tax act of 1989, the federal government took away the privilege of deducting the interest on most loans. The exceptions are mortgages and money that you borrow to make investments that are not tax-free. I advise against one temptation you might have to reduce your debt burden: a home equity loan to consolidate the debt. Because the government has eliminated the deductibility of interest for loans other than investments (such as margin accounts) and houses, many people are consolidating their debt by taking out home equity loans. I recommend a consolidation loan only if it's not a home equity loan—which is a second mortgage on your house. Although a home equity loan sounds all right, it's dangerous. You're putting your house on the line. Don't risk that. Even though you can lower your interest rate with a home equity loan, you're still in debt. You haven't cured the problem. You have to get rid of the debt.

Instead, shop for an unsecured loan that charges a lower interest rate than your credit card. Or shop for a different credit card. You can get a card today that has interest much lower than 18 percent. On some the interest is as low as 10 percent.

LIVING WITHIN YOUR MEANS

I want to stress that it's imperative to live within your means. If you've already shaved your expenses to the bone and are still mired in financial agony, look for a second job. Or change careers. You can't go on living in unrelenting debt. Like my friend Joe the artist, you might not have health insurance. Imagine the disaster a serious illness could wreak.

· If I still haven't convinced you, consider this:

Three Good Reasons to Save
Even If You'd Rather Spend

- To have an emotional and financial cushion.

- So you can buy items when they go on sale rather than wait till later because you have no cash and have tapped out on credit cards.
- So your long-term investments bring you money that you can spend when you're in a stronger position.

7

TAKING RISKS:
WHEN AND HOW

More than twenty-five years ago, my father saw that I was reaping high returns on my investments. He entrusted his investment money to me. Over the years, I put much of it in the stock market and earned him profits totaling hundreds of thousands of dollars. Despite that, he has always been reluctant to invest in stocks. He prefers bank accounts and certificates of deposit.

Some people are uncomfortable with any risk at all. Among them are people

- Who have lost their jobs or fear their jobs are on the line.
- Who have lived through the Great Depression.
- Who have seen neighbors lose their houses because the mortgage company foreclosed.
- Whose friends or relatives have lost a fortune through unwise stock investments.

With money, every action you take or don't take entails some risk. Some are obvious:

- Stock values can drop precipitously.
- Bond prices can collapse in the face of skyrocketing interest rates.
- Real estate prices can plummet because of nearby developments, demographic changes, or natural disasters.
- Life savings hidden under a mattress because you don't trust bankers can vanish in a fire or robbery.

The risk inherent in some financial actions is less obvious. You can put all your money in a bank or savings and loan insured by the Federal Deposit Insurance Corporation (FDIC) or Federal Savings and Loan Insurance Corporation (FSLIC), thinking it's safe. Then the institution fails and you find out that your account was insured only up to $100,000. Or that the principal was insured but the interest wasn't. Or that you will wait months or years to recoup your money.

This chapter shows how to evaluate the risks of investments. It also suggests when you should and should not take risks.

GOVERNMENT BONDS: MORE RISK THAN YOU THINK

The U.S. government borrows money in various vehicles: 90- and 180-day Treasury bills; one-, two-, and three-year notes; and ten-, twenty-, and thirty-year bonds. The people who lend the money are guaranteed to receive a set interest rate for the term of the loan.

U.S. government bills and bonds are often called the world's safest investment. After all, they have the full faith and credit of the United States government behind them. At the end of 1992, of course, that government was $4.2 trillion in debt, and interest on the debt costs the government more than $180 billion a year. But the government doesn't go broke, not in the United States. The government can print money to cover its debts—although the government would rather not, because it stimulates inflation.

What Inflation Does to Bond Values

In October 1992, when annual inflation was running about 3 percent, thirty-year government bonds yielded 7.4 percent. A month later, they yielded between 7.6 and 7.7 percent—that is, the interest rate paid on them was between 7.6 and 7.7 percent a year. Even in as brief a time as one month, their value had changed. Ten years earlier, by contrast, thirty-year government bonds were yielding about 12 percent. If inflation starts to rise, committing yourself to a thirty-year bond at 7.625 could be a bad investment. You *can* lose money on government bonds.

Here's how. It's true that if you buy a U.S. government bond, the federal government guarantees your interest. From the standpoint of guaranteed principal and guaranteed interest, it's about the safest investment you can make. Thirty years from now, Uncle Sam will give you back your $1,000 for every $1,000 you lent him, plus the agreed-upon interest rate. But there's a catch.

No one can predict what the cost of a telephone call or a first-class postage stamp will be thirty years from now. It could very well rise to two dollars. Interest rates fluctuate with changes in expectations about inflation, and the value of a bond is tied to interest rates. It will rise or fall depending on how interest rates fare.

Let's say you own a thirty-year bond paying 5 percent. If interest rates rise to 10 percent, would you be eager to buy a bond that pays 5 percent? You might—but only if you could buy the bond at a discount.

That's how the bond market works. When interest rates go up, bond values fall. Conversely, when interest rates decline, bond values rise.

So, if you have to sell before the maturity in thirty years, you could lose money. The longer the maturity, the more volatile the bond's price because of swings in interest rates. Thirty years means you'll have to put up with considerable changes in the bond's price. For example, if long-term interest rates on a thirty-year bond with a 7.5 percent coupon increase 1 percentage point, the value of the bond would fall almost 11 points, or $110 (each point represents $10 on a $1,000 bond). A 1 percent change on a five-year 7.5 percent bond would produce only a 4-point drop. You must be able to ride out those changes; otherwise you may incur a financial drubbing.

Suppose five years from now you need money and have to sell your bond. If interest rates have risen in those five years, a bond paying 7.6 percent might be much less attractive to buyers than a comparable one paying 12 percent. You would have to sell at a discount: you might get only ninety cents on your dollar. On a bond you bought for $5,000, you might receive only $4,500.

CDs: HOW SAFE ARE THEY?

If you're loath to take any risk with your investments, if your overriding concern is to safeguard every penny and avoid all price volatility, you can come close to meeting those goals. You can confine your investments to insured certificates of deposit (CDs). The federal government insures the principal on CDs up to $100,000 (it does not insure the interest). If knowing that helps you sleep with both eyes closed, fine. But...

Your earnings—the interest your CD brings—could be wiped out by inflation, and taxes can grab what little gain might remain. So even here, you're taking a risk; inflation may erode the value of your savings, and the government may pocket much of your profit. A better hedge against inflation, at least for some of your money, is common stock.

COMMON STOCK: A PLACE IN EVERY PORTFOLIO

Over the past sixty-five years, common stocks have returned an average of 10 percent a year. That figure includes (1) dividends and (2) appreciation in stock prices. Stock prices, however, can shift dramatically over days, weeks, months, and years. As I said in the discussion earlier in this chapter on government bonds, if you have to sell when the price is down, you can get clobbered.

Twice a decade on average, we hit a bear market. Although stock prices generally rose in 1991 and 1992, I can say with certainty that, sooner or later, a bear market will arrive. Instead of going up 25 percent, stocks could *drop* 25 percent. When that happens, cash looks pretty attractive, doesn't it?

The picture is much brighter if you hold a stock for three years or more. To be successful at long-term investing, you have to live with the short-term swings. You hold through the bear markets. Because I'm not smart enough to time the market (few people can with any consistency), I've never been able to buy at the bottom and sell at the top. Remember, it's how well you do that counts, not how well you could have done. Besides, I don't buy the market; I buy individual stocks. Ideally, I'd love to buy cheap and sell high. But as long as a company maintains its fundamentals—good management and good growth prospects—I stay with it. I'm never completely out of all common stocks, but when stocks are priced high, as they are now, I keep a reserve of cash (now 15 percent of my portfolio) to take advantage of friendlier prices in case of a sharp downturn. Try to look at the market as a market of stocks rather than a stock market.

The following chart, courtesy of Ibbotson Associates, shows how the likelihood of increases in stock prices correlates with the amount of time you hold stocks. Hold a basket of stocks for twenty years before selling it, and you're almost 100 percent certain to make money.

STOCK MARKET RETURNS OVER TIME

PROBABILITY OF MAKING MONEY

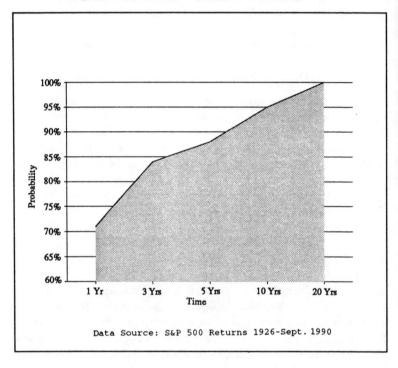

Data Source: S&P 500 Returns 1926-Sept. 1990

Everybody hears stock success stories. If you had bought $10,000 worth of Gap Incorporated in 1983 and sold it in 1992, your investment would have blossomed to $350,000. If you had bought $10,000 worth of WalMart in 1983, you would have seen it grow to $150,000 ten years later. Home Depot went from $1 a share in 1986 to $50 at the end of 1992.

But these are only some well-known examples. Investigate before you invest, and you too can find companies to grow rich with. You have to do your homework and be in the right stocks. For example, if you bought Philip Morris in the early 1980s, reinvested your dividends in the company, and held the stock for ten years, you would have earned seventeen times your investment.

Yet Philip Morris saw a 23 percent decline in the value of its stock in one ading session in early April 1993 after some negative news. The stock is year is down about 40 percent.

HIDDEN RISKS OF MUTUAL FUNDS AND FUND MANAGERS

Because of diversification, mutual funds offer increased safety over ndividual stocks. But mutual funds have several dangers you may be naware of.

When people comparison-shop for mutual funds, the first item they onsider is performance. They'll look at Magellan Fund and see that in the ate 1970s and early 1980s, it was one of the top-performing mutual funds n the country. But mutual funds have turnover—not only in stocks but in nanagers. The man responsible for Magellan's success was Peter Lynch. After Lynch took over in 1977, he beat the S&P 500 index by 20 and 30 percentage points for six years in a row. But that was when Magellan fund was much smaller and had much more flexibility. Today, Magellan is the largest mutual fund, a giant with $26.5 billion in assets. Lynch hasn't run the fund since 1990. Morris Smith, the man who came after him, left in the summer of 1992. You have to look at the management of a fund. Is it run by the same people who achieved superior results? And how did they go about doing that?

Another pitfall: Looking at performance records can be deceptive and self-defeating. Some mutual funds and money managers focus on a single industrial sector. Some, for example, buy only biotechnology stocks. In 1991, biotech was among the hottest sectors. A money manager or fund that focused on biotech stocks might have been able to boast: "For the year, I was up sixty percent." Investors see that and say, "Rubinstein is up sixty percent? Let's give this guy our money."

What they don't know is, Will Rubinstein stay with it or will he jump to another sector? If he stays in biotech, will biotech stay hot?

Investing all your assets in only one sector brings undue risk. Sector funds are okay as part of a diversified portfolio. I believe in diversification. In the early 1980s, some of the best results came from mutual funds that specialized in growth stocks. During the rest of the eighties, they were the biggest losers. "Past performance is no guarantee of future returns," say all the disclaimers. There's no guarantee they'll achieve the same success in the future.

For a while, fund managers who invest in a sector (say biotech stocks) before the sector gets hot can double the general performance of the stock market. But they have to be lucky; they have to be in the right place at the right time. They're taking a heavy risk: after going up, biotech stocks gc creamed.

Remember, stocks can drop in price faster than they go up. That especially likely in a highly speculative market, when stock prices hav been bid up too high. If a company issues a quarterly report that show earnings five cents below street expectations, its stock can fall 20 or 2: percent overnight. During the crash of October 1987, the entire stocl market lost 23 percent of its value overnight. The whole market Overnight.

So ask yourself these questions: How did the fund manager achieve hi: record? Did he do it through diversification? Did he do it by focusing on : hot sector? Will that sector stay hot? Are the same people running the func today? You have to know the answers.

GAMBLING: THE WORST RISK OF ALL

Ever since Resorts International opened in Atlantic City in 1978, I've followed the casino industry. If you don't think stocks are risky enough, casinos are the place for you.

In 1992, while much of the country struggled out of a long recession, the casino industry prospered. Atlantic City casinos racked up record revenues. I have the article (*Philadelphia Inquirer,* December 4, 1992) here: "Players lost $3.007 billion in the first 11 months of the year, the Casino Association of New Jersey reported." It was the first time the casinos' take exceeded $3 billion.

How did they do it? Simple. At the casino, the house wins. Millions of people like to gamble, and they usually lose. The odds say you will lose; that's why there's a casino industry. Would Donald Trump invest hundreds of millions in the Plaza, the Castle, and the Taj Mahal to put money in *your* pocket? The money goes into his. Although the odds are always tilted in favor of the house, we live in a society that not only tolerates gambling but promotes it. State governments encourage people to gamble. "Don't forget to play every day, because you could win any night," a Pennsylvania jingle ran. Lotteries are not a good bet. Payouts are generally in the 40 percent range, considerably lower than games at a casino. And lotteries hurt poor people more than anyone else. While governments criticize casinos, they spend tens of millions of dollars—yes, tens of millions—to induce citizens to buy lottery tickets. As of January 1993, thirty-six states had succumbed to lottery fever. That same month, the New Jersey Assembly was considering whether to legalize betting on football games and other sporting contests.

Unfortunately, gambling can become addictive. Don't think you're exempt from it because you live hundreds or thousands of miles from Vegas or Atlantic City. Strapped state and local governments are investigating gambling as a politically safe way to increase revenues without raising taxes. Besides promoting lotteries, many states are legalizing other forms of gambling. Connecticut permits native Americans to run casinos. Iowa, Illinois, Mississippi, and Louisiana allow riverboat gaming. Louisiana has also approved a land-based casino in New Orleans's French Quarter. Gambling is spreading and may soon be heading to a neighborhood near you. Don't be lured in.

MY FATHER THE RISK-TAKER

Remember at the outset of this chapter, I told you that my father has an aversion to stocks? In 1990, fearing a plunge in the stock market, he asked me to switch almost all his reserves into bank CDs. I didn't like that, but it made him more comfortable. Two years later, interest rates had plummeted. Suddenly, the 7 and 8 percent rates he had been earning on his CDs had dropped to 4 percent, and that was before taxes.

As I say, every move you make with your money brings risk. He decided to do what I had advised him. I thought he should buy some tax-free municipal bonds and collateralized mortgage obligations. I was able to get him at least twice what he was receiving from his passbook account and his CDs.

8

MODEL PORTFOLIO? FORGET IT!

In chapter 7 I talked about the risks of certain investment vehicles. Here I discuss decisions on how to divide your investments. Rather than a model portfolio, which some advisers and financial publications recommend, I give you a way to decide yourself how much of your portfolio to allocate to each type of investment.

A model portfolio suggests specific percentages of your funds to allocate to stocks, corporate bonds, government obligations, bank accounts, and other investments. Anyone who tries to prescribe one is fooling you. Blanket statements about portfolios are folly. There is no magic formula that says unequivocally and without fear of error: "If you're forty years old, earn $65,000, and have $50,000 to invest, put $30,000 of it in stocks, $10,000 in corporate bonds, and $10,000 in certificates of deposit."

You are unique. You could be one of three people sitting at my conference table. All three of you could be forty-two-year-old high school English teachers. You could all earn $50,000 a year. That doesn't make the three of you candidates for the same portfolio. Other factors come into play.

Although your two counterparts may have traits similar to yours, you are a one-of-a-kind mixture of ingredients: age, maturity, point in career, responsibilities, amount of savings, temperament, tolerance for risk, and other factors that determine how you can and should invest.

If you're so ultraconservative that you stash your cash under a mattress, I'd be lucky if I could persuade you to put 10 percent of your portfolio in stocks. If you travel to Atlantic City every weekend and enjoy throwing money on the blackjack tables, I might have to restrain you from putting all your investment money into stocks.

FACTORS TO CONSIDER IN DECIDING YOUR ASSET ALLOCATION

A sensible portfolio varies with circumstances. Only you can determine the asset allocation that's right for you. Important factors to consider are:

- Yearly income
- Expenses relative to your income
- Amount of money already invested and amount of additional money available to invest
- Debts
- Age
- Family situation, including whether you have children who may be heading to college, a mother who will be going into a nursing home, or an Aunt Matilda who may leave you a million dollars
- Health
- Stage in your career
- Tolerance for risk
- Amount of time and energy you want to spend tracking your investments

Age as a Factor

A nonagenarian's portfolio will differ from that of a teenager. I have clients ranging in age from twenty-two to ninety-three. The twenty-two-year-old who goes to graduate school in Denver has 25 percent of his money invested in the stock market. That will change when he graduates and gets a job.

For the ninety-three-year-old woman, I will put up to 25 percent of her money in stocks and 75 percent in fixed-income instruments. Typically, you hear that retired people should take little or no risk with their investments. Young people, you hear, can afford to take more risk.

Not necessarily. One of my clients, Harvey, is a lawyer in his thirties whose wife just had a baby and is expecting another. They're setting up the children's education funds. In the last few months, their situation has changed dramatically from what it was before they got married.

A while back, Harvey called me. "I wanted to tell you that my wife stopped working," he said. "I don't want you to shift away from growth completely, but when you weigh the considerations, just remember that she's not working anymore."

Because the family income has been sliced, he's saying, Let's alter the portfolio. Let's make it less oriented toward stocks that have the potential to grow and a little more toward stocks that produce income the family needs. A single lawyer the same age as Harvey may be much more interested in investments that will grow over time, because he has no family to concern him.

Some Elderly People Can Take Risks

Furthermore, some elderly people may be able to take plenty of risk. At lunch today, I met with two people whose eighty-eight-year-old grandmother lives in a nursing home that charges $60,000 a year. They're two of five grandchildren—between twenty-six and forty-one years old—who will inherit her estate when she dies. The grandmother has more than $2 million in liquid assets, and real estate worth even more than that.

Before the grandmother moved to the nursing home, she was averse to taking risks. She had twenty savings accounts (in those days, banks offered toasters, can openers, and other premiums to new depositors). Seven accounts were at banks within a block of a condominium she owns in Arizona.

Even though the grandmother's money flows to the nursing home at the rate of $60,000 a year, she has more than enough income to keep her principal intact. Because the money will eventually fall to her heirs, I felt that I could manage some of it as if it were already theirs. In my view, it was okay to invest up to 50 percent of it in stocks.

DIVERSITY IS THE KEY

Recently a client called about Roadway Services, in which she owned stock. The stock had fallen from $70 a share to $52 in weeks. "With the stock down so much," she asked me, "maybe we should buy more. What do you think?"

"Definitely, except for one thing. I don't want to put more than ten percent of your portfolio's assets in any one company. I try to keep it at about five percent, for diversification. I like the average portfolio to have between fifteen and twenty stocks."

Diversity is the key to a smart portfolio. Just as putting all your money into stocks is too risky, it's too risky to put all your stock money into one company.

No matter how comfortable or uncomfortable you are with stocks or any other investment, you should never have 100 percent of your assets in one investment, regardless of how safe it appears. Every investment has risk. If you allocate your assets in several places, you spread your risk and increase your odds of coming out all right even if one or several of your investments perform poorly. Look for balance.

A key factor is market conditions. If you can buy a ten-year CD for 14.6 percent, as I did in 1980, why put much money in stocks?

One former colleague in his sixties has about 40 percent of his money in stocks and the remaining 60 percent in municipal bonds and a money market fund. That allocation is fine for him. If he were forty, I would say he should have about 40 percent in bonds and fixed-income investments and 60 percent in stocks.

For many people, a ratio of 60–40 to 40–60 of stocks to fixed-income investments works well. Those percentages are moderate, not extreme. I usually advocate something near a 50–50, 40–60, or 60–40 split. I don't want 100 percent in any one type of investment.

Occasionally I meet with someone who's so afraid of risk that he's uncomfortable investing even 10 percent of his money in stocks. Because of stocks' proven strength as a hedge against inflation, I try to put at least 10 percent of every account in them.

I've told you about my cousin Darlene, who works part time as a bookkeeper. She has an account of about $100,000 with me. Although she can't afford to take much risk because her yearly income is less than $10,000, I wanted her to own some stocks as an inflation hedge. Rather than expose her to the risk of common stocks, I invested 25 percent of her money in convertible preferred stocks of selected companies. Convertible preferreds are hybrids. The dividends are fixed—as in a preferred stock— but if the common stock appreciates, you can convert to the common.

Because I'm monitoring her account closely and understand her situation, I'm running counter to my usual guidelines. Ordinarily, putting only $25,000 of a $100,000 account in stocks would be doing someone a disservice. You can't do much with $25,000; you just don't have the diversity.

STAY WITH YOUR ALLOCATION

Once you and any people close to you have settled on an asset allocation that makes you comfortable and that's sensible—given the amount of money you have to work with, your tolerance for risk, stage of life, prospects, market conditions, and the other factors we've talked about—it's essential to stay with the percentages. Only if circumstances change should you modify them. Just because a broker phones to tout the next "can't miss" stock, don't pull cash out of your bank account to buy it. You should direct future investments according to the allocation you've already settled on.

If you come into $5,000, $10,000, or some other large sum of money from an inheritance, insurance claim, legal settlement, or other source, what should you do? Park the money in a money market mutual fund (taxable or tax free, depending on your circumstances) or other short-term instrument (three- or six-month Treasury bills) until you can decide where to put it. At that point, you can stay with the asset allocation you're happy with, or adjust the allocation if this extra money gives you good cause to do so.

No matter how steady your life may be, you're subject to forces beyond your control. In the next chapter, I talk about how change affects you and how you should deal with it.

9

COPING WITH CHANGE

Once upon a time, IBM was the most glamorous stock on the New York exchange. It marched down Wall Street with the panache of a major in the Easter Parade. IBM hit its peak in 1987, when it sold for $176. In late 1992, over a period of just six months, it had dropped from more than $100 to $49. The bluest of the blue chips got black and blue, suffering a $30 billion or so reduction in market value.

Companies—and people—have to adapt to change. Otherwise they become dinosaurs. It's a new world. The Nikkei Stock Market index in Tokyo falls 3 percent. In seconds, investors know about it the world over. War breaks out in the Persian Gulf, and photos appear on network television within minutes. Events are compressed, and they're all seen live.

Change has been a mainstay of life, but today change comes faster and more dramatically than ever. Events that once took months or years to unfold now sometimes shrink into weeks or days. In 1970, Alvin Toffler wrote a book called *Future Shock*. Instant communication all over the world, Toffler said, means that change occurs much more quickly than ever before. In the nineteenth century, it took a week to send a story from

65

Europe to the United States. With the advent of undersea cables, people could telegraph messages in moments. Then Marconi invented radio, and voices around the globe could be heard instantaneously. Now you have immediate transworld pictures via satellite. Change piles upon change.

There was a time when IBM stock appeared to be heading in only one direction: up. Then IBM faced some unprecedented competition—although it is still the world's leading seller of computers and one of the largest corporations. IBM relied heavily on its mainframe business, which had been highly profitable. Without question, IBM was the world's dominant producer of mainframe computers.

But because of vast leaps in technology and miniaturization, computers have changed dramatically. In 1989, when I was still working at Janney Montgomery Scott, the firm bought me an IBM PS/2 50 desktop computer. It had an Intel 80286 microprocessor and a color monitor. The cost was $5,000. In 1992, I bought an IBM-compatible computer with an 80486 microprocessor and a much higher resolution color monitor. It cost $2,000—and it's far more powerful than the 286.

IBM slipped up in putting too few resources into the software end of the business, which exploded for other companies. Microsoft, which sells the operating system for most IBM-compatible computers, has done exceptionally well. Its founder and CEO, Bill Gates, was a multibillionaire before he was thirty. Intel, the maker of the microprocessor chips, saw its stock rise from $23 in 1992 to $61 in early 1993. You have IBM posting record losses, and Intel and Microsoft showing record profits. The stocks are moving in opposite directions.

IBM's story is a classic example of what can happen to a company that doesn't adapt to change. Other examples of once-dominant companies that fell are General Motors and Sears Roebuck. In 1980, Sears was the undisputed leader in the consumer retail business. But through the turbulent eighties, Sears removed its fingers from the pulse of the American shopper. WalMart surpassed Sears in sales and enjoyed record earnings. Its stock has done exceptionally—rising from 60 cents in 1982 to $33 in 1992. Sears saw its leadership position drop sharply, and its shareholders have not done nearly as well as the market.

THE COMPANY IS NOT ALWAYS RIGHT

Every company has to be in touch with the public pulse and the direction of its competitors. Companies can't make the same old product and expect to be successful forever. As Toffler said, changes, instead of taking a decade, can occur in one quarter. This is especially true in the electronics industry.

When a company expands, it can become so multilayered in management that senior executives lose sight of what's going on. Because of the layers of hierarchy and bureaucracy, larger companies often lack the agility to make decisions and changes as quickly as some smaller companies. In this way, behemoth companies can fall behind.

It wasn't many years ago that Eastman Kodak had about 90 percent of the photographic market. Now such companies as Fuji are making inroads on Kodak's market share, and who knows whether we'll even be using film in the twenty-first century? Film may still exist, but most people may be using electronic imaging. Massive changes in the photographic industry are occurring and will continue to occur. Which company will be on the cutting edge?

A difficulty that companies in some heavy industries face is the length of time it takes to bring products to market. If General Motors starts to design a new car today, it won't even know for three or four years whether or not it has a product that consumers will like—because of the time needed to design and manufacture. Yet even that lead time has been compressed. Japanese auto makers have said it doesn't take four or five years to develop a car. They say you can do it in three years. The domestic auto makers have also shortened the time.

COMPANIES, LIKE PEOPLE, CHANGE

Many of the thirty companies that composed the Dow Jones Industrial Average in the 1920s are not in the Dow today. Some no longer exist. Companies merged. Companies went out of business. Companies got dropped from the Dow. Industries that didn't exist in the twenties arose. The railroads were the growth industry in the twenties. Then came the airlines. More recently, biotechnology companies.

Environmental awareness put an end to some companies. Johns Manville had a thriving operation, but then the world discovered the hazards of asbestos. Johns Manville was on the receiving end of a lot of lawsuits. Then you have A. H. Robins. It was a big drug company, but it came up with a bad product, the Dalkon Shield, a type of intrauterine device (IUD). Multimillion-dollar legal judgments knocked the company out.

As an investor, you have to differentiate between the IBMs of the world, which are going through rough times but have the resources to adapt, and precarious companies like Manville and Robins. You yourself also have to be able to change. As I've said, the portfolio of a twenty-two-year-old who's just graduated from college will be entirely different from that of a sixty-two-year-old. If you're forty today and begin planning for when you're sixty-two or sixty-five, you must realize that the rules may change.

You may be counting on receiving Social Security, but twenty years dov the road, if people live longer, maybe Social Security will kick in seventy. You have to be able to shift gears and change your investme strategy with your changing circumstances: marriage, divorce, illne: education, all types of life experiences.

VACILLATING INTEREST RATES

In the early 1980s, interest rates were unusually high. I bought some te year CDs with a 14.6 percent yield. I wanted to lock up as much money I could for ten years, because I didn't expect rates to stay that high. I kne I would do very well.

With CD yields almost 50 percent higher than the 10 percent avera stock yield, why take risks in stock? With a federally insured CD, y know you'll get your money back. You may not get your money back w stocks. Even with the 2.9 percent CDs available in early 1993, you kne you'll get back your principal.

When CDs reach astronomical levels, it pays to lock them up for years as long as your bank remains in business. If your bank fails and is tak over by another, the new bank is obligated to pay your principal and interest that accrued to the point of the takeover. Federal law does require it to pay the old interest rates from that point forward.

When interest rates are low, you take a different approach. In ea 1993, money market yields fell below 3 percent. In effect, that's a negat return on your investment. Inflation can eat up all of the increase a more. Taxes take a bite too.

But long-term rates—thirty-year Treasury bonds—showed much l change. They began 1993 yielding 7.4 percent. That was identical to yield that thirty-year bonds offered at the beginning of 1992. Long-te rates didn't move much, because people were still reluctant to lend mor out for long periods at locked-in rates. They didn't believe that inflati was dead, and I didn't either.

STOCK MARKET JITTERS

The stock market does not tolerate uncertainty. In the face of changi markets and increased competition, how would IBM's profits fare? Tl uncertainty sent IBM stock into a tailspin. When a company says, "If hadn't taken these writeoffs in the fourth quarter, we would have brok even. And we really can't see any improvement in the first quarter, a who knows when we'll get back on track?" that's a troublesome messa for the market. It's why IBM stock lost half its value in a few months' tin

Like sheep, people on Wall Street usually follow the herd. Take money managers who work for a pension fund or a mutual fund. They all want to outperform the market, but deep down their number-one motivation is job preservation. When a company like IBM announces bad news in October, many fund managers pull the plug. They sell. In December, IBM announces another round of writeoffs, which creates even more uncertainty, and the market dumps much more of the stock. Money managers find it easier to admit making a mistake because everybody else has made it than to have acted individually, on their own.

IT'S A SMALL WORLD

Worldwide, uncertainty is the norm. But some places and times are more uncertain than others. The upheaval in Eastern Europe and the breakup of the Soviet Union in the late 1980s and early 1990s brought massive changes to the continent and to the rest of the world. The changes included not only uncertainty but opportunity.

In 1992 we began seeing American companies make major investments in Eastern Europe. Philip Morris, for example, bought tobacco companies in Hungary and other countries. CPC International bought small food companies in the Eastern Bloc. The Pan-European market has about 400 million people, which dwarfs the United States. Change brings dislocation but also tremendous opportunity.

Markets are becoming global and highly interdependent. Years ago, when the United States got a cold, Europe would sneeze. Now other countries often take off on their own. Germany and Japan went into recession in 1992, causing havoc around the world. People and countries are all reliant on one another. The United States is a big exporter and a big importer. So are Japan and many other countries. News that Japan's economy is slowing affects thinking around the globe.

In Japan, specifically, another trend is happening. After World War II, Japan was flat on its back—virtually a bankrupt country. Now it's a world leader. Over the years, Japan's economy has grown because its focus was on increasing Japanese companies' share of the market. For years, the Japanese did not worry about the bottom line. Pricing items such as VCRs and televisions very low, they attracted millions of buyers. They figured that if they increased market share, the bottom line would eventually take care of itself. Even though their margins were small, as long as companies were producing full tilt and kept on growing their market share, they would knock competing companies out.

Beginning in the early 1990s, that thinking reversed. For the first time since its ascendance, Japan began seeing deficits. The Japanese shifted gears: the focus is no longer on market share but on bottom line. What does that mean? Prices go up. Look at Japanese automobiles, and you'll see they're no longer cheap. They're more expensive than American cars. In 1975, by comparison, the Toyota Corolla was the least expensive car sold in America.

How do you as an individual investor deal with all this upheaval? How do you buffer yourself against all these changes? Stay with companies and investment products that you know and understand. Keep away from foreign companies unless you feel totally familiar and comfortable with the world currency situation, the environment foreign companies operate in, and the products they sell. In chapter 16, I show you how to evaluate companies and how to find opportunities amid the goods and services you know best.

DODGING THE HERD

As an investor, be wary of following the herd. When the market soured on IBM in 1992, I was buying it. Why? The company has many good points. It sells high-quality, dependable products. It has some of the most talented research and product development people in the electronics industry. It still has a strong balance sheet.

Can the company adapt? I think it can. I believe that IBM will be able to make the shift and be a strong company again. I bought the stock at less than half what it had been. At its peak, adjusted for splits, IBM stock was $176 a share. I bought it aggressively when the price dropped into the 50s. That might have been the best opportunity to buy IBM in thirty years.

When I came into this business, 80 percent of stock transactions were done by individuals. In the past thirty years, that has shifted completely. Now institutions dominate market activity. Every time you see volume on the New York Stock Exchange of 150 million or 200 million shares, 80 percent of that or better is institutional investors—primarily pension funds and mutual funds.

The change opens an avenue for the individual investor who thinks long-term. The herd instinct is short-term-oriented. Long-term thinking can create tremendous opportunity for you, as it did for some in the massacre of IBM. If you believe that a company makes great products, has solid research and a strong financial outlook, and if you believe in the company over the long term, you buy.

Most institutional investors, and many individuals, look only as far as the next quarter. (So do many companies.) If a company is performing poorly now, they get out. They don't care that the fundamentals are intact or that the management is first-rate. I'm the opposite. I don't care about the next quarter. I knew that IBM might not have a good earnings stream for a year or two. But I believed that the company's earnings stream would get a lot better, so I bought the stock at depressed levels. Bernard Baruch, investor extraordinaire and financial adviser to presidents, said, "The time to buy is when everybody else is pulling the plug." You'll never know when you've hit bottom until things have turned around, but so what? As someone said to the cowardly lion on the way to Oz, you need courage.

PART III

CHOICES

10

YOUR OWN MONEY MANAGER: TO BE OR NOT TO BE?

The award came to a million dollars. Nanette, who was all of nineteen and had never made more than $15,000 a year in her life, suddenly possessed a fortune from a legal settlement of a malpractice suit against her doctor. Yet because she doesn't trust anybody, she put the entire sum in the bank. She thinks everyone is trying to rob her of her money.

No question that she *should* be careful. People are coming out of the woodwork and calling her—stockbrokers, bankers, financial planners. When the world knows you've come into money, it marks you as prey. Relatives, old friends, and perfect strangers turn chummy.

Because Nanette trusts no one but herself, she is, in an odd way, a candidate to be her own money manager. But by being so cautious, she's not managing her money at all. She's mismanaging it.

By chance, she picked the right Philadelphia bank. CoreStates is a solid institution. But suppose she had put the million in PSFS just before it went under? She could have lost $900,000—all but the $100,000 the account was insured for.

Put yourself in her place. You've read stories about money managers embezzling movie stars' money and flying to Brazil. You're worried. You never had anything, and now you have a million dollars. You want to keep it. Preservation of capital is one of the most important priorities in managing portfolios. Appreciation is important, but preservation is paramount. In most cases, it took clients a long time to accumulate their money. I want to make sure they don't lose it.

So what should this nineteen-year-old do? Whom should she believe? She talked with me about the possibility of becoming a client. It happens that I've been managing her employer's money for six or seven years, first at Janney and now at Roffman Miller—and he seems satisfied with my services. Another fellow, who does a lot of business with the firm Nanette works for, has had me managing his money for twenty years. He's told her about me too. But she's been slow to come around. Meanwhile, the bank gets rich on her money. What should she do? If you were in her position, what would you do?

With a million dollars—with much less than a million dollars—the issue of how to handle your funds is crucial—and causes anxiety. It could be why you're reading this book. So read on for advice on deciding whether or not to be your own money manager.

TO BE OR NOT TO BE

First answer these questions:

- Do you enjoy changing the oil in your car?
- If you need a new washing machine, do you spend time in the library checking product reviews? Do you comparison shop to see who will give you the best value for your money?
- When your monthly bank statement arrives, are you eager to reconcile it?
- Do you follow the business news?
- When the financial pages show that the stock you sold three weeks ago at $11^5/8$ rose yesterday to $14^1/2$, can you smile instead of thrashing yourself?
- Looking at lists of stocks and bonds, can you figure out what to buy—and what not to buy?

- Can you assess your moves coolly and rationally, free of emotion?
- Can you change gears when your situation changes or when the economy shifts or goes haywire?

If you're the roll-up-your-sleeves type and answered yes to these questions (even if you answered no to changing your oil—it's a dirty, messy business), you might be a candidate for managing your money.

If you loathe comparison shopping, if you're as eager to reconcile your checking account as you are to speak with a life insurance salesman, if thinking about money makes you queasy, if you like handing a problem over to somebody else and just paying the bill, you're probably better off entrusting your money management duties to a professional. In the next chapter, I talk about how to choose one.

HAVE A MILLION DOLLARS?

When you have as much money as Nanette came into, my view is that you should have it professionally managed. I feel that way even if the amount is $100,000 or $150,000. With that much money, you have a lot to lose. Granted, I'm a professional money manager, so I have a bias in the direction of hiring a professional.

WHEN TO DO IT YOURSELF

When you have a relatively small amount of money to invest, say $5,000 or $10,000, should you do it yourself?

You might think there are two reasons to manage money yourself:

1. You love to do it, or
2. You can't afford a professional.

The truth is, you can afford a professional. If you're investing in a mutual fund, you *are* paying for and getting professional money management.

If you're leaning toward taking the responsibility yourself, can you live with your mistakes? I guarantee that you will make some. Even the most seasoned experts do. I certainly have.

The key is to live with your mistakes, minimize any damage they cause, learn from them, and move on. Don't get emotional. You want to express

your emotions? Join a local theater. Keep emotions out of your investing
Investing takes a cool head.

Here are actions you'll be taking if you serve as your own money
manager. After the list, I'll discuss each in turn. Do they appeal to you?

- Settle on your portfolio allocation. In chapter 8, I
  talked about determining how much of your
  portfolio you should put in stocks, how much in
  bonds, how much in such fixed-income instruments
  as CDs. This is the first step in managing your own
  money.
- Decide when to buy and sell.
- Select stocks or stock mutual funds.
- Select bonds or bond mutual funds.
- Know when to change gears.

DO YOUR HOMEWORK

Doing it yourself is okay, but I always say, Do your homework first. One of
your main tasks, if you want to invest in individual companies, will be to
decide which companies. I speak about selecting promising companies in
chapter 16. Look around. If you go to a Home Depot or a Gap store and see
that it's vastly better in design, execution, and service than competing
stores, you might have a find.

If you think you might like to invest in the company, you can request
information. You'll find the company address at your local library; ask the
librarian for help if you can't locate it on your own. *Thomas's Register* lists
many American companies, and other source books also have addresses
and phone numbers.

Write to the company and ask for the last three annual reports and the
last four quarterly statements. You get a feeling about a corporation by
reading the reports and seeing how the company is progressing. They go to
a mass audience and are written in relatively simple language that most
people can understand.

Most lay people won't understand a balance sheet, but the glossy
publications are things you can follow. Annual reports include graphs on
almost everything. From these graphs, you can see whether the company's
earnings have been rising or falling. Then you can go a step further. I
always ask for reports, called 10Ks and 10Qs, that are filed with the SEC.
These are more in-depth evaluations, don't have pictures, and aren't

rinted on slick paper. The 10Ks and 10Qs will give you some additional understanding.

What do you look for? Avoid companies that have more current liabilities than current assets. Look at how much cash the company has and how much debt. Then look at the shareholders' equity or book value—that is, total assets minus current and deferred liabilities and long-term debt. To me, a company whose capitalization is 60 percent in debt is highly leveraged. Many companies are even more indebted—70, 80, 90 percent debt. You should stay away from companies like that.

Then again, you have to look at the industry. Some industries are capital intensive. They need huge outlays of capital to keep going. Other industries are service-oriented; they don't need shipments from Fort Knox to supply their working capital. The average layperson won't know all these things. Few people can know them. You can only know them from years of experience or studying or doing accounting. But if you feel conversant with the material, you may very well choose to take on the task yourself.

STOCKHOLDER MEETINGS

As an analyst, one way I research companies is to meet with management and other employees of the company—from the CEO at the top to the floor sweeper at the bottom. You probably won't have many chances to meet face to face with the management of a company you're thinking of investing in, but you can do just that by going to the annual meeting. You can focus on companies near your home. At least once a year, you can meet with management by attending the annual meeting.

If you're thinking of buying a food stock and live in the Philadelphia area, as I do, you'll find Campbell Soup right across the Delaware River from Philadelphia in Camden, New Jersey. Company managers meet once a year with stockholders.

GO TO THE LIBRARY

Library research is another approach. I know of one man who became a full-time investor around 1980, after he retired from his job with a New Hampshire utility company. He spent hours at the library every day, reading news and business magazines, poring over annual reports, thinking about what new products might succeed. His research led him to

G. D. Searle, makers of Nutrasweet, a substitute for sugar. This fellow, who was in his sixties, invested thousands of dollars in Searle before Nutrasweet hit the market. He, in turn, hit the jackpot.

BUY HIGH-QUALITY BONDS

When you buy bonds, buy high quality. Inexperienced investors should not buy junk bonds. Don't seek unusually high yields; that entails too much risk. The purpose of a bond is secure, above-average income. So you should stay with quality. I like to buy only investment-grade bonds, those rated triple-B plus and higher. I don't want to go lower than that.

I also feel that a lay investor should hold a bond—not trade. Trading bonds is for professionals. Frankly, the chances of making money by trading bonds are slim. When I say making money, I mean improving your situation, because at any given time, a triple-A bond will have a certain yield. The only way you can get better yields is to go down in quality and take higher risk.

If you have $5,000 and want to buy a bond, be prudent. In early 1993, because inflation was low (although I didn't think it was dead), I didn't want to lock up money for thirty years. So I bought short-term bonds, with three- to seven-year maturities.

One of the last great tax shelters available today is tax-free or municipal bonds. I'm a strong believer in tax-free bonds, but only for people who are in the higher federal tax brackets—28 percent or above. (Proposals are on the table to increase the tax brackets even higher.) Some of these are triple tax-free: exempt from state, local, and federal taxes. If you're in the 33 percent federal income tax bracket and live in a state that has a 2 percent income tax and in a municipality that has a 1 percent local income tax, you would ordinarily pay 36 percent (33 + 2 + 1) on your investments. A tax-free bond would spare you those taxes. Tax-free bonds have lower yields than taxable bonds, but you often come out ahead. Here's how.

A 5.2 percent tax-free bond provides the same income as a taxable bond paying 7.8 percent. Let's say you invest $5,000 at 7.8 percent. After one year, your earnings will be $390. If you're in the 33 percent bracket, you'll pay $130 in taxes and be left with $260. If you invest $5,000 in a tax-free bond paying 5.2 percent, you'll receive $260 in earnings after one year and pay no taxes. If you invest in a tax-free bond paying more than 5.2 percent, you'll come out ahead.

If you're in a 15 percent bracket, on the other hand, you're better off buying taxable bonds. The tax savings you would get from tax-free bonds when you're in the 15 percent bracket are less than the greater interest paid by taxable bonds.

YOUR PORTFOLIO: COPING WITH CHANGE

As I've said, if you're sixty-five or older, you want a much higher percentage of your portfolio to be in bonds than somebody who's twenty-five years old. But in times of low interest rates, I tell clients not to go long-term. Stay relatively short-term, so that as these bonds mature, you can move money into longer-term bonds and then lock up the higher yields. Don't commit a lot of money to low-yielding long-term bonds. Even if it looks as if interest rates have bottomed out, you don't know that at the time. In 1993, CD yields dropped to below 4 percent and home mortgages to less than 7 percent. People hadn't seen such low interest rates since the 1960s and thought they'd never see them again. So who knows? Over the short term, no one has been consistently accurate in predicting where interest rates are headed. The best market experts don't know.

I've yet to meet a one-handed economist. Economists are always saying, "On the one hand this, and on the other hand that." Because people don't know where interest rates are going short-term, and because they don't know where the stock market is going short-term, I think long-term investors should invest mostly in stocks. I'd be a long-term investor in bonds if yields were much higher than they were in early 1993. But I don't believe that the 3 percent inflation that prevailed at that time was indicative of what inflation would be over the next five or ten years. The rates people were seeing then were anomalies.

That's why you have to be adaptable to change. As inflation increases, you may want to shift your portfolio and lock more money into bonds if yields are high enough.

You can buy a bond from a broker. You can buy U.S. savings bonds directly from your bank. I advocate buying bonds directly, rather than through a bond fund. (Although if you have only $2,000 or so, you're almost forced to go with a fund.) You need at least $5,000 to buy bonds directly. Otherwise, the commissions and other costs will eat up too high a percentage of your investment. If you have only $2,000 or $3,000, stick with bond funds, preferably closed end (see chapter 18).

Deciding whether to invest in stocks or bonds is perhaps not as tough as it sounds. If you're a young person building a portfolio, chances are you're interested in growth. If you're on the eve of retirement, when income is more important than growth, you already have more than $5,000. If you don't, you're in trouble. So most people who have a bond portfolio probably have more than $5,000 at their disposal.

TO BE YOUR OWN MANAGER OR NOT TO BE:
A SUMMARY

Having read all I've had to say, do you think you can perform as well as a professional, who devotes full time to the endeavor? Realize, for example, that Vanguard's Index 500 Fund, which is not managed at all, outperformed 70 percent of all managed funds over the past ten years. You can take that either way. You might conclude, "Well, I could hardly do worse." Or you might think, "Gee, if only 30 percent of the pros could beat the market, what makes me think I can?" Even if you think you can, is it worth your time and the stress you'll have to put up with?

In summary, here are a few questions to answer in deciding whether to be your own money manager:

- Do you have less than $5,000 to invest?
- Are you comfortable making your own investment decisions?
- Do you recoil at the idea of turning your money decisions over to someone else?
- Would you know how much of your portfolio to allocate to stocks? To bonds? To cash? To other investments?
- Unlike people who second-guess their decisions, can you move forward dispassionately?
- Do you remain calm when you find out that if only you had done something sooner (or later), you would have been much better off?

If you answered yes to most or all of these questions, you're a good candidate to manage your own money. Skip the next chapter and delve right into chapter 12. There I begin my discussion of what to do with your money. If you answered no and would rather entrust the money to someone else, turn to chapter 11 before reading the rest of the book. In chapter 11 (not the chapter 11 of bankruptcy, mind you), you'll find out how to select a professional money manager.

11

SELECTING AND WORKING WITH A MONEY MANAGER

It was a $900,000 account that Jacob handed me last week to manage. He had done his homework. Sitting at my conference table, he showed me his Philadelphia yellow pages and its listing of "Investment Advisory Service." Next to every adviser listed, he had a check mark. I don't know whether he had met with all of them, but he had called every one.

A broker at a local firm had telephoned Jacob, trying to secure the account. Jacob told the broker, "I've given it to Roffman Miller." The broker, whom I know well, called me and said, "Did you know that Mr. Jacob went to at least twenty different money mangers before he selected you? That should really make you feel good."

I tell this story to point out how one man went about what I consider a smart way to find a professional to manage his money. Because of your range of choices, the task is not easy; there are eighteen thousand money managers in the United States. If you, like Jacob, are looking for a money manager, you too should do your homework. This chapter is where you learn how: how to find a money manager, how to see whether you and the manager are compatible, how to work with the manager, and what other steps to take to ensure you're well served.

HOW TO FIND A MONEY MANAGER

As with other types of service professionals, such as doctors and lawyers, the best way to find a money manager is by word of mouth. Where do you get references? You can get them from:

- Bankers
- Accountants
- Brokers
- Lawyers
- Friends, relatives, and coworkers
- The yellow pages of your local telephone book

After starting our firm, my partner Peter Miller and I met with more than a dozen law firms and accounting firms in Philadelphia and told them our story. "We're conservative, long-term investors," we said. "If you come across someone you think we can help, please let us know." We've gotten business that way. We also have a listing in the yellow pages.

WHAT TO FIND OUT

Once you've put together a list of potential managers, call to find out a little about them. Ask:

- The minimum amount of money they'll take for an account
- How many clients they have
- Their investment philosophy: short-term, long-term, conservative, risky
- How often they change investments
- Whether you will deal with the principals or underlings
- Transaction costs
- Where they get their research
- How they make their money: from fees based on a percentage of money under management, percentage of profits, or some other arrangement

Call a manager whose praises others have sung—even if you don't think the manager is right for you—because secondhand reports are sometimes inaccurate. Yesterday we had a referral from an accounting firm. A woman called and said, "I'm a little nervous about the stock market, but I'm a strong believer in bonds. I understand from my accountant that you guys don't know anything about bonds."

"Absolutely wrong," I said. "Of the money we manage, probably more than half is in bonds. So, no, we are strong believers in bonds. It happens that right now we're not buying long-term bonds, not with rates like these."

She said, "Why don't you send me some information?"

Ask to speak with the principals who manage the money. Screen them. Ask: "What is your investment philosophy? What are you trying to do?" If they start boasting, ask for their record. If the record they boast about sounds fabulous, ask who ran the money when they achieved that record. Are the same people running it now as ran it then? Continuity is vital. You don't want to entrust your money to a company that's constantly changing portfolio managers or strategies.

Once you've done your initial screening by phone, make appointments to visit your top three or four candidates. Deal with them as if you're dating—as if you're seeking a mate for life.

Ideally, a relationship with a money manager, like a good marriage, should be long-term. The worst action you can take is to hop from one manager to another to another. If you do that, your portfolio keeps changing and your chances of making good money are slim.

Generally, after speaking with three or four managers, you should have a pretty good idea of who's right for you. If you don't feel comfortable after meeting with three or four, speak with as many as you need to before you start feeling comfortable.

BEWARE OF "FINANCIAL PLANNERS"

Watch out for "financial planners." (In some states, they are registered or certified.) Many financial planners are really insurance salesmen. They sell annuities, whole life insurance, and other products. The commissions on these products are usually very high. That's another conflict of interest: the salesmen can make big money by selling you something you may not need or want. You should buy insurance for protection, not as an investment. I talk about insurance in chapter 22.

Keep away from people who have these potential conflicts of interest. How can you tell who they are? You have to ask:

- "Do you participate in commissions at all?"
- "Are you licensed to sell insurance?"
- "Do you sell other products?"

A yes to any of these should raise a red flag. And if the person follows up with a sales pitch, look elsewhere. The proper relationship, I believe, is between an investor and a money manager who earns money from only one thing: *service*.

HOW DO THEY CHARGE?

Some money managers, including me, charge an annual fee based on a percentage of money under management. Generally, the fee is about 1 percent. Let's say you give the manager $125,000. Your yearly fee would be $1,250.

Compare that with a mutual fund. When you buy a mutual fund, you're hiring professional money managers, but your account is not custom tailored. You have no interaction with the managers, and you as an individual don't enter into the equation. Still, you pay the mutual fund a fee. The people who run the fund charge a management fee.

Management fees at mutual funds range from about 0.5 percent at Vanguard, which is one of the lowest, up to about 2 percent. Mutual funds also charge for the expenses of administering the fund and transaction fees. In total, the average mutual fund in the United States charges 1 percent plus expenses—the fund manager's salaries, heat, rent, electricity, promotion, publishing, and other costs of running the fund.

Independent money managers are on the same side as the investor. They have an incentive to keep transaction costs low, because costs affect performance. The less the transaction costs, the more money there is to manage. With some managers, the combined cost—management fee and transactions—is about 1.25 percent. That compares favorably with a mutual fund. It's like getting a custom suit at a rack price.

BEWARE OF MANAGERS WHO CHARGE A PERCENTAGE OF THE PROFITS

Some money managers charge on a different basis: a percentage of the profits. These managers typically charge you 20 percent of the yearly increase in the value of the account. No matter how much the account is worth at year end, your fee is based on the increase in the value of the account. If, for example, you had a $100,000 account at the beginning of the year and it is worth $110,000 at the end of the year, you pay the manager $2,000 of the $10,000 profit. If there's no profit in the account or a loss, you pay nothing.

I think that approach is problematic. It tends to do two things. One, it encourages the manager to take more risk, putting a higher priority on performance than on capital preservation. Two, it tends to increase your costs. If your managed investments do as well as the average stock— increasing in value 10 percent a year—you pay a 2 percent fee (20 percent of 10 percent) on the total value of the account. For average performance, you're paying double the average fee that money managers charge.

FIND A MANAGER YOU'RE COMFORTABLE WITH

Some money managers enjoy taking risks and turning over their portfolios frequently, trying to time when to buy and sell. Others invest for the long term. They look for stocks that have good potential for growth over a period of three to five years or more. These managers buy and sell infrequently.

Which type more closely matches you? Do you walk around with the *Wall Street Journal* in your back pocket and call your broker a half dozen times a day? If so, you'll never be happy with a conservative, long-term manager like me. Nor am I for investors who want frequent trading. Why? These people like action. They're like the folks who play the slot machines. They know they won't win, but they enjoy playing. Similarly, I've met people who can't make any money in the stock market. But they get pleasure from making trades and acting on all kinds of strategies.

My friend Norman is a perfect illustration. A brilliant fellow, one of the smartest people I know, he must have an IQ of 150. Norman worries about the cost of a postage stamp, but I've been with him to Atlantic City and seen him bet hundreds of dollars on a hand of blackjack.

Sometimes I take him to meetings with company management that I'm invited to. If the president of a company impresses Norman with a presentation, he'll buy the company's stock. At any given time, he may have a $100,000 account with twenty stocks—too many for him to track. What's more, he trades frequently. He buys and sells stock options.

I help Norman with advice. He listens, but he has to make trades himself. We've had this arrangement for twenty years. The long and short of it? His long-term performance is far from ideal. Still, he enjoys making the picks himself. He gets a thrill from playing.

Norman would love a money manager like Marty Zweig. There's action. Zweig, who also runs the Zweig group of mutual funds, is a market timer. He buys and sells frequently. He may have an annual turnover rate of 200 percent. That is, in the course of a year, he averages two purchases and sales of every stock in his portfolio. Yet I consider Zweig a genius. He has produced spectacular results.

Are you investing for the long term? Or are you looking for quick hits? Pick a manager whose philosophy matches yours. Choose someone you have a rapport with. You should feel comfortable with your money manager.

If you must have action all the time—the hot thing, the latest thing— fine. You can find managers like that. Most people, though, have worked hard for their money. They want to protect it. They want a conservative manager, and diversification. No money manager will be right all the time—not Marty Zweig, not Peter Lynch, not me, no one. If we were, as my partner Peter Miller says, we'd all be at the beach.

HIGH TURNOVER MEANS HIGH TRANSACTION COSTS

Actively traded portfolios produce higher transaction costs. Remember, every time you buy or sell a stock, you pay a commission. The higher the turnover, the higher the commission. For small individual investors, commissions can average about one dollar per share. That cuts heavily into your profits. For large money managers, commissions can be as low as three to five cents a share.

You can avoid transaction costs by buying stock directly. Some companies offer a way to buy their stock without going through a broker. I'll talk about these programs, called DRIPs or dividend reinvestment programs, in chapter 25.

When portfolios turn over frequently, they rarely earn high returns. Usually the managers are looking for quick dollars. If they hit a quick success, they have to find another quick one. That's difficult. Few managers can pull it off.

"MY WAY OR THE HIGHWAY"

Many money managers take only discretionary accounts. A discretionary account means that the manager has total leeway to make the decisions, without checking first with the investor. But some investors say, "Before you do something, I want you to call me." Other investors have guidelines they want you to follow.

A client came in with a $300,000 account. She brought a book, several inches thick, called *Being a Socially Responsible Investor.* She gave me guidelines. "No companies that are defense-related; I don't want anything that has to do with animal testing; I don't want anything with tobacco or liquor."

Some money managers say, "The hell with that. First of all, it affects our performance. Second, we must have total say." Other managers don't feel that way. Me, for example. I'm flexible. Every account is custom-tailored. I'm here to serve the client.

One of my clients is a young professor who wants me to call him about everything before making a move. I talked to him recently about Philip Morris, the tobacco company. Although tobacco companies have not lost a lawsuit yet, he fears that they are in for serious trouble because of government reports about the cancerous effects of secondary smoke. Maybe he's right. Before buying Philip Morris for him, I called him.

Some money managers wouldn't call. They would go ahead and buy the stock whether the client liked it or not. These managers won't let their performance be sacrificed for the fears or the scruples of the individual. They say, "It's my way or the highway."

I try to reason with clients. If they don't want to sell the stock Uncle Harold left, I'll talk it over. One man came to me with an unduly heavy investment in CBS (he works for the company). I said, "First of all, I don't follow CBS. We're responsible for everything in the portfolio, so if we don't follow it, we can't follow it just for you. But let's go one step further. Forty percent of this account is in CBS. That's imprudent. Even if we followed the stock, that's too much of your money in one basket."

He wound up selling a big chunk of it. In fact, after he sold out at 213, the stock dropped about 15 percent. The point is not that I was right. The point is that selling a top-heavy position was the prudent choice.

If he had said to me, "Under no circumstances do I want this stock to go," I'd have gone along with him. Of course, he had another alternative. He could have kept the stock himself, leaving it out of the account he gave me. But generally speaking, why go to a money manager and pay his fees if you don't intend to follow his advice?

You should deal with somebody who shares your investment philosophy, who's flexible, and who, recognizing that your needs change, will talk to you often. After all, investments don't necessarily come to fruition in a year or two.

ACCOUNT MINIMUMS

A union in Philadelphia was looking for someone to manage its $3 million pension fund. Before calling on Roffman Miller, the union listened to presentations from four other managers. I happened to hear a woman from the fourth firm speak. The firm was a large money management company that has about $3 billion under management. She was saying, "We're very happy to take small accounts like this." When it was my turn, I said, "For us, $3 million is a large account."

The Pitcairn Financial Management Group in the Philadelphia suburbs, run by the descendants of the founder of Pittsburgh Plate Glass, manages the family money as well as that of outsiders. Its minimum account is $2 million. Eddie Brown, who was a guest on *Wall Street Week with Louis Rukeyser* the same day I was, has a minimum of $1 million. The Glenmeade Trust Company's minimum is $1 million. At Roffman Miller, our minimum is $100,000, which is about as low a minimum as most professional managers accept.

Although $100,000 is a lot of money, many money managers view it as a small sum, because of the importance of diversification. In an equity account or a balanced account, ideally I like to see at least fifteen stocks. To get that diversification, you need at least $100,000. I'd prefer an account of a quarter million. But many other money managers have thresholds in the millions.

WHO TALKS WITH YOU?

One reason my firm attracted seventy clients in its first twenty months of operation is that few managers offer small investors—people who have "only" $100,000 or $200,000—the individual attention we give. When clients ask me questions or complain about how their investments are going, I give them all the time they want. A psychologist called and said she couldn't come into downtown Philadelphia, where my offices are located. I said, "Fine. I'll be happy to meet you at my house on Saturday."

Earlier I told you about a client who had a four-year car loan at 17.99

percent. Making that much on her investment money is unlikely, so I told her to pay the loan off. About two weeks ago, two sisters who have an account with us asked whether they should pay off their mortgage on a rental property. They were uncomfortable paying a 10 percent mortgage. They had the money, so I told them to pay it off.

We meet regularly with our clients. That should matter to you as you work with a money manager. Find out how often you will get to speak with the principals—only when they're trying to close the deal, or whenever you need them? I tell clients, "Circumstances change. We want to make sure we're on top of things. Stay in touch. Call any time."

WHO MAKES THE DECISIONS?

When you meet with money managers, they often try to lure you into their fold by boasting about past performance. You may hear, for example, "Our record for the past five years is 15 percent a year." Usually that's difficult to achieve, though it's not impossible. But find out:

- Who made the decisions? Who achieved that sterling record?
- How did they achieve it? Was the portfolio focused on biotechnology or other temporarily "hot" stocks?
- Is the manager too heavily concentrated in one area? (That's not healthy.)
- What was the turnover rate?

Make sure you're comfortable with the answers you receive. You'll be happiest with someone you feel rapport with.

WHERE DO THEY GET THEIR RESEARCH?

Research is critical in selecting stocks. By research, I mean due diligence in sorting out information about companies. At Roffman Miller we talk to the competition and, most important, we investigate how a company is managed. Good management remains our number-one priority in an investment decision.

Most money managers in the United States—perhaps ten thousand of the eighteen thousand—are small operations. They're one- or two-person shops that may manage $3 to $10 million. They may not have the resources to do their own research, so they go to brokers. And they read Wall Street reports, which are sell-side research. They're aimed at justifying sales, which generate commissions for the broker. Most research in this country is sell-side.

As you'll see, research analysts at brokerage houses are far from independent. They're subject to pressure from their employers to generate sales and avoid antagonizing corporate customers.

A big Wall Street firm such as Merrill Lynch has more than a hundred analysts on its payroll. Sell-side analysts, as I was at Janney, are under pressure: keep coming up with new names, rotate your recommendations, no negatives. Take their recommendations with tons of salt.

With the pressure that firms put on brokers to gather assets constantly, how can brokers closely follow research supplied by dozens or even hundreds of analysts? They can't. Here's a joke that made the rounds in 1993:

A Merrill Lynch broker is vacationing in New Zealand. Driving on a country road, he rounds a bend and finds the road blocked by hundreds of sheep. He gets out of his car and, seeing a potential client, begins talking to the farmer. He asks the farmer, "How many sheep do you have here?"

The farmer says, "If you can guess the exact number, I'll give you one—your choice."

The broker thinks for a minute and says, "I'll guess seven hundred thirty-nine." (That was the number of stocks Merrill Lynch had on its recommended list.)

The farmer says, "That's amazing, unbelievable. It's exactly right. Take your pick."

The broker goes into the middle of the flock, picks one of the animals, and comes out with his arms wrapped around it.

"How long have you worked for Merrill Lynch?" the farmer asks him.

"I never said anything about Merrill Lynch. How did you know I work there?"

"I have seven hundred thirty-nine wonderful sheep," the farmer says, "and you picked my dog."

WHO HOLDS THE MONEY?

Occasionally you read in the newspaper about an athlete or celebrity who's lost a fortune to an unscrupulous "investment adviser" or agent. Investment advisers of this type, who take money illegally, are rare. More common are those I caution you about in this book: brokers and managers who legally—though unconscionably—put their interests ahead of their clients'.

You can avoid getting taken. Ask your potential money manager how your money will be held. Will you make checks payable to the manager? Or to someone else? At my company, every account stays in the client's name. No member of my firm can take money out of the account. Checks are payable to either a bank or a broker, depending on which the investor is more comfortable with. Every month, each client gets a statement from the bank or the broker. In addition, most money managers issue comprehensive quarterly statements to their clients.

HOW ABOUT A MANAGER FAR AWAY?

The man who was my first account ever in the brokerage business, when I worked with Elkins Morris Stokes in the late 1950s, lived outside the United States. The president of the Insurance Company of North America in Europe, he lived in Belgium. He would see me two or three times a year. Now he lives in New York, and I still manage his money. We talk on the phone and we meet regularly, when he comes to Philadelphia.

Most of my clients, though, live in the Philadelphia area. Not that they must. Telephones and faxes provide instant communication. It's perfectly feasible to have a money manager who's far from walking distance of your house. Still, I think it's better to press the flesh. It's preferable to be able to go to the office. That way, you can see whether the manager is operating out of a garage, whether it's a professional operation.

SEE HOW THEY RUN

I don't think you should settle for speaking to your adviser by telephone, just as a doctor shouldn't diagnose an ailment over the phone. You should meet with your manager face to face. You benefit from seeing the people, the office, the whole setup. All these things give you clues. They all enter into the equation when you're choosing someone who provides you with a service.

Why visit in person? You're sitting in the manager's office. You look at the bookshelves. You look at his clothes, the way he dresses. You look at the way he keeps things. That tells you something about his personality. If he gets a call during the interview, listen to the way he talks on the phone. You'll pick up useful tidbits about his character.

I have one client whose account, worth about $2 million, actually belongs to her father. He lives in Alabama. The daughter sees me often, and she's told her father about my firm. I've spoken with him by phone, but I haven't met him. So I do have a client who lives more than a thousand miles away, but in general it's a good idea when you're entrusting people with a lot of money to go out and see them—at least initially.

WHEN TO CHANGE MANAGERS

Unfortunately, many investors focus so much on the short term that they'll say to their money manager: "The Dow was up four percent, and you were up five. That's a little better, but I know of managers who were up seven or ten percent. You're not so good. I'm going to leave you."

Say that over the past five years, the stock market gained 15 percent a year, but for some reason your manager has been off. He's up only 6 percent. When should you say, "Wait a minute, maybe I should change managers"?

My answer is simple. Don't rely on one quarter, two quarters, three quarters. Don't say, "He's down ten percent, the market's up five, I'm kissing this guy goodbye." That's not fair to any money manager—or to yourself. You can't judge a manager accurately over that short a time.

You create other problems for yourself, too. Take your account to another money manager, and he'll sell out the whole portfolio. Then he has to buy you a new portfolio. That costs you in commissions going out and back in. You're not giving yourself or the manager a chance.

Every money manager, I believe, should have an opportunity to show his or her stuff through at least one cycle in the market: three, four, five years or so—the time it takes to go through one bull market and one bear market. No matter whom you use, you should look at performance over a period of years.

But let's say the whole market cycle has occurred. In that time, the market was up 30 percent and your manager was down 30 percent. *Now* it's time to look for a new manager. Start the way I described at the beginning of this chapter. Screen several managers, interview them, go through the whole process again.

A DECLARATION OF INDEPENDENCE

Investors, I'm convinced, are best served by independent money managers—advisers who don't participate in commissions and who don't sell products. There's no conflict of interest when you're dealing with an independent money manager.

Look for someone who has integrity, someone you can trust. Someone who's competent. Someone whose investment philosophy matches your own.

Charles Schwab, the leading discount broker, estimates that by the end of the 1990s, 25 percent of investors will have professionals managing their money. Recently I visited my friend Howard. While I was waiting for an elevator, one of the salesmen I worked with at Elkins Morris Stokes, my first employer, saw me and said, "Boy, money management, that's the place to be, without a question." Brokers know it.

If you're hesitant to turn your money over to a professional, you can go in stages. You needn't turn over all of it at once. You can turn over part of it and manage the rest yourself. If you're happy with how the manager has performed over several years, you can entrust all your money then.

Even if you do have most or all of your money under professional management, don't lose your vigilance. You can use this book as a check to see how your money manager is managing.

12

THE BENEFITS
OF COMMON STOCKS

Some basic finance: When companies need money, they have several ways
to raise it. Among them are bonds, common stocks, and preferred stocks.
Bonds are a form of borrowing. They obligate the company to pay a set
rate of interest until the bond matures. *Stocks* give investors a share in the
ownership of a company. For that reason, they are sometimes called
equities.

Companies often pay dividends in exchange for the money they receive
when they issue *common stock*. Companies always pay dividends on
preferred stock. The percentage of the stock price that the dividend
represents is called the *yield*.

Common stocks, over time, have outperformed almost all other forms of
investment. Since 1927, they have returned twenty-two or twenty-three
times as much as U.S. Treasury bills. They have outperformed passbook
savings accounts and certificates of deposit. They have advantages over
sometimes spectacular investments like real estate or art. They also build
America.

No matter what stage of life you're in, stocks probably belong in your
account—because of their power in fighting inflation and enhancing
wealth. Here I make the case for having a portion of your portfolio in

equities. I also introduce you to some alternative stock types that you may hear about.

COMMON STOCKS ARE FOR ALMOST EVERYONE

Unless you need to safeguard every cent because your income barely pays your expenses and you can't afford to take any risk at all, I maintain that common stocks belong in your portfolio. The benefits of stocks outweigh the risks—as long as you invest for the long term, three to five years or more.

Over hundreds of years, America has had inflation. I think it's here to stay. As I write in 1993, inflation is at an unusually low point, because the economy is weak. But the economy will pick up, and, I believe, inflation will return. The greater the threat that inflation poses, the more you need a hedge. My favorite hedge is common stocks.

What is the probability of making money in stocks? The chart on page 56 showed that if you invest in stocks, your probability of making money rises with time. If you hold stocks for only one year, those twelve months could be part of a bull market or they could be part of a bear market. The chance of making a profit with a one-year investment is only about 70 percent. When you invest in stocks for twenty years, assuming you are diversified, the probability is nearly 100 percent.

Now consider the chart on page 98. For the years between 1926 and 1990, it shows the average growth of one dollar invested in various vehicles: U.S. Treasury bills, long-term government bonds, and the five hundred common stocks in the Standard & Poor's 500. Because it's adjusted for inflation, the 0 line across the bottom is tantamount to the cost of living. As you can see, savings accounts and CDs do no better than hold even with the cost of living. U.S. Treasury bills fare a little better. But common stocks are the clear winners. Over time, they compound to a growth rate of more than 10 percent a year.

Can some other investments bring you a better return than common stocks? What about the big-ticket items that some high-rolling investors favor, such as rare coins or stamps, paintings by old masters, antiques, jewelry, gold, or real estate? These can earn the staggering sums you sometimes read about in the paper. But they also have drawbacks.

To succeed with these investments, you need a professional's understanding of their respective markets. You also need to understand something of the objects themselves. Rare coins, for example, fluctuate in value according to the metal they're made of. Their worth also depends on condition, according to arcane grading systems that make extremely fine

Stocks, Bonds, T-Bills

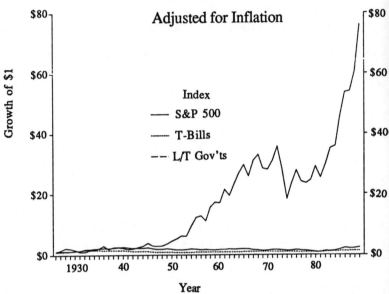

distinctions. Another problem with coins—and with stamps, jewels, and oriental rugs—is the enormous dealer markup. Buy a coin for $100, then turn around and try to sell it the same day. You might get only $50 or $75 for it. If you buy an oriental rug and try to sell it, you'll be lucky if you get half what you paid.

Artworks—even museum pieces—have risks. Even a rare and valuable piece, a painting or a tapestry, can drop in value. We're seeing that happen now, with Jackson Pollocks and other masters. They can drop perilously. Just ask the guy who paid $55 million for Van Gogh's "Irises" and saw the demand and prices for other Van Goghs plummet.

For years, people thought real estate was a nearly foolproof way of making money. The downturn in housing values in the late 1980s and early 1990s showed it ain't necessarily so.

Gold has proved to be a strong hedge against inflation, but its value doesn't always hold up. In the early 1980s, gold was more than $800 an ounce. Now it's about $370. Over the past ten years, gold has been a terrible investment.

Another drawback: objects don't earn interest. Also, you have to lay out money to ascertain their worth. Art, coins, stamps, and antiques must be appraised. Gold must be assayed. And you have to keep objects in some safe place. Chances are you don't want to put them under your mattress. So you incur storage and insurance costs.

Stocks have key differences from these other items. If you buy a stock today and sell tomorrow, chances are you won't take a beating. The stock market offers liquidity. *Liquidity* means you can sell on a moment's notice. You don't have liquidity in real estate; you don't have liquidity in art or any of those other investments.

Another advantage of stocks is that you can hire experts, at reasonable rates, to make your choices for you. You can't do that with the other investments. If you enter the art world, for example, commissions and other costs are onerous.

The following table summarizes the problems in the investments I've talked about. After it is a table showing some benefits of common stocks.

DRAWBACKS OF SOME TYPES OF INVESTMENT

Rare coins	Value fluctuates markedly; dealer markup is enor-
Rare stamps	mous, meaning that if you buy and immediately
Gold	sell, you'll lose much of your money; they return no
Jewelry	interest, dividends, or other earnings while you hold
Antiques	them; you must keep them in a safe place; you need
Oriental rugs	to insure them.
Works of art	
Real estate	Value fluctuates; high costs to buy and sell; much less liquid than stocks.

ADVANTAGES OF COMMON STOCKS

- They're highly liquid.
- Many pay you dividends while you hold them.
- Commissions, though sometimes higher than they could be, are far less than dealer markups on coins, stamps, and other objects.
- You incur no storage or insurance costs.
- Advice is available at relatively reasonable rates.

PREFERRED STOCK: I'D STAY AWAY

Preferred stock generally pays a higher dividend than the same company's common stock, but it has less potential to appreciate in value. The main reasons are:

- The dividend on a preferred stock remains constant.
- The market for preferred stocks is much smaller than the market for common stocks.

In early 1993, Ford Motor Company issued a new preferred stock that paid a dividend of 8 percent. Eight percent at the time was very attractive, because most other investment instruments had yields as low as 2 and 3 percent. But I was not attracted to it, and I'll tell you why. When you buy a straight preferred stock, the dividend always remains the same. It cannot increase. I think you're better off buying a common stock that yields 5 percent and is likely to raise its dividend every year by 5 or 6 percent.

Say you buy a preferred stock that cost $100 a share and has an 8 percent yield. Every year, the company will pay you $8 per share. When interest rates are low, the stock is attractive. But if interest rates rise three or four years hence, the price of the stock will drop. If interest rates rise to 12 percent, for example, the price of that preferred stock might be 67 instead of 100.

If, on the other hand, you buy a utility common stock with a 5 percent dividend—a growth utility—the company is likely to increase its dividend every year. If the 5 percent dividend increases 4 to 6 percent a year, it won't be long before you see substantial growth. Because of the dividend growth, moreover, the value of the stock is likely to appreciate—as opposed to the drop in the value of the preferred.

So why would anyone buy a preferred stock? Because the interest rate climate can be such that people recoil from yields of 2.5 and 3 percent in savings accounts and certificates of deposit. Even long-term bonds may not offer as high a yield. In early 1993, a thirty-year Treasury bond was paying about 7.2 percent—less than Ford's preferred stock dividend of 8 percent. People desperate for income may be willing to buy the preferred for the dividend and forgo the growth potential. Compared with almost every other investment available in early 1993, 8 percent was a high yield. Preferred stocks, on the other hand, do have great appeal to corporate buyers, because they offer tax advantages. In most circumstances, corporations are exempt from taxes on the first 70 percent of dividends they earn each year. The exemption can go as high as 80 percent.

If you're sixty-five or seventy and insist on a high yield because you need it to live on, every percentage point counts. Buy a preferred stock, and you can be reasonably sure you'll receive the promised dividend yield. Only if the company folds might you suffer. Even then, holders of preferred stock are paid dividends before other expenses are paid, such as dividends on common stock. That's why they're called *preferred*.

CONVERTIBLE PREFERRED STOCK

Between preferred stock and common stock is a hybrid known as *convertible preferred*. This is a preferred stock that you can convert—at prescribed times or prices—to the same company's common stock. You can convert some convertible preferreds share for share; that is, for every share you convert, you receive one share of common. With others, you convert the preferred to a percentage of a common share. Delta Airlines offers a convertible preferred that gives you 0.7605 share of common stock for every share of the convertible preferred.

Generally speaking, convertible preferreds have much higher yields than the common stock. Delta's common stock sold for $50 a share in February 1993, and it paid an annual dividend of 20 cents. That comes to a yield of about four tenths of one percent. Delta's convertible preferred paid 6.5 percent. Along with the trade-off I mentioned—you get a higher yield with convertible preferred shares, but you usually can convert them to only a portion of a common-stock share—convertible preferreds have several other trade-offs:

- When the common stock goes up in value, the convertible preferred goes up much less—even if it's convertible into common stock share for share. With the convertible preferred, you don't participate in the advance of the stock price nearly as much.
- When the common stock goes down in value, the convertible preferred's price holds up better. It doesn't go down the same percentage as the common stock, because the higher yield helps prop up the price.

Convertible preferreds differ from one to another. The Delta I cited has an issue convertible into 0.7605 share of common stock. General Motors has a convertible preferred that's convertible into one share of common.

Because the yield on the convertible preferred is higher, the market puts a premium on the convertible preferred. While General Motors common was selling at 37, the convertible preferred was selling for 41. If the value of the common went up, you'd do much better on the common than on the convertible preferred because the convertible preferred was already selling at a premium. So as the price of the common went up, the premium on the convertible preferred would start to disappear, because the yield on the preferred would come down.

Another kicker is that some convertible preferreds have forced conversions, known as *PERKs*. In the General Motors example, GM can force you to convert your convertible preferred shares into common shares in July 1994. No matter what the price of the common stock was at that time, you'd have to convert.

I believe in convertible preferreds. I like Delta Airlines. It's out of favor right now, but I think its common stock will show good growth in two or three years. If you want to buy the common stock and take the low yield in exchange for possible appreciation down the road, fine. But if you can't accept the low yield that the common stock offers, the convertible preferred gives you a happy medium: participating somewhat in the company's future and earning a higher yield than you get with the common stock.

You may want to buy Delta, for example, but can't stomach a yield of 0.4 percent. The convertible preferred gives you a way to buy Delta *and* get a higher yield—6.5 percent. If the common stock goes up, your preferred stock won't do nearly as well. So there's a compromise.

To benefit from convertible preferreds, you have to do some work. A common stock is a common stock. But many factors enter into convertible preferreds. You have to find out what provisions the company has about forcing the conversion and how much common stock it's convertible to. Sometimes it will be one figure at first and change to another figure after a certain number of years. You have to read the prospectus carefully. *Read the prospectus.*

13

FULL-SERVICE BROKERS

The first clue was a statement from the stockbroker. The second was a 1099B. That's an income tax form on which a payer reports miscellaneous income to the IRS. This 1099 was from a broker, and its receipt prompted one of my clients to call me.

In January 1992, my client, a widow in her sixties, had taken her life savings of $150,000 to the broker, who works for a major regional brokerage firm. She has no job and no income other than what the account generates. In November, she called me because she didn't understand what was happening to her. The broker's statement she had just received showed that her account had dropped from $150,000 to $130,000. When she showed me the stocks in the portfolio, I recognized only one name. They were $4 and $5 stocks.

She switched the account from the stockbroker to me in November, so she had had it with the broker for eleven months. Later she got the 1099B. To the Internal Revenue Service, the brokerage firm had reported sales of $281,000. During the first eleven months of 1992, then, in an account originally worth $150,000, the broker had stock sales of $281,000. He had $260,000 in purchases–which don't appear on the 1099. (The 1099B shows sales only, not profits or purchases.)

Between sales and purchases, the broker had totaled $541,000 in trades. Remember, the broker earns money from commissions on sales and purchases. He had *churned* the account to generate commissions on trades. In eleven months, I estimate that his commissions totaled about $10,000.

The brokerage house had $10,000 more in its coffers, while the widow's account was $20,000 poorer. It wouldn't have mattered to the brokerage house if her account was $20,000 richer. On $541,000 worth of transactions, the brokerage house would have received the same commission, regardless of whether the client made money or lost it.

There's a fine line between churning and trading. Suppose that instead of being down $20,000, the account had been up $20,000. The broker would still have got $10,000 in commissions, but the average investor wouldn't think of it as churning. That kind of activity is churning, however, whether there's a loss or a profit.

Let me underscore that this broker's motivation could not have been profits for the client. It was commissions from trades. As long as stocks are traded, the broker makes money. You can see why the broker yearns to trade.

How did the broker have the nerve to do what I've described here? Did he think he'd get away with it because the client didn't know what was going on?

The answer, I believe, is that the broker hoped his stock picks would do well and earn the client a profit. If they had, their performance could have masked the high volume of trades the broker churned and the commissions the broker made.

Does the story make your blood boil the way it does mine?

Not all brokers—but far too many—have only their own interests at heart. The client suffers. In this chapter, I detail the conflicts of interest that many brokers succumb to, and the horrors they cause investors. Much of what I tell clients appears here. These are ways the average investor gets exploited. I'll tell you, for example, about:

- Deals that make companies rich but leave investors with worthless paper
- Brokers who sell too soon
- Brokers who get inside deals
- High-priced wrap accounts

Don't misunderstand. I'm not saying that Wall Street is all bad. The market's purpose, after all, isn't merely to trade and make money; it creates industries. Wall Street raised the capital for industries such as personal computing and biotechnology. If we ever end cancer or pollution, Wall Street will play a big part in that. It makes funds available for research and development. That's the beauty of Wall Street: good ideas can go to the market and become great ideas.

BROKERS ARE SALESMEN

Wall Street has two sides, buy and sell. Brokers are on the sell side. They're called *brokers,* but they're *salesmen.* In an article published in the mid-1980s, Merrill Lynch said, "We're going to sell things that are profitable to us." But brokerage houses are rarely that honest.

The 1980s spawned a spate of corporate takeovers. One of the top takeover artists, Donald Trump, bought a sizable position in Holiday Inn. Fearing a takeover, Holiday Inn executives wanted to increase the debt on the balance sheet and make the company a less attractive target. Holiday Inn, whose stock was selling at about $70, paid a huge one-time dividend of about $65 a share.

A salesman where I worked asked me, "If I buy the stock now, will I get the dividend?"

That's basic stock market lingo. Every salesman at every brokerage should know the answer. If you buy the stock after the dividend went into effect (called *ex-dividend*), you do not qualify for the dividend.

"It's very simple," I told the salesman. "When the stock goes ex-dividend, the seller—not the buyer—gets the dividend and the price will decline by the amount of the dividend. The price of a stock (with a large dividend payment) will show when that happens."

Holiday Inn's debt exceeded $2 billion, and the value of the stock dropped precipitously, as expected. Trump sold his stock at a profit. But what struck me was that a brokerage salesman was ignorant of an item right out of Wall Street 101.

COMMISSIONS: AS AN INDIVIDUAL, YOU PAY A HIGH PRICE

When the federal government deregulated brokerage fees in the mid-1970s, it precipitated dramatic changes in the industry. It helped facilitate the flip-flop between individual and institutional trading that I talked about before. Thirty years ago, 80 percent of the trades on Wall Street were made by individuals. Only 20 percent were made by institutions, mutual funds, pensions funds, public authorities, and the like. Now the situation has flip-flopped. Eighty percent of the transactions, maybe more, are by institutional holders.

Moreover, before deregulation, commissions were fixed. If you bought a hundred shares of stock, the commission was roughly 30 cents a share: $30. If you bought two hundred shares, the commission was 30 cents a share: $60. Above three hundred shares, the commission would come down a little. But basically, brokerages couldn't cut commissions. If you went to Merrill Lynch, or to Elkins Morris Stokes, or to Goodbody and Company, the commissions were similar. Brokers opened their little Standard & Poor's book and read the commissions right out of the book.

No matter how great their financial clout, institutions had little leeway in negotiating favorable commissions before deregulation; the rates were virtually unalterable. Now institutions have the clout to negotiate commissions at a lower level than is available to individuals. Institutions are paying as little as 3 cents a share commission. Meanwhile at full-service firms, a small account is paying about a dollar.

BOND FUNDS

One investor whose million-dollar portfolio I saw had an account with a well-known national brokerage. Her broker had about $300,000 in municipal bond funds. For someone with a small amount of money (say $25,000) to invest, bond mutual funds—especially no-load funds—make sense. But with as much money as this woman had, she should have purchased the bonds directly. She could have paid a sales charge of as little as 0.25 percent—$750—rather than the broker's fund commission of 3 to 8 percent—$9,000 to $24,000—and avoided the funds' approximate 0.75 percent annual management fee.

PRODUCTS: WALL STREET REINVENTS THE WHEEL

Pretend I'm a broker. How can I make a living if you, my client, have stocks and bonds but don't trade? To increase the yield to the broker, Wall Street has created so-called products. It used to be that all or most of a broker's paycheck was commissions from stock trades on the New York Stock Exchange. Not anymore. Now many brokers make most of their money from these special products. As a bonus to the brokers, the commissions on special products are much higher than commissions on traditional stocks and bonds.

Wall Street likes to make investing a complex process. In trying to reinvent the wheel, it has come up with products the average salesman can't even understand. I've read prospectuses so thick that they were obviously written by lawyers and M.B.A.'s from Harvard. To justify the huge salaries they were making, the M.B.A.'s conceived all kinds of new things. The average broker can't understand them, but many brokers push the products to make commissions.

If I'm a broker extolling tax-free bonds, for example, I can sell you a product that would pay me a 0.5 percent commission, or a product that pays a 4 percent commission, or even one with as much as an 8 percent commission. It depends on which product I sell you. You can easily see why I might push the one with the high commission.

Remember, the people who invented these products did not ask themselves, What is in the best interests of our clients? but rather, What will sell? Real estate sold (before the decline of the late eighties). Oil sold, so they put together oil partnerships. They came up with collateralized mortgage obligations, CMOs, some of which are so complex that even I can't understand them. They came up with STRPS (Separate Trading of Registered Interest and Principal Securities), TIGERS (Treasury Interest Gross Receipts), CATS (Certificates of Accrual on Treasury Securities), lots of catchy new products that people had never heard of before.

Why, you ask, does this happen? Why does the public accept it? Fear and greed. Those are the forces that motivate the public to buy and sell. Wall Street asks, What's going to inspire buyers? How can we create products that will exploit their fear and greed? They come up with answers and work backward.

The government lets Wall Street get away with all this. Why? How many congressmen were getting campaign contributions from savings and loan heads like Charles Keating? The public was greedy as well and went where it could get the best deal. People thought, "I stayed with my local bank and got an eight percent return. But my neighbor bought a CD from a bank in Kansas and got eight and a half." So what if the bank couldn't pay? So what if the savings and loan bailout costs the taxpayers half a trillion dollars?

In summary, the public got higher yields; it was greedy. Wall Street got higher commissions; it was greedy. Bankers were greedy. And there was no cop around to say, "Hey, boys, you can't do this."

It's like the tulip craze in Holland in the 1600s. People started bidding up the price of tulip bulbs to astronomical heights. Then somebody said, "Who needs a tulip?" And the prices came crashing down.

DO YOU UNDERSTAND THE PRODUCT?

Some people who talk to me have accounts with many limited part nerships. Partnerships were a vehicle that Wall Street invented during the 1980s to generate commission business. Some partnerships paid the broker an instant 8 percent commission. I speak more about limited partnerships in chapter 25.

Underwriting new stock issues pays particularly attractive commis- sions. They can easily be 5 percent, 6 percent, or even more. On my desk I have a prospectus for a new stock underwriting that pays the brokerage 10 percent. I quote from the prospectus, which fills more than a hundred pages: "Price to the public: $10 million. Proceeds to company: $9 million." Ten percent of the stock proceeds goes to brokers' fees.

Later in the prospectus—PRINTED IN SMALL CAPITAL LETTERS—comes this intriguing point: "This offering involves substantial investment risk, and units should be purchased only by persons who can afford the loss of their entire investment." Their entire investment. But who the hell reads this thing? It's more than a hundred pages.

New investments are required to send you a prospectus, but prospec- tuses are often so daunting that most people don't fully read them. Who will go through a hundred-page document in legalese?

I've seen prospectuses on breakups, especially in the 1980s, when leveraged buyouts occurred almost every week. I've been in this business for more than thirty years, and I couldn't understand what they were talking about.

I have a rule that I don't buy into complex stories. If an investment isn't simple, I avoid it. I let the Ph.D.'s buy it.

I told that to a psychologist who consulted me. She said, "But I am a Ph.D."

Unfortunately, she's a Ph.D. in the wrong field.

Municipal bonds offer brokerage firms low commissions. That's why many sell *unit trusts*, which are pools of many bond issues. Unit trusts can pay them four or five times the commissions they would get selling municipal bonds. Instead of selling you a bond whose commission is $2.50 to $10 per thousand, brokers would much rather sell you a unit trust paying $40 or $50 a thousand. Yield to the broker.

Payouts on Wall Street Products Give Brokers Even Greater Incentives

When I discussed that 10 percent commission on the new offering, did you think, "Wow, what a high commission"? It is. Realize, though, that the broker doesn't receive the whole 10 percent. The broker's firm may get 60 cents of each dollar, and the broker may get 40 cents.

With incentive like that, brokers will sell the product. Not only do they get a higher-than-usual commission, but at some firms the payout ratio calculated to the brokers is much higher on the product than on a New York Stock Exchange stock, which is likely to be 25 to 40 percent. Furthermore, at all firms, the higher the broker's commissions, the higher the payout percentage. A broker who produces $500,000 in gross commissions may get a 40 percent payout. A lower producer gets a much lower payout. Many firms have a policy that gives the broker no credit for a sales commission when the commission falls below a certain point. The policy discourages brokers from handling small transactions and discourages discounts on small orders.

The Sales Contest: Earn High Commissions, Go to Europe

My old firm had a yearly sales contest. The winners were the brokers who generated a certain level of commission business. The prize was a trip—to Europe or some other appealing destination. When the firm calculated the commissions, it didn't count commissions on stocks listed on the New York Stock Exchange. Most commission calculations were for product.

In other words, the contest was based on the sales of Wall Street product, or in-house inventory, which had a much higher yield to the brokerage firm than did stock transactions on the New York Stock Exchange.

"You want a trip to Europe?" the brokerage firm asked the broker. "Go out there and sell products that produce high margins for the firm." It's perfectly legal. But what does it do? It pressures the broker to sell the product with the high commissions, whether it's in the client's best interest or not.

End-of-month Flurries

Every brokerage firm has a date when commissions stop for the month. Then it pays the brokers. It is no secret that year in and year out, a broker's commission business is highest in the last commission week of the month. Why? Is it because market conditions are better then? No. It's because, in the last week of the month, brokers want to reach their quotas. They start to panic.

A broker was scheduled to come to my office for a meeting but canceled the appointment. He explained: "It's the last commission week. I can't leave my desk. I don't even go out to lunch. I'm too busy trying to do business."

Round-trip Discounts

Some brokerage firms promote trading with what they call the round trip
Here, the commission you as the client pay is sliced in half if you sell a
security within thirty days of buying it. In other words, if you sell it in tha
time, your commission rate drops in half on the sell side of the transaction
The structure encourages you to buy and sell.

It fosters activity in your account. Then you can reinvest the sale into
another buy, so the brokerage gets two commissions. They love it. It's more
profit to the firm.

Wrap Accounts: Too Expensive

Recognizing that investors are wising up to Wall Street's shenanigans,
Wall Street has jumped on the bandwagon. As individual investors have
shied away from full-service brokers and flocked to mutual funds and
money managers, brokers have been fighting back. One way brokerage
houses have lured individuals back into their fold is by devising an all-in-
one money management program called a *wrap account.*

If you have assets of at least $100,000, you can establish a wrap account
at any of the large brokerage firms. To me, a wrap account for a small
investor is like a mutual fund: a group of stocks that a money manager
manages. Many managers pool investors' money and buy a diverse
portfolio of stocks. The wrap account covers all transactions, so you pay no
commissions. Instead, you pay a yearly fee—usually 3 percent a year. The
average mutual fund charges about 1 percent.

Wrap accounts are a rapidly growing field for full-service brokers. Tens
of billions of dollars have flowed into wrap accounts. That's an enormous
amount of money, and it sprang up from nothing just a few years ago.
Recently Charles Schwab announced that it would offer wrap accounts at a
substantial discount. Schwab thinks people are overpaying. I agree. The 3
percent fee is too high.

Let's say the stock market over time shows 10 percent yearly growth.
Take three percentage points off the top, and you turn 10 percent into 7.
That's just too high a cost. To cover that cost and equal the 10 percent
average return, the manager has to outperform the market by 30 percent.
Only the best-performing money managers could dream of a 13 percent
annual return year in and year out. I don't recommend wrap accounts at
all.

BROKERS ARE EXPENDABLE

Brokerage firms remind brokers of their priorities. Many tell brokers what to sell. Merrill Lynch says to brokers, "You've got so much of this stock to put out today or so much of this mutual fund" or whatever the product is.

At large firms, brokers whose gross commissions are less than $200,000 a year are in peril of losing their jobs. The company will kick them out. It will give a broker a couple of years to get up to that level, and then gone! At Merrill Lynch, if you're not producing $250,000 in annual commissions after four or five years, the company doesn't want you. You're taking up a desk where somebody else could be generating big money.

My friend Sam worked at the Merrill Lynch branch in Philadelphia. One morning at ten o'clock, the Merrill Lynch branch manager walked into Sam's office and asked, "What do you have to show me today?"

Sam hadn't done any sales yet. The branch manager walked out of the office, said, "You're not paying the electric bill around here," and turned out the light.

WHAT SECURITY ANALYSTS AND RESEARCH DEPARTMENTS ARE REALLY ABOUT

Brokerages have research departments that produce reports analyzing the prospects of companies that issue stocks and bonds. These departments, made up of security analysts, also forecast companies' earnings (a significant factor in the value of a stock), and they issue recommendations on whether to buy or sell.

Supposedly, analysts' forecasts and recommendations are based on mathematical analyses of sales, profits, the company's ratio of earnings to debt, the ratio of the stock price to earnings, and other measures. Too often, though, what comes out of analysts' offices are not the unbiased words the public thinks they are. Security analysts at brokerage houses are far from independent. Wall Street creates pressure for analysts to say to a client, "Your stock has gone up. Why not sell it and buy something else?" It's the churn-and-burn mentality I discussed earlier.

In theory, a "Chinese Wall" separates the research department from the rest of the brokerage firm. In reality, that wall is as thin as tissue paper. My boss at Janney always told me, "Marvin, the research department is not a profit center. We're here for the sales force."

Analysts are often pressured to produce favorable reports on companies whose stock the brokerage house is underwriting. Brokerage firms may punish analysts for bearing bad news. Negative comments from an analyst could offend a major corporate client or potential client. A sell report on a company could prevent the brokerage from participating in underwritings, which are a high-commission product. The lifeblood of an analyst is company contact. Such drying up of information undermines the position of analysts, till they're like journalists without sources.

In July 1990, after I was fired, *Institutional Investor* did a cover story on the hazards of negative research. Sixty-one percent of the analysts surveyed said they had been asked to temper or modify a negative opinion at least once in their careers. The other 39 percent? Job preservation must have been a factor in some of their answers.

In 1986, Janney hired a new analyst to cover the banking industry. She had little experience as an analyst. After being on the job for some months, she issued her first major report, on Mellon Bank Corporation. Full of charts and graphs, it was a long, comprehensive report, one of the longest the firm ever put out. The report recommended Mellon as a purchase. The stock was then trading at about $60 a share.

Within six months, the stock began falling precipitously—first into the 50s, then into the 40s. At our weekly research meeting of all analysts, when the stock was around $40, I said, "I have quite a bit of stock in Mellon. With such a fall, I'm concerned." I asked the analyst directly: "Is Mellon Bank a buy, hold, or sell?"

"It's a sell."

Jim Meyer, the director of research, said, "It's a *what?*"

The analyst repeated, "It's a sell, Jim."

Company policy has always been that as soon as a stock recommendation changes, the analyst must issue a report. By the next week, no report had been forthcoming. But I said nothing at the sales meeting. The stock kept falling.

The week after that, I still hadn't seen any report. By then the stock had fallen into the mid-30s. I said to Meyer, "Two weeks ago in this very chair, I asked whether Mellon Bank was a buy, hold, or sell. The analyst said it was a sell. There hasn't been any report issued, and it continues to fall."

Meyer said to me, "Marvin, it's none of your business. We'll handle this in our way and in our time."

In another case, Janney did an underwriting for a company that made training films. The company's stock went from about 5 to about 2. I visited the company and came back not liking the story. I told Meyer that I didn't want to write a report about it. He said, "You don't have to recommend it. Just write an 'information' report."

"If I put my name to something," I said, "even if I don't recommend it, people will take it the wrong way."

"The firm wants a report," he replied. "Don't you want to be a team player?"

Every December, Janney asked all its analysts to pick their stock for the new year. This was the stock each analyst thought would outperform all others he or she followed. On the first business day of January, Janney published its monthly letter, which featured the stock picks of the year, including a page on each stock by each analyst.

My favorite was Consolidated Foods, which later changed its name to Sara Lee. That was my stock pick for the year, and it did well. If it wasn't number one in performance, it was probably number two among the stocks the analysts picked. I also picked it the next year. Jim Meyer said, "You can't do that. You picked it last year."

"Jim," I said, "you asked me what stock I thought was going to outperform all my other stocks for the year. I think Sara Lee will."

He said, "Maybe it will, Marvin, but you can't pick it again." I finally got him to agree. I listed it for the second year, and it did extremely well. It turned out to be one of the best-performing stocks of the 1980s.

The third year, I picked it again. Meyer blew up.

One year, I recommended General Mills, and it did well. Meyer said, "Marvin, why don't you recommend a switch to Hershey Foods and nail down the profits? Then we can go buy Hershey." He wanted another name to generate more commissions.

In 1989, I wrote a report on Paramount Communications, which had made a bid to buy Time Incorporated. I recommended that investors interested in Time proceed with caution. My boss crossed out the cautionary line and wrote: "At this price, these shares are a suitable holding for those investors with a risk arbitrage mentality."

Several months earlier, on a Saturday in April 1989, the former chairman of Campbell Soup, John Dorrance, died. The day before, Campbell stock had sold at 33¼. On Monday, the stock went up 6 points. I wrote a report that day, saying that the Campbell hat had been tossed into the takeover arena.

Within a few months, the stock had risen to about 60. It was selling at 30 times earnings, double the norm for a food stock. Clearly, the price

reflected a possible takeover. If that didn't happen, I wrote in the draft o
another report to go out on the company wire, the stock could well swing
down. Owning Campbell stock now, I said, would be like riding a rolle.
coaster.

I showed the report to my director of research, because the issue wa:
sensitive. Campbell Soup stock was controlled by the Dorrance family, and
Janney Montgomery Scott had several Dorrance connections. Samuel
Hamilton, an account executive at Janney, was married to Dodo Dorrance,
a director of Campbell Soup. Another senior Janney person, George
Strawbridge, was also married to a Dorrance.

Months later, Campbell stock rose sharply, and Dow Jones called me to
ask for a comment. Using the words my boss had written before about
Time, I said, "At this price, Campbell Soup stock is a suitable holding for
those investors with a risk arbitrage mentality." At a weekend party soon
afterward, Janney's CEO, Norman Wilde, was sitting next to a member of
the Dorrance family. The woman said to Wilde: "I own X million shares of
Campbell Soup. Do I have a risk arbitrage mentality?"

When I got to work the next Monday, my boss called me into his office
and told me what Wilde had heard. "Jim," I pointed out, "those were your
words, not mine."

"Marvin," he said, "they may be my words, but they were not meant for
the media. You know how sensitive any negative comments on Campbell
Soup would be to people connected to the Dorrances."

How Accurate Are the Earnings Forecasts?

Another concern about analysts who work for brokerages is the accuracy of
their earnings forecasts. This has consequences. Often I speak with the
managers of pensions and mutual funds. Many say, "We don't trust Wall
Street research anymore."

One manager told me: "The only part of a sell-side analyst's report I
look at is the upper right corner." That's where a stock recommendation is
summarized as a buy, sell, or hold. "I interpret a hold recommendation as
a sell. I've heard of a buy ticket and a sell ticket. I've never heard of a hold
ticket."

Brokers are not trained in analysis, although New York Stock Exchange
tests for brokers require that they be able to read a balance sheet. The test
reminds my partner, Peter Miller, of a boxer's weigh-in. It only means the
boxer is alive; it doesn't mean he can fight.

I Recommended Selling Casino Stocks— the Industry Foamed

Resorts International, the first casino in New Jersey, debuted in 1978. In the summer of 1980, I made a presentation at the Atlantic City Country Club. Janney had opened a branch office in Linwood, ten miles outside Atlantic City. Casino stocks were flying high, new customers were coming on board, and the firm saw a great opportunity to put on a seminar. So Janney invited clients and potential clients to the Atlantic City Country Club to hear the gaming expert talk about gaming stocks.

They had buyers in there, people who had bought casino stocks that day. I got up on the podium and told people, "Sell all your casino stocks."

The brokers went nuts! One of them called Norman Wilde, Janney's CEO, and said: "Fire him. I have all my people there and I've sold them all these stocks, and he's coming out with negative things."

Actually, I was right. The stocks had peaked. At its top, Resorts was more than $200 a share. By 1981, though, Atlantic City reached a point where much new competition was coming on stream and the economy was slowing down. Instead of showing giant gains, casinos were starting to show losses. The bubble burst, and casino stocks started to tumble.

Janney didn't fire me then. But the management then was the old guard, before the Penn Mutual Insurance Company bought the company in the mid-eighties. Later, after Donald Trump threatened to sue Janney for negative remarks I made in the *Wall Street Journal*, the director of research said, "Marvin, remember, we're owned by a life insurance company. Life insurance companies don't like waves. They don't like negatives. And they don't like lawsuits."

"Congratulations, Marvin, You're the New Airline Analyst"

In the third week of February 1990, I was at a food conference in Florida. Lou Marckesano, the analyst at Janney who followed the airline industry, had retired. I called the office and spoke with Meyer. He said to me, "Congratulations, Marvin, you're the new airline analyst."

It takes years to learn an industry. "Jim," I said, "what do I know about airlines?"

He said, "You were friends with Lou. Pick his brain. You don't have to be real strong in this thing. All we want is somebody to cover it."

As soon as I got back to the office, United Airlines faced a management buyout. I had to make a comment on it, but what did I know about the airline industry? It had taken Lou Marckesano twenty years to learn, but suddenly I was the airline analyst people looked to for comments.

HOW BROKERAGES ABUSE STOCKHOLDERS: DOGS AND PONIES

My partner, Peter Miller, used to work at Drexel Burnham. He describes what they called the dog-and-pony show. A week before bringing out a bond, they would gather their brokers and tell them what a great deal it was. They got the brokers interested, but the morning of the offering they would say, "No retail distribution." That was at 9 A.M. The market opened at 9:30. Five minutes later, they would announce on the loudspeaker: "These bonds are now available. We can't offer them at the original asking price, but we'll sell them at one thousand fifteen dollars."

In other words, although each bond had a par value of $1,000 and should have been sold at that price, the firm would sell it at $1,015.

An honest broker would say, "I'm not buying it. Why should my client pay a premium?" But some brokers hated to lose a paycheck, so they went along.

MORE ABUSES: THE OVER-THE-COUNTER MARKET BRINGS YIELDS TO THE BROKER

In the over-the-counter (OTC) market, the difference between *bid* and *ask* prices can include attractive markups to the brokerage firm. A stock may have a bid price of 27 and an ask price of 30. That means you could buy it for as much as 30 but sell as low as 27. The price could include a spread as high as three points to the broker, which they don't tell you. On a stock, one on which few shares are traded, I've seen a two-point spread, even for a stock selling at $11 a share. The investor could be paying 2 points to the broker on a stock costing 11—a 22 percent markup.

MORE CONFLICTS: WALL STREET POLICES ITSELF

If you do business with a member firm of the New York Stock Exchange and you have a grievance, you can't take the firm to court. You have to go to arbitration. Who do you think appoints the arbitration panel? The New York Stock Exchange. The people who work as arbitrators are paid by the exchange. Do you think they like to give out generous awards?

CONFLICTS ON WALL STREET: A SUMMARY

- Because brokers' pay depends on commissions, they have incentives to generate lots of transactions.
- Wall Street creates products that increase profits to brokers.
- Bad brokers focus on the yield to the broker, not the yield to the client.
- The corporate finance department does not work for the investor: it works for the firms it underwrites.
- Research analysts at many firms are compensated on the basis of commissions they generate, not on their forecasting acumen.
- Wall Street and corporate America don't like negatives. Research analysts who write negative reports on companies can be cut off. One well-known firm has been quoted in print: "Don't say negative things about our corporate clients. We can lose them."

LET THE PUBLIC BEWARE

How well known are these conflicts and abuses? Though many are hidden from the public, brokers know all about them. Brokers who have left firms or retired sometimes talk about them. They're well known in the industry.

As for the public, from years of dealing with brokers and losing money, some investors know. And many investors do sense that full-service brokers can be an expensive way of doing business. Other than that, the public is sadly unaware of the problems.

SOME GOOD WORDS

Peter Miller tells this story: "At Janney in the nineteen eighties, the hotshot brokers went to Marvin. He sat there and kept doing his old-fashioned investing. One guy kept coming in and saying, 'Marvin, tax shelters; Marvin, options; Marvin, junk bonds.'

"At the end of the decade, Marvin counted his marbles and beat all the hotshots. He never accepted all that newfangled stuff."

Here's some stuff I *have* accepted. I've talked a lot about how brokers exploit their clients. Now I offer advice on how to avoid being exploited and allow yourself to come out ahead.

- *Fortunes are usually made with patience, over time.* Buy stocks in solid companies and hold them through lean years. Look for growth over the long term.

- *If your broker plies you with requests to sell, Ask why.* Usually there are only two reasons to sell a stock: (1) The company's fundamentals have changed—perhaps because of a shakeup in management, a drastic increase in debt, or a lawsuit over the flagship product. (2) The price of the stock has been driven up much too fast, with no solid reason for the run-up.
- *Trust yourself more than anybody else.* Ask tough questions. If you don't understand an investment that a broker recommends, say you don't understand it. Let somebody else buy it.
- *Examine your motive for buying any investment.* Is it fear or greed? If so, how much fear? How much greed?
- *Sit down and think about any broker's suggestion for a couple of days before deciding on it.*
- *If a broker guarantees something, forget it.* Other than investments backed by the government, there are no guarantees. True guarantees don't give you great rewards. To attain great rewards, you have to take risks.
- *If you buy bonds, make sure they have assets behind them.* Don't buy based solely on expectations. Don't buy junk bonds.
- *Beware of relying on patterns in stock prices.* As soon as you think you identify one, the market will fool you.
- *Open all financial correspondence immediately.* Mail from brokers may contain transaction statements, which could clue you in to churning. Monthly or quarterly statements show you the performance of your investments—vital information for the do-it-yourself investor.
- *Check statements for accuracy.* Notify your broker of any discrepancies immediately. Mistakes can create problems for you or become time-consuming and expensive to clear up.

14

ARE DISCOUNT BROKERS
THE ANSWER?

Outraged by the abuses I just catalogued? Tired of costly and ill-chosen advice from some full-service brokers? Fed up with high commissions? Sick of hearing about partnerships or the latest insurance gimmick? Concerned about doing better with your money? Well, then, consider discount brokers.

The Securities and Exchange Commission abolished fixed brokerage commissions on May 1, 1975, a date the industry came to call May Day. Fixed commission rates had prevailed since 1792. Since deregulation, individual investors have deserted full-service brokerage firms and flocked to discount brokers and mutual funds. No wonder. Along with conflicts of interest, full-service brokers charge individual investors high commissions—as much as a dollar a share, versus the 3 or 4 cents they charge large institutional investors. That's why Wall Street has been losing out. That's why many brokerage firms have consolidated. That's why several hundred thousand fewer people work on Wall Street today than before the crash of '87.

According to the Securities Industry Association, the United States has about 200 discount brokerages. The top three—Charles Schwab, Fidelity, and Quick & Reilly—have an estimated 82 percent of the discount brokerage business. About 20 percent of the nation's brokerage accounts are in the hands of discount brokers. Discounters have about 12 percent of the total commission dollars.

FULL-SERVICE BROKERS HAVE A PLACE

You get a tip: "Buy Consolidated Feather." If you want more information on the company, you can do it yourself or you can go to a full-service broker. Full-service brokers can find information on a company quickly. They can help analyze financial conditions that affect the company. They can tell you of current developments and negatives. Full-service brokers who work with you this way earn their pay and are entitled to higher commissions.

If, after hearing the tip, you decide to buy the company without getting professional advice, you can buy it through a discount broker. In such instances, the only item that a full-service broker gives you that the discount broker doesn't is a higher commission.

DISCOUNT BROKERAGES HAVE ORDER-TAKERS, NOT BROKERS

Discount brokerages don't have salesmen who pounce on you. They don't have fancy, high-risk products to sell. Discount brokerage firms lower commissions and raise investors' hopes for fair deals.

Discount firms can trade at reduced rates because they don't have brokers and they don't pay analysts to do research. They have order-takers. You've done your research or gotten advice elsewhere, you phone in your order, and an order-taker takes it and transacts it. Order-takers don't work on commission. They're paid a salary.

DISCOUNTS AREN'T ALL THE SAME

There are discount brokers and deep discount brokers. Deep discounters, such as Brown & Company, are no-frills operations. They handle transactions and not much more. Discount brokers, such as Charles Schwab, offer more service and let you place orders twenty-four hours a day. Schwab has IRAs guaranteed to have no fee to the investor for the investor's lifetime. Schwab also lets clients buy and sell no-load mutual funds for a small fee.

Discounters cut fees at least 50 to 60 percent off full-service brokers' rates. Deep discounters offer less service, so they can cut fees as much as 90 percent.

SELECTING A DISCOUNT BROKERAGE: COST ISN'T EVERYTHING

Discount broker doesn't have to mean discount service. I've found the service at some discounters to be better than that at some full-service firms. For example, one discount broker whom I use tape-records all conversations. If there's ever a mistake, it's easy to find out how it happened and to correct it.

WHERE TO GO

The best way to find a broker is through recommendations. If someone you trust recommends a discount brokerage and you're impressed with the literature they send you, give them a try. Remember, price isn't the only consideration.

Many discount brokerages are large firms that operate nationwide and have offices you can visit. Others are local firms, either independent or affiliated with financial institutions such as banks.

The following list gives names and telephone numbers for some of the country's leading discounters.

Charles Schwab	800/435-4000
Quick & Reilly	800/222-0437
Fidelity Brokerage	800/544-9697
AccuTrade	800/762-5555
Brown & Company	800/822-2829
Fleet Brokerage Securities	800/221-8210
Olde Discount	800/872-6533
Seaport Securities	800/732-7678
Muriel Siebert & Company	800/535-9652
Waterhouse Securities	800/765-5185

Given what I've said about discount brokers, is there any reason to work with a full-service broker rather than a discounter? Yes, for research on specific companies, for information on financial conditions, and for advice. Many brokers are well worth what they earn in commissions. If you already know what you want to buy or sell, you may do better with discount broker. You may get better service with the discounter, you'll b under no pressure to buy high-commission products that bring yo excessive risk, and you'll pay lower commissions too.

Are discount brokers the answer? In many cases, yes!

15

MUTUAL FUNDS:
NOT A PANACEA

You want a diverse portfolio and professional management, but you don't have enough money to diversify. Somebody in Oshkosh has the same considerations. So the two of you, and thousands of other investors, get together.

That's a mutual fund. Many investors pool resources to buy many stocks or bonds and to hire a professional manager. You needn't be present at the beginning, or active in forming the fund. Thousands of funds already exist and would be happy to count you among their number.

Mutual funds are good for people who have limited resources, who alone can't achieve the diversification needed to protect against the vagaries of individual stocks or particular sectors of the economy. You can't reach that diversification with small amounts of money.

How much is a small amount of money? For investing in individual stocks on your own, I'd say the minimum you need is $25,000. With less than $25,000, it's difficult to get enough diversification.

That principle is the guiding force behind mutual funds. They offer the protection of diversification and the professional management to pick good companies.

MUTUAL FUNDS EXPLODE

More than four thousand mutual funds are available today—greater than the number of stocks on the New York and American exchanges combined. Mutual funds have exploded. Investors have grown more and more savvy. They're eliminating brokers and biased research departments by hiring the professional money management that mutual funds offer.

Recognizing the trend, the *Wall Street Journal* expanded its coverage of mutual funds beginning February 2, 1993. The amount of money in mutual funds, the *Journal* said in that issue, had grown from $95 billion at the beginning of the 1980s to $1.6 trillion in February 1993.

TYPES OF FUNDS

Because of the great number and variety of funds, knowing which to pick takes work. There are mutual funds for people seeking:

- Current income
- Growth over time
- Investment in one sector of industry, such as high technology or health care
- Investment in small companies
- Short-term bonds
- Long-term bonds
- High-yield (junk) bonds
- Municipal bonds
- Investment in a particular region of the world, such as Europe or Mexico
- A combination of stocks, bonds, and cash (these are called *balanced funds*)
- Investment to match the performance of a broad range of stocks (these are *index funds*)

I cover bond mutual funds in chapter 18.

Some mutual funds charge a sales fee when you buy them. These are called *load funds*. Ordinarily, you pay the load up front. Some funds charge the load when you sell; that's a *back-end load*. Load funds usually sell through brokers. Other funds, called *no-load funds,* charge no sales fee. You usually buy them from the mutual fund directly.

Note that all mutual funds—load and no-load—have *administrative fees,* which pay for the costs of running the fund: rent, postage, utility bills, and the like. Most funds also have *management fees*: the money paid to the person or company that runs the fund, along with the commissions on transactions. These costs can be low or high. *Read the prospectus.*

Besides these fees, the government allows mutual funds to charge *12b-1 fees*. These let funds pass on the costs of publicity and advertising. Both load and no-load funds may charge 12b-1 fees. They even allow no-load funds to pay brokers sales fees year after year. How do you know whether a fund charges the fee? *Again, read the prospectus.* Always read the prospectus.

Most mutual funds start with a certain amount of money (their capitalization) and buy stocks for that amount. As the number of people investing in the funds grows, they buy more stocks. Such funds are called *open-end funds*. Their value rises and falls with the values of the stocks in the fund. They continue to grow as the money invested in them grows. Conversely, when investors want to sell, an open-end fund's manager can be forced to liquidate the portfolio at inopportune times—if he doesn't have enough reserves on hand to meet redemptions.

Closed-end funds start with a specified capitalization that never changes. You can't buy closed-end funds directly from the funds themselves. You buy and sell them on a stock exchange, just like individual stocks.

HOW TO CHOOSE

How do you choose from the complex array of mutual funds available? Do load funds (those that charge sales fees) have any advantages? What about funds sold by brokers? Are you better off buying funds on your own? Here I answer those questions and present criteria to follow as you decide on the mutual funds that are best for you.

As with hiring a money management firm, you have to match yourself with a mutual fund that meets your needs. It's like going to a dating service. The main difference between buying a mutual fund and hiring a money manager is that the fund is not interactive. The fund doesn't talk with you to find out who you are or what you want. It does take your money and invest it according to the mission set out in the prospectus.

With so many mutual funds to choose from, you may be overwhelmed at trying to pick the right fund or funds for you. The business is so complicated that some companies do nothing but study the thousands of mutual funds to see how they perform. Some of these firms publish newsletters that you can subscribe to. Others counsel you individually for a fee; you pay their fee on top of the administrative and management fees you pay when you own a mutual fund, so it's expensive.

INVESTMENT PHILOSOPHY

You want a fund whose philosophy matches yours. If you're looking for current *income,* you want a fund with little risk. Usually funds like that invest primarily in companies that pay high dividends. If you're looking for *aggressive growth,* you want a fund that takes more risk. Such funds often invest in small companies that have little or no current earnings but great potential. If you're looking for some growth and some income, you want a fund with moderate risk. Or you can choose multiple funds, say one income fund and one growth fund.

If you want risk, you'll like a fund that buys and sells speculative stocks. If you're conservative, you'll prefer a fund that focuses on established companies.

Some mutual fund managers buy and sell stocks often. This high turnover means high transaction costs, with no guarantee that the results will exceed (or even meet) those of a fund with low turnover. Low turnover means low transaction costs. All other things being equal, lower transaction costs mean more money in your account.

PERFORMANCE RATINGS: NOT ALL THEY'RE CRACKED UP TO BE

How do you pick mutual funds the do-it-yourself way? One way is to follow the *Wall Street Journal*'s expanded daily coverage. Every day, the *Journal* publishes not only each fund's current price but also its investment objective, sales charges, annual expenses, dividends, and performance from the beginning of the year. On certain days of the week, the *Journal* publishes more detailed information: initial sales charge, annual expenses, performance over the past four weeks, thirteen weeks, twenty-six weeks, thirty-nine weeks, one year, three years, four years, and five years.

Another source is *Forbes* magazine. Each February 15, Forbes publishes its Honor Roll. It shows the top-performing mutual funds in many categories and contains a wealth of other useful information.

In addition there are services, Morningstar and Lipper Analytical, that evaluate mutual funds. These are the most detailed sources of information about mutual funds and are available in some libraries. The list published by the *Wall Street Journal* uses Lipper statistics.

One plus of the *Journal*'s coverage is the details on expenses, which are useful to investors. But the listings also have a strong negative. On Tuesdays, Wednesdays, Thursdays, and Fridays, they show performance: how funds have fared for the year to date, and other periods going back to five years. Although performance can be a useful tool, it can also be misleading. I think the *Journal* is doing investors a disservice by stressing performance over short intervals. I also frown on the *Journal*'s pros-versus-darts feature. The *Journal* compares the performance of professional money managers with that of a portfolio of stocks selected by throwing darts at a piece of paper with stock names on it. In such a short time, anything can happen. Don't buy and sell mutual funds for the short term.

If you happened to have bought a biotech fund in early 1991, you could have been up 60 percent for the year, a tremendous return. But if you kept the biotech fund, or if you bought it late in the year, you would have had a disaster in 1992. The ups and downs of the market make it unwise to expose a high proportion of your assets in only one sector.

A man I spoke with recently had been sold a bill of goods to buy a mutual fund specializing in health care. I told him not to. He replied that the broker had pointed out how well the health care industry had done over the past five to ten years. Although that may be accurate, it's not the whole story. Take pharmaceuticals as an example. I just got a $900,000 account, of which 28 percent was in pharmaceutical stocks. That's an inordinately high percentage, and I said so. To show how poorly you can do: from January 1, 1993, till the beginning of March, when the account came in, pharmaceutical stocks as a group had declined in value 15 to 25 percent. It's a perfect illustration of why your investments should be diversified.

Also, as you've undoubtedly heard, the past is no indication of how a fund will do in the future. A fund may have been lucky, showing big gains by loading up on a hot sector. Health care stocks did great for five years, so you should buy a health care mutual fund, right? Biotech was a big winner in 1991; stay with biotech, right? Wrong. Performance over the short term makes investors shortsighted.

The X Fund was up 22 percent over the past thirteen weeks, you read in the *Journal*. So you're thinking, "I should take my money out of my bank account, or the mutual fund it's in now, and invest in the X Fund." Maybe, maybe not.

For one thing, in a period of rising stock values, many mutual funds do well. But how does the X Fund do in down markets? How strong are the companies it invests in? How sharp is the fund's management? Where does it get its research?

If you constantly switch from one fund to another, you will rarely hit the hot ones. Usually those statistics are known only in retrospect. Some fund managers perform well year after year, and they're the ones you should seek.

WHO'S MINDING THE STORE?

During the 1980s, Fidelity's Magellan Fund was one of the best-performing mutual funds. So if you want a good mutual fund now, Magellan is the one to buy, right?

Not necessarily. When Magellan was posting those impressive totals, it was run by Peter Lynch. Lynch left Magellan in 1990 to devote time to writing books and pursuing personal interests. He no longer runs the fund. The man who followed him as the Magellan Fund manager, Morris Smith, stayed a little over two years and then left too. Long hours and the stress of managing a portfolio worth hundreds of millions or billions overwhelm many managers.

When you look at performance statistics, it's vital to know who achieved the impressive record. Are the same people running the fund now? Is there continuity? If not, why buy that fund? I recommend sticking with funds whose managers are the ones who achieved the fine records.

How do you find out who's running a fund? The prospectus. By law, mutual fund companies are required to list their managers and directors.

SECTOR AND SPECIALTY FUNDS

Earlier in this chapter, I talked about the sudden run-up and subsequent run-down in biotech funds. Do you see how you can get into trouble with a narrow focus and a short time frame? Investors get excited about a company or a whole industrial sector, buy it, and inflate the prices. Then an unfavorable news report comes along, or another new industry, and investors lose enthusiasm. The sector nosedives.

In the early 1980s, some of the best-performing mutual funds were those that invested in gold. That was a time of immense inflation, when gold performs well. But in the calm, low-inflation times since then, gold stocks have been in the doldrums.

It's human nature to respond well to novelty. Those who make their living by selling know the value of buzzwords. By that I mean the words that symbolize hot, new items. Mutual funds and Wall Street are marketing-oriented, so they too come up with buzzwords. In the mid-1980s, junk bond funds were the big thing. Soon after, junk bonds proved a disaster. Now they're back. More junk bonds were sold in the first six months of 1993 than in any other six-month period in history.

Another buzzword now is *small cap*. Small-cap stocks are companies whose market capitalization is between $100 million and $250 million, depending on which institution is looking at them. They are back in vogue, but three years from now may take a back seat to big-cap stocks. Investors will flock to something else.

INDEX FUNDS

At the beginning of this chapter, I mentioned that a mutual fund consists of a group of investors who pool their resources to hire a professional money manager. That's true of most mutual funds but not of all. There's an important exception.

Index funds have—and need—no professional management. Rather, they attempt to duplicate the performance of a particular group of stocks. They can never beat the index, because mutual funds have transaction and administrative costs that the indexes themselves don't. Also, to give themselves flexibility, index funds can't be 100 percent invested in stocks all the time. They must retain cash for overhead and for room to maneuver because of additions to or deletions from the index, or when fund owners liquidate.

Common indexes include:

- The Standard & Poor's 500, a group of 500 stocks representing a cross-section of large-capitalization American companies.
- The Russell 2000, which emphasizes stocks of small-capitalization companies.
- The Wilshire 5000, which embraces all common stocks traded on the New York Stock Exchange, the American Stock Exchange, and the NASDAQ over-the-counter market. Because it includes a greater number of small companies, it's tilted toward higher risk and reward than the S&P 500 or the Russell 2000.

An index fund buys all the stocks in a particular index. An S&P 500 index fund, for example, has all five hundred stocks in the S&P 500. It buys and sells the stocks according to the proportions of outstanding shares (stock that has been issued) relative to all other stocks in the S&P 500. If Xerox has 1 million shares outstanding (it doesn't) and Unisys has 500,000, the index fund would have twice as many shares of Xerox as of Unisys.

Index funds turn over only in the proportion of the stocks in the index.

No management and low turnover means their costs are the lowest of all mutual funds.

Some investors yawn at index funds because they avoid timing and stock selection. So what? Do you want excitement or do you want profit? You never have to worry about a manager's performance if you're buying an index fund. You needn't trouble yourself over stock selection. If you believe in stocks and have a small amount of money, index funds could be your best bet. They give you high diversification, the administrative expenses are low, and they're a good way of approximating the performance of the market.

Index funds, however, are betting on the whole market. My philosophy is to invest in individual companies. With index funds, you can't beat the market. With individual funds, you can. To differentiate themselves, some index funds have added bells and whistles. Some, for example, try to time the market. This departs from the point of an index fund. Why would it appeal to you? If I were shopping for mutual funds, I would buy individual funds that match my investment philosophy.

THE CASE FOR CLOSED-END FUNDS

The value of a closed-end fund rises and falls with the respective values of the underlying stocks in the portfolio. But it also varies with the vagaries of the stock market and investors' interest in the fund's manager. Investors may want to buy a closed-end fund because of their view of the manager. If a manager is highly regarded, great demand for his fund may cause it to sell at a premium compared with the underlying value of the stocks. Yet because of inefficiencies in the stock market, some closed-end funds sell at a discount. When a fund sells at a discount, you get a higher dividend yield than you would from owning the stocks themselves. Because of that, and because closed-end fund managers do not have to buy or sell stocks in response to moves by their investors, I think closed-end funds selling at a discount may be your best choice in owning a fund. You get the diversification and professional management that mutual funds offer—without the outside pressure that can force managers' hands.

MUTUAL FUNDS: SUMMARY

Although you can use the *Wall Street Journal*'s performance records as a guideline in picking mutual funds, you have to go further. Here are some important points to keep in mind:

- Don't focus on a fund's performance for the year to date or the past thirteen or twenty-six weeks. Look at three- to five-year records to see how the fund does in both good times and bad.
- Many investors don't receive the return that funds advertise. Although the Barracuda Fund might have grown 15 percent for the year, it could have grown 30 percent in January and February and then dropped during the rest of the year. If you bought it in March and held it the rest of the year, you would be down.
- Make sure you know what the fund's costs are. All other things being equal—and many things are—low-cost funds will serve you better than high-cost.
- Don't be a slave to performance ratings; invest for the long term. Choose solid funds and stay with them as long as the managers who achieved good records are running the store.
- Call to find out who's running the fund. Make sure there's continuity in the fund's management.
- Mutual funds give you diversification. To achieve even more diversification, consider buying several mutual funds.
- Index funds are a relatively safe, sound way to achieve diversification and growth. You can simplify your selection of mutual funds by using index funds. Being unmanaged, index funds have very low costs and outperform about 70 percent of all mutual funds.
- The main selling point of some mutual funds is convenience. As with the local convenience store, you could be paying substantial money for the lack of hassle. Is it worth it to you?

16

PICKING STOCKS:
BE A FINANCIAL
SHERLOCK HOLMES

In the early 1980s, a client asked my partner, Peter Miller, about investing in Liz Claiborne, the clothing manufacturer. She was a woman of taste who had been buying Liz Claiborne clothes. She liked the clothes, liked everything she saw about the company.

Peter didn't know Liz Claiborne, so he asked a colleague, the director of research at a Philadelphia brokerage house.

"Why do you want to get involved with a rag company?" the director asked. "The garment business is a rag business." Peter went back to the client and said, "Don't do it."

Although the woman knew much more about Liz Claiborne and about clothing than Peter or the director of research—neither knew anything about fashion—she let them talk her out of buying the stock. By not going with her instincts, she missed a great investment.

The key to most successful investing, I believe, is knowing how to pick stocks. If you already think you're capable of doing that, read this chapter as a double-check. If you think you're incapable of picking stocks well, read the chapter for suggestions. You may find that it gives you all you need to begin.

THE SECRET TO PICKING STOCKS

In deciding on companies to invest in, I'm strictly a fundamentalist. I use fundamental analysis—looking at the underlying strengths of companies and the projections of their future earnings. I pay no attention to the matters that fascinate *technical* analysts: such items as the volume in which a stock trades, highs and lows, price patterns, and thirty-day moving averages.

I'm interested in the company itself. I study the financial statistics found in company reports. I scrutinize trends in earnings and profit margin improvements. From experience, I know that the price of a stock reflects expectations of the company's future earning power and future dividend payout. Not past or present earnings and dividends, but future. A stock needn't pay a dividend now. If earnings are growing at a healthy pace, investors believe that the stock will pay a dividend eventually. That increases their demand for it.

One of the first companies I wrote up as a stock analyst was Crown Cork and Seal, manufacturers of metal cans. In 1964, I had gone to a meeting of the Financial Analysts of Philadelphia. John Connelly, the company chairman, made a presentation that impressed me. I called the company to find out more about it and to request the annual and quarterly reports. I asked to speak with Mr. Connelly. I was surprised to discover that Connelly answered his own telephone calls.

We arranged a meeting. When I interviewed him, I noticed that behind his desk was a big picture of him with President Kennedy. Going through the plant, I was struck by several features: the physical layout, the company atmosphere—Connelly answering his own phone—the high degree of respect for employees that was evident, the cleanliness of the plant.

When I wrote the report, in April 1964, the company had a net income of $9.5 million in 1963 on sales of $205 million. The stock was selling at $31 a share. (Adjusted for splits since then, that would be well under $1 a share.) The company had so much confidence in itself that it had a continual program to buy back its own shares. It still has never paid a cash dividend. Rather, management keeps plowing money back into the company. It's a stock I've stuck with. In the past ten years alone, it has gone from 2½ to 40.

After gathering numbers, I crunch them. Using a computer model, I project company earnings several years down the road.

Selecting companies is like weaving a quilt. It means stitching many pieces together. The number crunching I do, which is part of fundamental analysis, is important—it's the way I made the prediction about Trump's Taj Mahal that cost me my job. But number crunching is not the top criterion for the investment decisions I make. To me, a more important analysis is qualitative. The secret to good companies, I believe, is good management.

Audiences I speak to ask, "What is good management? How do you know it when you see it?" From interviewing executives, I've seen all types. I've met executives who bend the truth, those who exaggerate, those who believe their own press notices. I've met executives and managers ranging from dynamic and forceful to completely inept.

One executive who impressed me with his style and grace was Walter Hoving. I paid a visit to the corporate offices of Tiffany and Company, jewelers, on Fifth Avenue in New York. At the time, Hoving ran the company and was its chairman. He owned about 17 percent of its stock. When I visited him, the stock was selling at about 10.

To get to his office, you had to walk through Tiffany's store. As soon as I walked in, I noticed the courtliness of the employees and the service they provided. Some assistants escorted me to Hoving's office. By then he was in his upper seventies. On his lapel was a pin that read, "Try God."

Hoving and I had a two-hour interview. An old-fashioned, gentle fellow, he said, "Tiffany will never sell a diamond ring for a man, because I think it's in poor taste."

After the interview, he said, "I never meet with analysts." Excited by Hoving and his policies, I wrote up the stock. Less than three years later, it had quadrupled in value.

Of course, executives can have superb taste and still be poor managers. Some executives jeopardize their companies by taking them beyond their areas of expertise, or outside the areas they know best.

In my hands I hold a copy of a memorandum I wrote on a company in the early 1960s. I can see it dates from a long time ago—it's a carbon copy. Photocopying was still off in the future. Then 3M developed a machine that made copies on thermal paper, which turned brown and crinkled.

Xerox entered the picture, and photocopy machines as we know them revolutionized the office. Great demand arose for companies supplying copy paper, one of which was Patterson Parchment Paper. Patterson saw its earnings begin to rise.

I went to visit the company in Bristol, Pennsylvania, twenty-five miles from my office at Elkins Morris Stokes. I was there till eight o'clock one

ight. I spoke with employees and noted their devotion to the firm. Then I
met with the chairman. I was about to leave when he said, "If I could tell
you the whole story, you'd really be impressed."

"What's so exciting?" I asked.

"We're going to start making our own copy machines."

I left thinking, "Here's a company where the stock will probably go up
at first. It can prosper in its own field, but it will never have the resources
to succeed in the competitive photocopier industry."

Even though I thought the stock would rise in the short term, I never
recommended it. The stock did well for some time, but then the company's
earnings suffered from the decision to manufacture photocopy machines,
and its shares fell precipitously.

After many years of success on Wall Street, I'm confident that I know
how to pick well-run companies—the cornerstone to stock winners. I'm a
bit different from most money managers, because of my extensive
background in fundamental research. Many of the eighteen thousand
money managers in this country are one- or two-person shops or relatively
modest operations that don't conduct their own in-house research. They
don't visit companies and interview management. I don't make a stock
recommendation unless I meet with management or see the company
myself—kick the tires, if you like. I firmly believe that an analyst has to
visit the company and talk to the top executives.

The stories you hear in the boardroom, however, are almost always
favorable. They're often too good to be true. So I try to meet with as many
employees as I can—from the mail room to the factory floor to the loading
dock. I speak with middle management and the financial officers. I
especially seek out competitors. People like to talk, especially about the
competition.

When Peter Miller worked in the brokerage industry, he heard some
questionable stories about a bank in New Jersey. One of his clients, who
worked for a competing bank, told Peter he had sold his shares in the
bank's stock. He thought the bank was violating banking rules. He said to
Peter, "Maybe they know more than I do. Maybe they've figured out a new
way of banking, but I want out of the damn thing." The bank stock didn't
just go down; it went completely broke. The Resolution Trust took the bank
over. It doesn't exist today. You often learn more from talking to
competitors than you do from hours at the company itself. It's like
industrial espionage, but perfectly on the up-and-up.

One company that invited me to do research on them sent a chauffeured
limousine to pick me up. Peter Miller hopped in the back seat and enjoyed

the television set, the company phone, and other amenities. I sat in the front and spoke with the chauffeur. The company was a forty-minute ride from my house. All the way, I was quizzing the driver. He'd worked for the chairman for twenty years. By the time we arrived, I knew quite a bit about the firm.

We were asked to wait before meeting with the chairman. I wandered off to the plant. I spoke with the people there. To a fellow at the loading dock, I said, "Gee, it's kind of slow today. Are you usually more busy?" You can learn a lot by watching a product go out the door. If he said, "I used to ship two hundred cases a day, but in the last couple of weeks I've been sending out only twenty-five a day," that would tell you more about the company than you'd hear from the man in the boardroom.

When you talk to people, you can get a feel for how they view their jobs. Speaking with a chairman in his office, you look at his fingernails and his desk. You see how organized he is. You listen to how he talks to callers on the telephone and how he addresses his employees.

Peter finally caught up with me and said, "I've been looking all over for you, Marvin. Come on, they want us upstairs."

I said, "I know there's a good story in the boardroom, but I'm learning more about the company here on the factory floor. There's no way we'll buy this stock. I don't like what I've seen."

The Franklin Mint began in the 1960s as a manufacturer and seller of coins, medals, and other collectibles. In late 1969, I met with Joseph Segal, the mint's founder and chairman. I consider Segal to be a marketing genius. I like his business acumen. He came up with the idea of making medals and medallions, and later branched into books and porcelain figurines. Out of nothing, he created a rapidly growing, successful company. I saw the stock go from 1¼ in 1967 to 57 in 1970.

In December 1990, I was working on the launch of Roffman Miller. I wanted to talk with Segal about his becoming an investor in my firm. I went to see Segal at his new company, QVC. QVC sells products via television. Shown into his office, I immediately noticed the television monitors all tuned to QVC. He was watching QVC's programs on closed-circuit television.

The stock had gone public in the late 1980s and had quickly almost doubled in price, to about $20 a share. "I don't like the stock market," Segal told me. "I just put $1 million of my own money into QVC." In 1991, QVC stock dropped below $4 a share and Segal was disgusted. But by 1993, the stock had risen to 63.

In his lifetime, Segal has started more than thirty companies and is one of the most successful entrepreneurs I have ever met. He has always put money not into other stocks but into his companies, which he knows best of all. The best investments you can buy are those you are most familiar with.

As an amateur, you probably lack the entree to companies that a professional analyst has. Later in the chapter, I suggest steps you can take to simulate this type of research.

WHAT CONSTITUTES GOOD MANAGEMENT?

So what is good management? What am I after when I visit a company? What am I trying to find out about management? I'm looking for good management that permeates an organization. Here are the basic points I've learned.

Concern for Employees

Good management, I'm convinced, *motivates employees* and takes care of them. People are everything. If you don't treat your people right, they'll never do their best for you. You have to motivate your people, and you have to be good to them.

To encourage employees to work harder and give them more of a stake in their work, well-managed companies have programs for employees to become shareholders. Many companies match employees' outlays for purchases of company stock. Many also reward executives whose performance is outstanding. A good example is Promus Corporation, which recently outlined plans to give up to 10 percent of the company's stock to employees who excel.

As you can imagine, I see hundreds of annual reports each year. Many are ho-hum, but in 1972 an annual report that came across my desk caught my attention. It showed a young child eating a peanut butter sandwich. Published by Flowers Industries, a baking company, it was one of the best annual report covers I'd ever seen.

Shortly after I read the report, W. H. Flowers spoke before the Financial Analysts of Philadelphia. I told Mr. Flowers, the company's chairman, that I wanted to check out Flowers Industries in the hope of doing a report. "I'd like to meet as many people as possible," I said.

Flowers met with me and had arranged for me to speak with several mid-level executives. I spent a week studying the company. I went to almost every plant. In Atlanta, I spoke with Amos McMullian, who was head of the Atlanta bakery. I also toured plants in Florida and Spartanburg, South Carolina. The man who showed me through the Spartanburg plant was Heeth Varnedoe III.

At the time, Flowers Industries had sales of less than $100 million a year, but the people impressed me. Everyone was highly respectful of everyone else. Varnedoe had the enthusiasm of a teenager. I had an intuitive positive feeling about the company, and I came away from every facility I visited with the same feeling.

Recommending the company was a "no-brainer." When I wrote my report in 1972, Flowers was selling at 13. Adjusted for splits since then, that 13 would be 1.12. In May 1993, Flowers stock was worth 19. The company's sales, less than $100 million in 1972, have grown to $950 million. According to Value Line, Flowers is the fifth largest producer of bakery and snack food goods in the country. Varnedoe, McMullian, Robert Frazer, Martin Woods—people who were mid-level executives when I interviewed them twenty years ago have risen to the top positions in the company.

Adapting to Change

Another feature of good management is that it *adapts to change*. Companies that are well managed not only adapt to rapidly changing conditions at home and around the globe; the best-managed companies take advantage of change. In today's volatile world, change is a given. Companies must adapt to it or risk going out of business.

When I speak with a chief executive officer, one of the first items I'm interested in is what the company is doing to stay contemporary. How does it keep its products fresh? How is it filling the pipeline with new products? How will it grow into the future? A company can't be successful two, three, or ten years from now unless it adapts to change. No matter how prosperous a company may be, it can go out of business if it rests on its laurels and thinks no one can build a better mousetrap.

A Harvard business school case study is Bally Manufacturing. When I began following the gaming industry in 1979, Bally was the country's leading manufacturer of slot machines. It had about 80 percent of the slot machine market in the United States. Because Bally's management failed to put money into the company and adapted to change sluggishly, Bally lost its huge market share.

Bally stock had been selling at $29 a share but dropped to $12. Janney's salesmen kept calling me. "Marvin," they said, "this stock's got to be a buy. It's got to be a buy." And investors were buying Bally bonds. At sales meetings, I kept on saying, "Don't buy Bally bonds. They're bonds for the brave. Avoid them." The bonds lacked a strong company behind them.

What were the changes Bally failed to adapt to? There were changes in customer demand and interest, as well as new technology—the switch from mechanical to electronic machines. Bally forgot how to make machines and games that have appeal. A small, upstart company called International Gaming Technology (IGT) made gigantic inroads. Today in Nevada, which has about 153,000 slot machines, IGT commands 75 to 80 percent of the market. Bally Manufacturing has a tiny share of the total U.S. market. Again, Bally lacked good management and never adapted to change.

National Cash Register would be a minor player today if it hadn't adapted to laser-beam scanning, which revolutionized point-of-sale retailing. Western Union *is* a minor player today because of fax machines, credit cards, and other technologies that eliminated the need for people to use telegrams and to wire money. Western Union could have decided to enter the fax business or the credit card business. It didn't, and it fell behind. Companies must adapt to change.

The Long-Term View

In 1914, when only the rich could buy cars, Henry Ford doubled his employees' pay to the then-unheard-of sum of five dollars a day and reduced the workday from nine hours to eight. The *Wall Street Journal* criticized him, but the strategy paid off. Ford, who in other areas could hardly be considered enlightened, made the changes for two reasons. The first was to create loyalty among his twelve thousand employees. The second was to let them afford to buy cars. It was a brilliant move, because it created a whole new market for his own products. Later Ford gave his employees Saturday off, so they had more leisure time to go out and drive their new cars.

The *long-term view* is another factor that differentiates good management from middling management. Good management looks beyond the next quarter. Poor management can't see more than three months ahead. If a company tries to make its earnings grow 15 percent this quarter—but therefore eliminates funding or research for the future to make the current financial statement look better—that's poor management. In the pharmaceutical industry, for example, it often takes well over a hundred million dollars and eight to ten years to bring a drug to market. Without devoting that much time and money to new products, a drug company is unlikely to prosper.

Too many leaders of corporate America are so conscious of focusing on next quarter's earnings that they're unwilling to make necessary investments. They say, "We can't undertake this capital project now. It'll take away from our earnings-per-share growth. Let's defer it."

Wall Street has a killer instinct today. It wants immediate solutions. If the person who runs a company hasn't shown a 10 or 20 percent increase in earnings since last quarter, stockholders cry, "Get rid of him! Off with his head!" As if anybody could transform a company's situation in a month.

This short-term attitude is typical of far too many American companies and investors. It's a prime reason America has lost out in this highly competitive world. Contrast it with the attitude typical in Japan. Japanese companies say, "We don't care if we invest money for ten years with no payback. We want market share. Ultimately we'll dominate the markets and raise prices." The Japanese have gained market share in the United States because they're patient and look toward the future. They've invested billions in basic research that can last ten years or more with no payback.

Basic research differs from research and development. Basic research means following paths whose end points you do not know. The effort may not bring a payback for five years, ten years, or more. During the 1930s and 1940s, American companies devoted tons of money to basic research. That's how they pioneered television. That's how they pioneered the laser. Basic research has produced many of the prominent ideas and products of this century.

Since World War II, however, America has lost one industry after another. How many video cassette recorders are made in this country? How many cameras? How many watches? More than 99 percent of all video recorders and video cameras are made outside the United States. When I bought my first TV set in the 1960s, the United States had dozens of television manufacturers. Today, we have one: Zenith. Now even Zenith is beginning to manufacture televisions beyond our shores.

Some people explain away this trend by saying, "America no longer has a manufacturing economy. We're a service economy." Do you see that change as positive? Service jobs pay much less than manufacturing. The service economy is wiping out American cities. The wage tax in Philadelphia, where I work, is so high that firms leave the city to escape the tax. Lawyers can pick up and move their firms across the city line. You can't move a manufacturing plant so easily.

Protecting the Balance Sheet

Good management *maintains control*. It doesn't plunge the company into precarious levels of debt. Borrowing excessively to achieve growth is poor management. Debt can turn a company's destiny over to people outside the company. Or it can prevent the company from investing the funds needed to make fundamental changes. Good management guards the balance sheet and holds on to control.

Not that adapting to changing circumstances and maintaining control is easy. When a company as large as IBM needs to change direction, it can't maneuver like a rowboat. Redirecting IBM is like turning the *Queen Mary* around.

In late 1992 and early 1993, IBM stock lost almost half its value. Yet the company had a strong balance sheet. When IBM cut its dividend in half— 55 percent—the stock rose. Why? The dividend saving kept one billion dollars within the company.

Also, between 1987 and 1993, IBM closed 25 percent of its manufacturing capacity and laid off 110,000 people—of a total work force of more than 400,000. In spring 1993, it announced 25,000 more layoffs and more plant closings.

Although IBM failed to keep pace with changes in the computer marketplace, it never stopped putting billions of dollars into basic research. It has one of the best research laboratories in the world. IBM never had to dip into heavy debt. Its balance sheet remains strong. With all the basic research IBM does and with new, imaginative leadership, this restructured company has a chance to grow its earnings again.

General Motors, on the other hand, was mismanaged for years. It saw a long erosion of market share because it was making products that customers didn't like. To continue operating, General Motors management had to spend billions of dollars in company reserves. Borrowing billions and depleting the balance sheet severely hurt the company. General Motors could no longer self-finance its growth. So it had to raise capital by selling costly preferred stock to keep going, to design new products, and to give the public what it wants. Its finances are a shadow of what they used to be. General Motors now has new management, and it is taking aggressive steps to become much more efficient.

Even if IBM went from a triple-A credit rating to double-A minus, it's still a strong company. General Motors' rating is triple-B plus. The big gap between double-A minus and triple-B plus reflects the difference in how the two companies handled their balance sheets.

Beware of Companies That Pay Their Executives Astronomical Salaries

In the early 1980s, Janney did an underwriting for a firm that handled data processing for other firms. It also had a school that taught data processing. A week after the initial offering, Peter Miller was in a restaurant in Somers Point, New Jersey. He saw the chairman of the company having dinner, apparently in a celebratory mood.

The chairman had received the check with the proceeds from the offering. He now had a public company and was worth millions on paper.

"I'm a broker with Janney," Peter told him. "We just did your offering last week."

"Yes," the chairman said, "I've had a wonderful day. I'm celebrating because I picked up my check and I just bought a new Bertram boat."

"It was a quarter-of-a-million-dollar boat or so," Peter says. "That was the tip-off. I should have sold the stock that night. Within a year the stock went completely bust."

Greed and avarice are rampant among the people who run corporations today. Earlier in the chapter, I talked about the dismal performance of Bally Manufacturing's stock. Yet while the stock was tumbling in the late 1980s, Bally's top executive was staying in a suite in the Waldorf Towers in New York City. Bally held directors' meetings in places like Switzerland. In 1987 the man in charge of Bally's casino operations, Dick Gilman, had a total compensation package of $10.4 million. It was great for him but a terrible disservice to Bally shareholders, who saw the company's profits erode.

In 1989, before Time Incorporated merged with Warner Communications, Paramount made a $200-a-share bid for Time stock. That was well above the market price, which was then about $115. Time's management refused to let the shareholders vote on the proposed buyout. Instead, they let the buyout take place. The deal had golden parachutes for management but left out the stockholders. Four years later, the stock was still selling at 30 percent below Paramount's generous offer.

In early 1993, after IBM's stock fell precipitously, the company chairman, John Akers, resigned. That was a good move for the company, I believe. But Akers was given a pension of $1.2 million a year for the rest of his life.

So great have salaries and pensions for those at the top become that they have even attracted the attention of the SEC. The SEC is now concerned about executives raping and ruining their companies. Don't wait for the SEC to act. Avoid companies that pay their executives outrageous salaries and give them golden parachutes for retirement.

COMPANIES THAT DOMINATE THEIR MARKETS

One promising strategy is to invest in companies that dominate their markets. Such companies can raise prices in difficult circumstances to maintain their profits and remain ahead of the competition.

In the food industry, the big profits go to the companies that have the number-one and number-two positions in a category—such as breakfast cereals. If you're number three in a category, you're not a price leader. You can't command those markets; you're too subject to moves by your competitors. You can't raise prices when you're a smaller player, and profit margins can be considerably lower when you don't have the volume of the market leader.

Number one and number two in the breakfast category are Kellogg and General Mills. Those two companies control 65 percent of the market. All the other companies split up the remaining 35 percent. Which companies do you think have the highest margins, the most say over pricing, and the most clout in getting shelf space to launch new products? Established brands are like cash cows. They provide the capital to introduce new products and keep the companies contemporary and growing.

Remember, the single most important factor in the success or failure of a company is management. If a company overborrows and loses control of its destiny, that's poor management. If a company alienates its employees and their productivity diminishes, that's poor management. If a company defers basic research, that's poor management.

Companies that thrive are the ones that take care of their employees, focus on the long term rather than the short, plan, and adequately fund research and development programs. They're the ones that maintain a strong balance sheet and constantly seek to grow through new products, geographic expansion, and increased productivity.

Good Management:

- Motivates employees and takes care of them.
- Adapts to change.
- Initiates change.
- Takes advantage of change.
- Looks beyond the next quarter.
- Maintains control: it does not overly leverage the balance sheet and plunge the company into desperate levels of debt.
- Compensates executives properly, not with astronomical salaries.
- Encourages employees to become shareholders.

UNCOVERING GOOD COMPANIES

Even in hard times, successful companies abound. But how do you scope out companies when executives won't meet with the average Joe or Josephine? How do you spot promising companies and trends?

The answers are all around. Some are in the most unlikely places, such as your local supermarket's bathrooms. Some are clues you never notice, such as the light bulbs in a department store.

Picking stocks calls for some detective work. You have to act like a financial Sherlock Holmes. If you intend to invest, investigate. One of the great investors of this century is Peter Lynch, the former manager of Fidelity's Magellan Fund. Lynch believes that amateurs can make their own investment picks. Anybody who's been to a shopping mall in the last five years, he says, has seen stores such as The Gap, The Limited, or Home Depot. You walk into these stores and know that something special is going on. It doesn't take a genius to figure that out. In layout, atmosphere, selection, service, you can tell they're well ahead of their competition. Unlike a Sears. You walk into a Sears store, and it's fairly depressing.

Some of Lynch's best investment ideas have come from firsthand experience—simple contact with store employees or exposure to innovative store designs and products. One of Lynch's big investment successes was L'eggs. His wife had gone to the supermarket to buy pantyhose and spoke highly of the pairs in the egg-shaped containers.

Pretend you're a professional Wall Street analyst. On second thought, pretend you're not. As you've seen, most analysts are under strong pressure to buy, to sell, not to stay with investments. Many analysts become number crunchers to such an extent that they don't understand personalities. They don't weigh factors like management. With them, everything is numbers. That's not enough.

Don't overlook small clues. You go into a Dunkin' Donuts, taste the coffee, and know that it's vastly superior to coffee you buy in most restaurants or diners. I shopped at WalMart for the first time a few weeks ago. It amazed me. I found some splendid buys. I liked the whole concept, and right away I knew why the chain is successful. I used my common sense, which merits a prominent place in all investing.

So you can be your own judge. Or you can ask people who know. Want to learn about the athletic shoe market? Ask your kids. Chances are they're experts. They probably know much more about it than you do. They probably know all about basketball shoes, running shoes, aerobic shoes, cross-training shoes, and the rest. At a hotel, ask the bellhop how busy the place is.

One company that a friend asked me about is WordPerfect, makers of word-processing software. In early 1993, WordPerfect announced it would go public. My friend had used the software for years and thought it was superb. He said the telephone support was incomparable. "Is WordPerfect," he asked, "an example of what you're talking about?" It's a perfect example. You look for trends and trendsetters. You see something that you know is a special product or company, and you invest in it.

Here's an example of what a shopper can find out. A week ago, I bought a can of WD-40 oil. When I put the nozzle on, the valve broke in half. Yesterday I went back to the store where I bought it, Home Depot, although I couldn't find my receipt.

"Oh, get another one," the clerk said. That's typical of Home Depot's employees, who are invariably helpful. If you ask where an item is, they take you there. When I was in the checkout line, I saw a miniature Alberta spruce selling for only $9.99. The cashier saw me eyeing it and said, "Why don't you get one? I'll hold your place."

Look for things that are out of the ordinary. When you're in a car, pay careful attention. You can usually tell when you're in the presence of something special. You can almost feel it when a car is superior to the competition. If this happens again and again with a company's cars, you may have found yourself a stock pick.

Once you find companies you think you might invest in, write and request some information. Request—and study—the last three annual reports and the last four quarterly statements. Then you can check to see whether the company is delivering on its earlier promises.

DISCIPLINE

Like a company, you as an investor must adapt to changing times. You also need the discipline to look long-term. You shouldn't telephone your broker five times a day. You have to live with short-term swings in the market. You shouldn't make buy or sell decisions on stocks for periods as short as two months or six months or a year down the road. That's too short a time. You never know what will happen to the overall market or to your companies in so short a period.

Roadway Express is one of the nation's premier trucking companies. It has a pristine balance sheet, no debt, wonderful management, a fine record. In March 1993, it announced that its earnings for the first quarter would be below expectations because of an accounting change. Earnings for the full year would not match those of the previous year. One reason was that the company was proceeding with a capital program to gear up for the future. That reinvestment would affect the earnings performance in 1993. In two days, the stock fell from $70 a share to $61. I interpreted the announcement as a positive sign. But the market disagreed. Wall Street is so shortsighted that it saw the news as negative.

At about the same time, two analysts said they doubted that H. J. Heinz could make the $2.60 a share in earnings that it had forecast. The analysts said maybe Heinz would earn only $2.55 or $2.50. As soon as that happened, investors dumped the stock. Measured by return on equity, growth, many fundamentals, Heinz has one of the best performance records of any company in America. Suddenly, because it's five or ten cents short of its earnings projection, investors are dumping it. The trend makes no sense, but that's what's happening today.

Every decision you make about the stock market should be based on a three- to five-year horizon at least, not three weeks or three months. There is no sure way to get rich quick. Don't believe the stories that say there is. It takes time and patience to make money.

AN INVESTING PLAN

I suggest a plan in which you force yourself to allocate a certain percentage of your savings to regular investment. Use dollar-cost averaging, which I described in chapter 5. Dollar-cost averaging gives you the discipline to buy when the price of your stock is depressed, which is when you should be buying.

With discipline, you will demur or at least think twice when your broker calls and says, "Listen, XYZ has gone up ten points in three weeks. Do you realize that works out to a three hundred percent gain annualized? Let's nail down that profit and move on to the next one." Or when your broker says, "XYZ is heading way down. Let's get out before it falls some more." Brokers pressure you to sell and buy something else. It's the churn-and-burn approach I've decried.

If a company's fundamentals remain intact, you shouldn't merely ride out downturns in the market. You should view downturns as buying opportunities to accumulate more stock at favorable prices—as long as you don't commit too much of your portfolio to one issue. As I've said before, I regard 5 percent as the ideal limit in any one stock. In some circumstances (such as heavy sell-offs), I might raise my position as high as 7 or 8 percent. I would never go beyond 10 percent.

If you thought a stock was a good value at $25 and nothing fundamental has changed, it's an even better buy at $15. Selling at the first decline doesn't give your investments enough time to mature. Nor does selling at the first rise. An old Wall Street cliché says, "Bulls and bears make money; hogs get slaughtered." Don't succumb to greed.

EVERYBODY MAKES MISTAKES

If I had to leave you with only one message in this chapter, here's what it would be. Don't let your mistakes prevent you from investing. No investor—not the seasoned pro, not the novice, not those in between—is always right. If you invest with enough frequency, some decisions won't work out. Investing is an art, not a science. You will make mistakes in your picks. Don't let them jade you. Don't let them turn you off from the stock market. As I said in chapter 1, you can always come up with reasons not to invest. That's a worse mistake than most stock investment mistakes you'll make.

17

TIMING? NOT NOW,
NOT EVER!

Which statement makes more sense to you?

"Buy low, sell high."

"The ideal period to hold a stock is forever."

Both make sense to me, but one is much easier to adhere to than the other.

Many investors make the mistake of trying to buy when stock prices are low and sell when they're high. Never mind that it's almost impossible to achieve this aim with any high degree of consistency. Up or down? In the short term, no one knows where stock prices are headed. I don't trade in and out of stocks. Why not? Because I can't time the market. I don't know where the market is going in the short term. Neither does anyone else.

People think they know, and stock market gurus don't hesitate to make predictions about market directions. But events in the United States or halfway across the world can occur and drive prices in ways no one expected just hours earlier.

Remember seeing products boasting that they were "advertised on

TV"? Being on TV gives people credibility. I watch CNN every morning, and I watch CNBC. Almost every day, they have someone saying something like, "Well, I think the market's going to thirty-six fifty before the end of the year; and then sometime in January or February, we should be up to thirty-eight hundred." Viewers think, "I guess they wouldn't be on if they didn't know what they were talking about."

The public wants to believe in something. The public wants gurus, but gurus know little. In my career, I've seen almost every major guru get in trouble.

I've already talked about Joe Granville. In the late 1970s, Granville would predict that something would happen in the market, and it did. Then in the early 1980s, he called for everyone to sell. He not only got bearish, recommending that investors sell their holdings; he recommended that they sell some issues short—to sell borrowed shares of stock in anticipation of a drop in price, buying back in at what the investor hopes is a lower price to replace the borrowed shares. In other words, selling short enables an investor to profit from a decline in the price of a stock. For many years, he stayed in that bearish mode, during one of the greatest bull markets in history.

My old firm has its own technical guru, one of the nicest guys you'd ever meet. But his performance in timing the market is something less than perfect. Every morning he makes a market comment; and every day I was there, I monitored his performance. Before the stock market crash in October 1987, he had clients buying; and in the midst of the crash, he recommended selling—just the opposite of what they should have been doing.

On Friday, October 16, the market dropped about 100 points. On Monday, October 19, it dropped 508. After three o'clock on Monday afternoon, when the market was in free fall, the analyst got on the speaker phone and said, "This market's going a lot lower. Sell." So what happened after that? By early 1988, the Dow was higher than it had been before the crash. In 1993, it passed 3,500.

The analyst is still a guru and is often quoted, offering his technical viewpoint of where the stocks and the market are going. People forget how badly off course he strayed.

My point is, to trust in gurus is folly. I don't want to say gurus are phonies, but short-term predictions of stock market movement are junk. Yet the media promote gurus, and people believe them. It's a circus. It's all a bunch of—let me put it this way: He who lives by the crystal ball ends up swallowing glass.

If you think you can succeed where so many have failed, think again. Gurus are professionals. They have full-time jobs following the stock market and economic trends. What makes you think that you, an amateur, can do better than they can?

When you try to outguess the market, you usually guess wrong. A perfect illustration is a stock I've mentioned often, IBM. When IBM was selling at about 49 at the end of 1992, I read in the paper that Wall Street experts were calling it an aggressive sell. (Three months earlier, it had been an aggressive buy.) The stock will fall into the 30s, they said. Today the stock is selling at 58.

STOCKS ARE FOREVER

Consider the thinking of Warren Buffett, one of the top investors of the twentieth century. Someone asked Buffett, "What's the ideal period to hold a stock?" He said, "Forever."

That doesn't mean buying Western Union, locking it in a vault, and forgetting about it. At one time, Western Union was a blue chip. But that was a long time ago. Today it's been eclipsed by more forward-looking companies.

What Buffett was getting at—and I concur—is that one key to successful investing is buying stock in good companies and having patience. If you lose patience, if you try to time the market, you can cost yourself dearly—even with good companies that are well managed.

Well-managed companies will prevail in the long term; but over short periods, anything can happen. A perfect illustration is Motorola, a high-technology company that makes computer chips and electronic equipment. In December 1992, a man sued Motorola, alleging that his wife's use of a Motorola hand-held cellular phone had led to her death from brain cancer.

When the story broke nationally in January 1993, Motorola stock was selling for $61 a share. Three trading days later, it had dropped to 48⅝—a 20 percent decline. But within two weeks, the stock was back to its previous price. It later passed 90 and reached an all-time high for the stock.

There's always something. If it's not this lawsuit, it's another. Almost every major company faces hurdles that cause quick changes in its stock price, changes that no one could predict.

Drug manufacturers, for example, can be slapped with lawsuits from people who are dying, which can cause their stock to crumble. Other factors cause unexpected drops.

In February 1993, Merck was in the doghouse. It was selling at $37 per share. Not long before, it had been selling at $55. Then early in February, *Barron's* magazine had an article quoting a money manager who said that Merck was not only a sale but a short sale. The article was published on a Saturday. The next Monday, Merck stock dropped a point and a half. Tuesday, it was off another point and a half. In two days, the stock had lost nearly 10 percent of its value.

Because portfolio managers in institutions—mutual funds and pension funds—are concerned primarily with preserving their jobs, they go with the flow of trends. Even before the article came out, institutions were negative on Merck and other drug stocks. So what happens? Investors sell the stock or sell it short. Someone at one institution says, "Hey, wait a minute, look at all this selling. This stock is going to get killed. We can't hold it. Let's sell it. It's down from 57 to 38; it'll go to 30. This guy's saying it'll go to 30, sell it short." Some institutions start the first wave of selling. Remember, there are more than four thousand mutual funds and thousands of investing institutions. They don't all act at once. So a second wave of selling hits. A third and fourth wave can hit. Over two weeks, the company's stock could plummet still further.

There was nothing wrong with Merck. Nothing fundamental had happened to the company. Its earnings were continuing to rise. Merck's earnings have been growing 17 or 18 percent annually, year after year. Yet the stock fell from 55 to 37 in only a few months. Why?

Fear, mostly. After Bill Clinton was elected president, many on Wall Street began thinking that the new administration would aim to reduce medical costs by controlling the prices that drug companies charge (even though drugs account for only 6 percent of the country's total health care bill). Drug companies, investors feared, would be forced to lower their profit margins. But even if the investors were right, is that a good reason for Merck stock to lose a third of its value?

No one can kill the stream of new drugs. What pays for new drugs is high prices on old drugs. Will the American public stand for price controls that stifle the arrival of new drugs?

Let's say investors' fears materialized and Merck stops growing at 18 percent. Maybe it grows at 14 percent or 12 percent. It's still a phenomenal company, with a high rate of growth. We're talking about one of the top companies in the country, if not the world—a consistently profitable company, with billions of dollars invested in basic research, and one of the biggest streams of new drugs of any company in its industry. Not only that: Merck's chairman has been voted one of the ten top executives in the United States.

We're in a communication age. Some television stations broadcast stock prices all day long. The media focus on catastrophic events. Some people are so concerned about this hour's market movements that they carry portable units that flash stock prices. They're too oriented to the short term.

It's not just institutions and private investors that fall into this short-sighted trap. Corporate America has been hewing to the short-term line for years. That's why so many American companies are laying off employees and seeing their profits vanish.

Fundamentally strong companies recover from short-term swings. They adjust to sweeping change. In my opinion, the Merck scenario I'm describing was an opportunity to buy, not to sell. Instead of paying a 30 percent premium to buy Merck, you could buy it at a price-earnings ratio equal to the market's overall ratio, or "multiple." When the stock dropped like that—and a few months earlier who could have predicted the drop?—investors should have been buying it. But it takes courage to buy an out-of-favor stock.

Much more typical are the actions of a doctor I know. On Monday, October 19, 1987, while the market was shedding 500 points, she called Fidelity to sell all the shares she had in the Magellan mutual fund. Her shares were worth about $55,000. She had bought it two years earlier for $80,000. Like so many other investors, she was afraid the market would continue its plunge.

"I panicked," she says. Within weeks, the market had turned around. It recouped all it had lost and then some. She was sitting on the sidelines. She could have bought rather than sold on that "Black Monday." She missed a grand opportunity to buy low that day and sell high later.

Most investors act the way she did. You don't know—until afterward—that prices have bottomed out or peaked. In predicting where the market's going, I saw a study that said the best prognosticators in the business are right only 65 percent of the time. So even the top market timers are often wrong.

An old story in the industry goes like this: A broker tells his client, "Such and such a stock is one dollar—buy it," and the client does. The next day, it's $2. The client says, "Buy more." The day after that, the broker says, "It's three dollars." The client says, "Buy more." Finally it gets to 6. The broker says, "I think you should buy more." The client says, "No, sell it." And the broker says: "To whom? You're the only one who's buying."

WHEN TO BUY

Having said so much about the difficulties of timing, let me give a few pointers that can help you.

Don't insist on reasons not to invest. You've checked the financials and you see that the price of your selected company has shot up tenfold in the past two years. "I may be too late," you think. "The stock's already had its big run-up."

Maybe it has and maybe it hasn't. If the company is well managed, it will continue to stay abreast of changes and ahead of its competition. It could still be an excellent buy opportunity. Its best years may be ahead of it.

You can take a technical view of the overall market and come to the same conclusion. You may say, "On paper, the market looks awfully rich here. Prices are too high. I'm not going to buy stocks; I'll buy money market funds." So you stay out of the stock market.

Then the market caves in. Stocks get even cheaper. But you know what? Again you might say, "I'm not buying now. This market is going a lot lower." After the 1987 crash, when stocks dropped 23 percent in one day, people like the doctor I mentioned earlier said, "I'm not buying now; this thing is going through the floor."

Maintain that attitude, and you'll always miss out. You'll never enter the market at the right time. You may never enter it at all.

The point is, you must have the discipline to weather up and down cycles. Nobody is smart enough to be totally out, totally in, totally out, totally in. That is, totally out of the stock market when prices have peaked and totally in it when prices have bottomed. If you think you can't invest unless you hit those points precisely, you'll never invest in stocks.

Don't be afraid to buy out-of-favor stocks, as long as the companies are well managed. In the quarter ending June 1992, bank stocks were one of the best-performing groups. For years before, they had been hit hard and were one of the worst-performing groups. One investor I know made thousands of dollars buying airline stocks when they were out of favor and selling them when airlines recovered. Then airlines went out of favor again. That's what happens. Companies and whole industries flourish, flounder, and flourish again.

A common investment mistake is to follow the pack consistently. Sometimes it's better to be a contrarian—to buy when everyone else is selling and vice versa.

Initial public offerings (IPOs) can be risky. I've said a stock price generally reflects the expectation of future earnings and dividends. Initial public offerings and rampant speculation defy the conventional thinking.

Both established companies and start-up companies can issue new stock in IPOs. Investing in IPOs of start-up companies or companies without adequate track records can be risky. No matter how promising they may seem (a new company could announce a breakthrough cure for AIDS, for instance), many IPOs are for sophisticated investors and people who can afford to take big risks. I myself prefer to invest in companies that are established and that have track records and proven good management. They too can have IPOs, so make sure you read the prospectus to see how long the company has been in business.

Unbridled enthusiasm for almost all IPOs can be a danger signal. It's often a sign that a bull market is overheating and close to a top.

Speculation is another red flag. Casino gambling—on land and on riverboats—is spreading in many parts of the United States. An entrepreneur sees its popularity and declares, "I'll build a riverboat for fifteen million. I can make a lot of money." Sure enough, some casino stocks explode. Speculative fever hits. Investors get carried away.

In 1991, the price of International Gaming Technology stock rose fivefold. In 1992, it doubled from that. In early 1993, it went up another 30 percent. The stock was selling at $64; in early 1991 it had been $3½.

Investors see the success of IGT or Promus (another casino company) and think no casino stock can miss. "All these secondary companies are coming alive," they say. Casino Magic came out in late 1992 at $5 a share; seven months later, it was $81. As a group, gaming stocks soared—some with little or no profits. That's an overreaction. As competition heats up, poorly run and financially weak casinos will have difficulty competing. Although I regard casino gaming as a growth industry for the foreseeable future, failures will occur. Anytime Wall Street falls in love with a group, the floodgates open and everybody wants to run a casino. Wall Street raised billions in 1993 for two dozen new gaming issues. Today about sixty public companies are involved in gaming, compared with little more than a dozen a decade ago. I believe great rewards lie ahead, but there is a sea of sharks out there. How can you safely participate in all this growth? That's where a sector fund can serve as one segment of a diversified portfolio.

As soon as Wall Street picks up on something, you hear a buzzword. Today, *information highway* is the buzzword. When I came into the investment business in the 1950s, the buzzword was *bowling*. Bowling companies were the hot stocks. Where are they now? Other buzzwords were *nuclear* and *television*. Then nuclear became anathema. Television fizzled.

Invest for the long term. People experienced at investing know that what counts is the score at the end of a long-term period—three, four, five years or more. Recently, a casino stock sold for $2 a share. A client came in and asked for my opinion. "Betsy," I said, "the stock will go up." Two weeks later, it had doubled, to $4. She thinks I'm a genius. Yet I didn't buy it for any of my accounts. It was too speculative. I don't want speculative. Three years down the road, the stock could be worth zero.

At Elkins Morris Stokes and Company in the early 1960s, I worked with someone who was part of a group that had bought a large block of stock in a mining company, New Jersey Zinc. Listening to his explanation, I liked the company's prospects. I bought the stock myself. It cost $30 a share, if I recall correctly, and I bought fifteen shares.

One day I saw on the office broad tape that New Jersey Zinc had been taken over by Gulf and Western Industries. Gulf and Western, whose primary product was automobile parts, was a conglomerate. It took over so many companies that Wall Street jokingly called it Engulf and Devour. Among its other acquisitions were Consolidated Cigar Corporation, Paramount Pictures, Prentice Hall, and Simon and Schuster publishers. Although conglomerates were the in thing in the late 1960s, they lost that status in the seventies to companies that were "focused." Beginning in 1983, Gulf and Western began to dismantle (now called restructuring). It sold off dozens of companies, but Paramount Pictures remained one of the core businesses. Later the company changed its name to Paramount Communications.

Having become a shareholder, I went to New York to speak with Gulf and Western's chairman, Charles G. Bluhdorn. He could read a balance sheet better than anyone else I ever knew. Later, on an airplane flight back from the Dominican Republic, Bluhdorn died of a heart attack. He was only about fifty years old. For his successor, the board passed over the company's president and selected Martin Davis, who was then executive vice president. I had known Davis for years and thought he was the ideal choice.

Over the decades, I kept on buying the stock. It became a major holding of mine. I held it through the terrible decline of 1974, when it went from $65 a share to $9. I held it through the crash of '87 and the minicrash of '89. I weathered all those downturns. Today it's worth many times what I paid for it.

Balance and timing. Some of my clients want their portfolios to be 100 percent invested in stocks at all times. I believe in more diversity. Bonds should be in a portfolio to add a measure of safety and income. And cash isn't always trash. There are times when stocks are overpriced. As I've told you more than once, I'm not a market timer. But in late 1992 and early 1993, I was nervous about the stock market. Historically speaking, stocks were expensive. The outlook for the economy was uncertain. The market cannot tolerate uncertainty. It likes predictability.

The main factor pushing the market to new highs in the first half of 1993 was low interest rates—the lowest in two decades. Investors lacked high-paying alternatives to stocks. As the senior vice president of Janney Montgomery Scott said to me years ago: "Where does money go? It seeks higher returns." When CD rates drop as they did in 1992 and 1993, people search for higher yields. One source of higher yields is stocks and bonds, which can be risky. So instead of making a safe 3 percent on their money, they could lose 20 percent over the short term. Even though markets are close to record levels and stocks are not low-priced compared with historical norms, there are plenty of attractive buys for long-term growth. Sooner or later, though, the market will shift gears from bull to bear. Remember, it's a market of stocks, not a stock market. You have to live with the short-term swings.

Don't buy on takeover rumors. Never make investment decisions based solely on rumors that a company is about to be taken over by another. In the late 1980s, takeover rumors arose almost every day. A good illustration is Hilton Hotels. Hilton stock got caught up in the takeover frenzy. The stock went from the low 40s to 115 in a little more than a year. All of the rise was based on expectations of a takeover. Then the junk bond market collapsed—it became difficult to raise money—and Hilton pulled the plug. Baron Hilton said, "We are not for sale." No takeover offer materialized. The stock dropped to 26$\frac{1}{2}$. You shouldn't make investments because of rumors. Don't buy on takeover speculation.

To summarize buying decisions:

- Buy stock with the idea of holding it long term.
- Pay more attention to fundamental aspects than technical ones. Monitor how the company's earnings are progressing and compare it with similar companies in the measures of price to earnings, price to dividend, and price to book value. Buy a company because of its underlying fundamental strength.
- Consider companies that dominate their markets, but make sure they have the inclination and wherewithal to adapt to change.
- Don't be afraid to run against the pack. Don't hesitate to buy out-of-favor companies, as long as they're well managed.

- Don't buy a plummeting stock solely because you think it has hit bottom.
- Don't buy a stock just because it's risen from 50 to 60 and you think it's heading to 70.
- Don't buy a stock just because it makes the most-active list every day.
- Be wary of IPOs of start-up companies or companies with no earnings.
- Be wary of stocks that are the subjects of speculative fervor.
- Don't buy a company just because you've heard rumors that it's about to be taken over.

WHEN TO SELL

Deciding when to buy is easy. When to sell is tough. I've already quoted Warren Buffett, who said that the ideal holding period is forever. Ideally, a company remains contemporary, stays on a growth track, and you keep it. Holding a stock doesn't mean marrying it. It means monitoring it.

In general, holding is preferable to selling. In 1992, I sold only three stocks—out of about forty that I follow. Events are so volatile today that I tell every client, "As a long-term investor, you have to live with the short-term swings. Stay the course." History doesn't repeat itself, but humanity always does. Stock cycles will start again, as they always have.

I sell a stock for one of only two reasons:

1. The fundamentals change.
2. The stock gets way ahead of itself.

Fundamentals are the important measures of company performance I've talked about so often: price to earnings, price to dividend, price to book value, and so on. When they change or something else happens that leads me to think the company's earnings can no longer grow, that's when I consider selling.

For example, the company suddenly loses good management because of death or because of dissatisfaction among the board of directors. New management comes in that I'm skeptical of. Or competition is making serious inroads in market share and profits. Responding to competitors' advances or some other circumstance that makes it vulnerable, the company can make panicky changes in direction.

Companies must be attuned to their environment. If you're in high technology, your flagship product can become obsolete in six months. Personal computing is becoming a fiercely competitive commodity market where brand names matter less and less and profit margins are tiny.

By *ahead of itself*, I mean that a stock price has been driven up too fast.

In 1992, I bought USAir at 8⁷/₈. Within two months, the stock had doubled, to 17. It had moved to the point I thought it would be two years later. My two-year expectation was based on a better economy and greatly improved earnings.

Thinking that the price had gone up much faster than it should have, I sold my entire position in USAir. Then the stock fell down again—to 11 and a fraction—and I bought it again. I'm not a market timer; timers focus on technical aspects of the market, not on the fundamentals of a company, such as earnings or dividends. But sometimes when a stock doubles in a short period for reasons other than the fundamentals, I'm not afraid to take a profit. In early 1993, I sold out USAir for the second time, at a little more than $19 a share.

Your fundamentals can change. When your own fundamentals change, that may also be a time to sell. If you're getting married and buying a house, for example, you may need cash. If your three children are soon to enter college, you may need even more cash. As you approach retirement, you may want to change your portfolio allocation so that it's less aggressive. These could be times to sell.

Stop-losses. Some advisers suggest selling a stock when its value drops 15 percent from the price you paid for it, or its high, or anywhere in between. The idea is to stop your loss—to protect you from steeper losses if the price drops further.

But if a company's fundamentals are intact and the stock is being buffeted only by today's news or undue investor nervousness, the "paper" loss could be short-lived. If you sell just because the stock has dropped, you could be making a mistake. You'll never benefit from the growth of a company like WalMart. WalMart's prices fluctuate considerably. You'd have sold out—based on the 15 percent stop-loss guideline—and missed out on the big growth that came later.

Do your homework. Owning a stock takes some effort. After making a purchase decision and buying a stock, you have to do your homework. As a shareholder, you'll receive quarterly reports and annual reports. Read them. If you're smart, you'll call the company. Most public corporations have an investor relations department or other contact. You should call investor relations and ask basic questions.

What should you ask? The exact questions, and what you make of the answers, depend on the company. If you're calling an airplane manufacturer, such as Boeing, you want to find out about backlogs and order trends. If it's a food company, you're interested in unit growth—whether gains in sales revenue are being achieved by increases in price or by volume.

Let's say General Mills' food revenues are up 10 percent this year. How much of that growth is price increase and how much of it is volume—tonnage gains? If the growth is due to price increases that are too aggressive, General Mills could lose market share. Unit gains, in contrast, could indicate a gain in market share.

So ask intelligent questions and look at the answers critically. How much are costs going up? Is the company absorbing costs by keeping prices steady? Are its costs increasing faster than its prices? If so, the company's profit margins are shrinking. What's happening to corporate debt? If interest rates are coming down, is the company refinancing its debt? What about productivity gains? Most important, review product introductions and capital expenditures. How much is the company investing in new facilities and equipment?

When it's time, it's time. Never be greedy when you conclude it's time to sell. When you've decided to sell, sell. Don't try to squeeze that extra eighth or quarter of a point. Don't think, Well, it's gone up six points already this year; by tomorrow it could be up to eighty-four. Almost invariably, your efforts will end in disappointment. In thirty years on Wall Street, I've seen that happen hundreds of times.

Clear plastic bottles made of polystyrene represented a new technology in 1970, when I met with the president of APL Corporation in New York. Competitors made plastic bottles of polyvinyl chloride (PVC), which was heavier and more expensive.

APL's bottles looked remarkably like glass but were much lighter and more resistant to breaking. As I left, they gave me a pound jar of Vaseline in one of their bottles. When I returned to the office, I told a colleague about the product. With great force, I threw it against the floor—with such force that it shattered. Still, it was tougher than glass.

In May 1970, I recommended the stock when it was selling at 14. One client bought a thousand shares. It ran up to 30. Believing that the stock had gotten way ahead of itself, I said, "Let's sell." He said, "I'll sell it when it gets to $31\frac{1}{8}$," and he put in a stop-limit order at that price. The stock hit 31 but never reached $31\frac{1}{8}$. It started dropping. He kept waiting for it to go back up, but the stock kept tumbling. He finally sold it at 4.

The difference between selling a thousand shares at 31 and selling a thousand shares at $31\frac{1}{8}$ is only $125. The difference between selling a thousand shares at 31 and selling a thousand shares at 4 is $27,000. Don't try to wring another eighth or quarter point out of a stock.

Similarly, with an investment that's gone sour, don't hold on to it until it reaches the price you paid. The fallacy is, "It's a lousy investment. I don't want to be in it, but I can't sell it at a loss, so I'll keep it till it comes back."

No. The market doesn't know what you paid for the stock, and the market doesn't care. When it's time to sell, sell.

Don't make tax consequences a major part of an investment decision. You have to be aware of them, but don't make them a major factor. One of your stocks can get way ahead of itself. It's November and you think, I want to nail down my profits, but I'll wait another two months so I won't have to pay capital gains tax till next year.

If fundamentals point to unloading a stock, don't delay selling it till next year. That could be the biggest mistake of all. While you're waiting for the new year, you could get clobbered. For example, in late 1992, IBM fell 50 percent in less than six months. If you had decided to sell, you would have lost far more by delaying the sale into 1993 than you would have paid in capital gains taxes.

TIMING WITH MUTUAL FUNDS

When you buy a mutual fund, you buy professional management that's making the buy, sell, and hold decisions. In general, you should stay with mutual funds. You shouldn't switch funds or sell out wholesale. A select few people, such as Marty Zweig, have a highly successful, proven track record of market timing. They know when to hold them and when to fold them. I can't do that. It's a gift, like music. Some people can play a Chopin polonaise. No matter how hard I try, I'll never play it. That's why I bought a digital piano player. I don't have it in me to be Vladimir Horowitz, but I enjoy hearing him play and benefiting from his skill. Unless you have Zweig's gift for timing the market, stay with the mutual funds you own. Let the fund managers make the buy and sell decisions.

PART IV

ALTERNATIVES

18

BONDS: CORPORATE, U.S. GOVERNMENT, AND MUNICIPAL

Companies need money to operate—to build factories, to pay salaries, to rent space, to advertise—and they're willing to pay money to get it. A bond is a corporate IOU. In return for the money you lend, they'll pay you an agreed-upon interest rate. Almost all bonds pay interest semiannually. They return principal at the bond's maturity.

To protect yourself against violent swings in the market, you must diversify. Ideally, bonds offer secure, above-average income—a safer and lower-performing avenue for investing than stocks—that is part of a balanced portfolio. In this chapter, I discuss three types of bonds—those issued by:

1. Corporations
2. The United States government
2. Municipalities and state and local authorities

DO BONDS BELONG IN YOUR PORTFOLIO?

Absolutely. As gung ho as I am on stocks, I firmly believe that no one should invest 100 percent of their assets in stocks. The risks, the volatility, the uncertainty are too great. Instead, I favor balance. I think you should have some of your portfolio in stock, some in cash (for emergencies and for flexibility), and some in fixed-income instruments such as bonds. How much you allocate to each depends on your inclinations and circumstances. (I talked about asset allocation in chapter 8.)

So what sorts of bonds should you seek, what research should you do, and from whom should you buy them?

DON'T GO LONG WHEN RATES ARE LOW

Interest rates fluctuate, of course. Bond prices vary with interest rates, their maturity, and the quality of the bond. As I write this in the spring of 1994, interest rates are at their lowest levels in a generation. Short-term bank CDs (those shorter than a year or two) are paying 3 percent or less. After inflation and taxes, that's a negative return. Short-term bond rates are about 5 percent, and thirty-year government bonds are yielding 6 percent.

You don't want to lock up money at those rates for three decades. Neither do I. So I'm staying relatively short term. By short, I mean up to five, six, or seven years. Seven years would be the maximum I would commit on new purchases of bonds. I'll follow that strategy until inflation returns and interest rates rise. For now, I won't go out beyond five to seven years, because the yields are so low. The time to lock in rates is when long-term yields approach the total returns available from stocks. Don't worry about anyone else. When the rates are good for you, lock in. You have to put yourself into the equation. Remember, though, that no one can predict interest rates with any consistency.

PREMIUMS AND DISCOUNTS

Companies usually issue bonds with a *face value* of $1,000. That's the amount the company will pay when the bond matures. In the meantime, the bond has a *coupon*, the interest rate it pays each year.

You can buy bonds as new issues, or as existing issues on the secondary market. Like stocks, many bonds are traded (although they have important differences, which I discuss later in the chapter). Bond prices are expressed as a percentage of the face value. They are based on several factors, notably:

- *Strength of the issuer*—what's behind the bond
- *Yield*—how much the bond pays in interest
- *Maturity*—when the bond pays you back

When a bond sells for exactly its face value, it's said to be trading *at par*. But bonds often trade at more or less than par value, especially during periods of changing interest rates. If interest rates have risen since a bond was issued, the bond is likely to trade at a discount from face value. Investors won't pay full price for a bond yielding 7 percent if new bonds are paying 10. Conversely, investors will pay a premium (more than par) if a bond is yielding 9 percent when new bonds are yielding 5.

U.S. TREASURY OBLIGATIONS

The United States government finances part—too big a part—of the more than half a trillion dollars it needs annually to operate by issuing Treasury obligations. Short-term bills and notes and long-term bonds let you lend the federal government money without taking any risk. They're the safest investment vehicle you can get. They're backed by the full faith and credit of the United States government. Unless the federal government goes under, it will repay your money and the interest it promised.

You're not one of those people who believe that the U.S. government will go under, are you? If so, give me your idea of where your money will find a safer place.

My belief is that the U.S. government will always be there. If the government runs short of money (which it has every year but one since the 1960s), it has three options: print more, borrow more, raise taxes. Typically, the government does all three. Yes, the government will always be there, and it's likely to continue issuing Treasury bills, notes, and bonds. Some pay fairly decent returns, especially given the low risk. Later in the chapter, I show some of the advantages that U.S. Treasury obligations offer bond investors.

STATE AND MUNICIPAL GOVERNMENT BONDS

States, cities, municipalities, school districts, and some quasi-governmental authorities also issue bonds. The interest rates on those bonds are generally lower than the rates on corporate bonds or other fixed-income investments, but that's not the whole story. The interest on municipal bonds is usually exempt from federal taxes and exempt from taxes in the state or municipality that issued it.

For example, if you live in Los Angeles and buy a state of California general obligation bond (GO), the interest you earn will be exempt from taxes of the federal government, the state of California, and the city of Los Angeles. If you live in Philadelphia and buy a California bond, you will have to pay taxes on the interest to Pennsylvania and to Philadelphia.

SELECTING BONDS: BUY QUALITY

On the corporate side, stick with investment-grade bonds—those rated triple B or better by Standard & Poor's or Moody's. You can find these bond guides at the local library. In corporate America, companies rated triple A are rare. There are fewer than a dozen. Below investment grade, you enter a realm of too much risk. Remember, the purpose of investing in bonds is secure, above-average income.

When I buy corporate bonds, I look at the company behind the bond— just as I do with stocks. I do my homework. Look, too, at the ratings on municipal government bonds. Stay with investment-grade.

In municipal bonds, I recommend that you confine yourself to your own state. Don't buy municipal bonds issued elsewhere. Stay with general obligation bonds, because they're backed by the full faith and credit of the state. If the state runs out of money, it has the power to raise money by raising taxes.

Despite the taxing power, the general obligation bonds of some municipalities are risky. Remember New York City in the mid-1970s? Bridgeport, Connecticut, in 1991? Philadelphia? My hometown hasn't gone bankrupt, but its bonds did drop to junk status. The investment community has had doubts about the city's ability to cover its debts. Taxes aren't the answer. With its high taxes, Philadelphia has already chased hundreds of thousands of residents and businesses across the city limits.

WATCH OUT FOR AUTHORITIES

Another type of government bond, called a *revenue bond*, has no pledge of a government's full faith and credit. Instead, it's paid from revenues of an activity such as an airport, sewer system, or hospital. During the 1980s, brokers raised money for hospitals, industrial authorities, and the like by issuing tax-exempt revenue bonds. Some of those organizations, having no power to raise money, went under. Here in Philadelphia, Metropolitan Hospital couldn't meet its debts, and the people who held its bonds lost their money.

Be careful of industrial revenue bonds. You have to do your homework, which is difficult, and their interest can be subject to the alternative minimum tax. Stick with investment-grade general-obligation bonds.

HOW AND WHERE TO BUY BONDS

When buying bonds, you have three main choices:

1. Individual bonds available through a broker
2. Bond funds—both open-end and closed-end
3. Bonds sold directly by the U.S. government

Buying individual bonds has some key advantages and some pitfalls, which I describe below. If you have less than $10,000 to invest in bonds, or if you don't want to face all the pitfalls that buying bonds can strew in your path, you may want to buy bonds via a bond fund. I talk about that approach later in the chapter. I talk about buying bonds directly from the U.S. government in chapter 19.

INDIVIDUAL BONDS

The only way to buy bonds individually is to shop. That's not as easy as it sounds. Buying bonds is not like buying stocks. When you buy a stock listed on the New York Stock Exchange, the price is the same at every broker. The commissions may change, but the price is the same. Bonds are a different story. Bonds listed on the New York or American exchange have very much the same price everywhere—although on small orders, $5,000 to $10,000, you will pay more or sell for less than for orders of $25,000 or more. On tax-exempt and unlisted bonds, you may find considerable variation in the prices of bonds from one broker to the next.

Also, the commissions on unlisted bonds, including all tax-frees, are different from other commissions, but they're commissions nonetheless. Called *markups*, they're built into the bond prices. Markups depend on the type of bond you buy, how available it is, and the amount you buy. At full-service brokers, the markup on a municipal bond, for example, generally ranges from 0.25 percent to 3 percent of the bond price. The more you invest, the lower the markup.

Much more skill is involved in buying unlisted or tax-free bonds than in buying stocks. It's harder work. That's why some people buy bond mutual funds: someone does the work for them.

Many brokerage firms, particularly discounters, don't keep bonds in inventory. When you place a buy order, the broker takes to the street to buy the bond. Larger firms have bonds in inventory, because at any given time, client A may have to sell because of sickness, death, or some other reason, while client B wants to buy. The bonds are crossed in-house—the broker does not have to go out and buy them. In that situation, the sale is usually done at an advantageous price.

Let's say a mutual fund that owns a large position in bonds wants to sell them and put more money into the stock market. The fund goes to a large broker such as Prudential and shows them the bonds. If you're a large, well-capitalized brokerage firm, you're always being shown different bonds. So these firms tend to have the most inventory and the best selection. They don't have to go outside to buy them.

Because the prices of bonds vary, I shop the street whenever I buy bonds. I check with two or three different brokers to make sure I get the best price. Bonds can have markups of $30 or $40 per $1,000, and I like to buy at friendly prices. Because I buy in volume, I can buy a bond for a commission of $2.50.

Discount brokerages such as Charles Schwab handle bonds, but they don't maintain inventory. They have to shop the street to buy, just like an individual. That's why you have to be very, very careful. It's better to call several brokers. Get prices from three or four firms and compare them. How do you know which broker to go to? You don't. You have to check around, unless you're dealing with a broker you really trust.

Some brokers make a good living by putting large markups on bonds they trade. Investors generally are not aware of how much brokerage firms make on bonds, or how much they're marking them up. On small orders, it's not unusual for bonds to have a 3 or 4 percent markup. See why I say you'd better shop around?

When you do your comparison shopping, you might experience something like this. You phone one broker, perhaps at Dean Witter, and say, "I want to buy a bond that matures in five to seven years that's double-A or better." Dean Witter may have such a bond. Then you call another firm. They might not have the same bond, so you're comparing apples and oranges. You have to know your product. It's tricky. You really have to go by several things: the bond's rating, yield, maturity, price, and call protection (see below). Make sure you're getting comparisons of identical items.

ANOTHER CHOICE: LISTED BONDS

One exception to the complex story I just outlined are bonds listed on the New York Bond Exchange. Hundreds of those bonds exist, and their prices are the same no matter which broker you go to. For prices, you can check the *Wall Street Journal*, in the New York bond section. When you do that, though, you may be wondering to yourself, How are these bonds rated? The *Journal* listings don't have ratings.

What I would suggest is this. Go to a library or any broker, and consult the *Standard & Poor's Bond Guide*. Look in the guide for bonds listed on the New York exchange (they're the ones that have dots before their entries). Move your eyes across the columns till you find the rating. As I said earlier, focus on investment-grade only.

CHECK THE NUMBER OUTSTANDING

Another item to watch for is the number of bonds outstanding in a particular issue. If it's a small issue, like $25 to $50 million, chances are the bond will be traded infrequently. Even if it's listed, most of the issue is probably in the hands of institutions, and they will rarely trade it. When you see a large outstanding figure—some AT&T bonds, for example, have $250 million outstanding—those bonds are traded relatively frequently. The larger the bond issue, the higher the liquidity. That's important, especially if you have to sell the bonds before they mature.

IS IT CALLABLE?

Your homework has not yet ended. Make sure you know the bond's redemption provisions. Some bonds are *callable*; others are not. *Calls* let the issuer refinance at lower rates—just as you can with your mortgage. Why pay 10 percent on a bond if the prevailing rate has fallen to 7? The issuer calls the bond. *Call protection* prevents the issuer from calling the bond for a specified amount of time or till maturity.

The *Standard & Poor's Bond Guide* has a column for redemption provisions. Some bonds are callable at par—that is, when they call the bond, they'll pay the face value. The next question is, When are they callable? One bond whose listing I'm looking at is callable beginning September 15, 1993. Its price is 99¾ (that is, 99¾ percent of the face value). In 1992, the price of this bond went to 110—10 percent above par. Suppose you had bought it at 110 in December 1992, and it was called—at par—in September 1993. Mistake. For every $110 you paid, the company would pay you back a mere $100.

CMOs: NOT BONDS EXACTLY, BUT SIMILAR

My father is a conservative investor, but even he doesn't like one-year certificates of deposit at 3 percent. So last year I bought him a series of collateralized mortgage obligations, CMOs. These are similar to bonds, in that they're debt. But instead of being corporate or government obligations, they consist of mortgages. They're packages of mortgages put together by brokers, such as Prudential, and other companies. My father has become a mortgage holder. In effect, he lends money to people who borrow it for mortgages, and he receives interest as the mortgages are paid off.

One CMO we bought was to pay 9.75 percent till the year 2018. We bought it for $1,005 a bond, a premium of $5 over face value. He bought nine of these CMOs on December 21, 1992. As of March 10, 1993, three of them had already been called at par. It was obvious to me that as interest rates came down, more of them would be called. If they were called at par four months or six months after he bought them, he would lose $5 a bond (the premium over par). But the 9.75 percent rate, minus the $5-a-bond loss, would still amount to a yield of about 6 percent. That's a hell of a lot better than the 3 percent he was getting with CDs.

Dad will get at least double what he could get anywhere else, with no risk. Actually, there's always risk. The risk here is that the bonds could all be called tomorrow. But that's unlikely. I have a computer program that helps me with calculations, and I figure that the average life of these bonds is two years. In January 1993 it was four years, but interest rates have plummeted since then. As the rates are coming down, the life expectancy of the bonds will drop.

Statistically, if interest rates are at a certain level and mortgage rates are at a certain level, I know how fast the mortgages will be paid down. As mortgage rates drop, the pace of refinancing accelerates. On average, these bonds will be called in two years. I would gladly accept 9.75 percent guaranteed for the next twenty years (what my dad would get if the bonds were never called). But they will be called, because people will pay off their mortgages. Still he'll get a much better return than he would in a bank.

In times of low interest rates, people have to find ways to protect their money. What the average person did in the low-interest period of 1992-93 was to take money out of CDs and put it in the stock market. Stocks, of course, carry much more risk than CDs. CMOs—what my father is doing—have almost no risk. How, you ask, can they pay 9.75 percent if there's no risk? Isn't it too good to be true?

The answer is, these trusts were created years ago, when interest rates were in the 9 and 10 percent range. In 1989 or so, that was the rate that people who bought mortgages were paying. As interest rates drop, people pay off their mortgages, and that's why the bonds are likely to be called.

Some can be called every six months. Others have different provisions. There are literally scores of types of CMOs. Some brokers who handle CMOs charge big markups. To buy these CMOs, you have to know what you're doing. Some investors, not understanding what they're all about, get a lower return than they expected.

Because I know how to buy them, I'm buying them at attractive prices. I deal with brokers who make only $2.50 for every thousand dollars' worth of bonds. Most brokers will not work for that. The average broker would probably charge the average investor $30 or $40 a thousand.

CMOs are for professionals. They're tools we use to increase high-quality yields substantially over what we could get somewhere else. I bring them up not to suggest that you buy them but to illustrate the point about callability. Most investors, I believe, should stick with stocks and bonds, investments they understand.

CURRENT YIELD VERSUS YIELD TO MATURITY

One column in the bond guide shows you the bond's current yield. The next shows yield to maturity. It's important to understand the difference, because it can be significant.

With some bonds, the current yield is higher than the yield to maturity. With other bonds, it's lower. The difference depends on the bond's current price. If the price is below par, the current yield will be lower than the yield to maturity. If the price is above par, the current yield will be higher than the yield to maturity.

Yield to maturity is a complicated calculation. It encompasses the years remaining until the bond matures, the annual interest payments, and the profit or loss that you get at maturity.

GOING OUT AND BUYING

Once you have some listed bonds with solid ratings and decent yields, and once you know about their call provisions, go back to the *Wall Street Journal*. For each listed bond, you'll see a bid price and an ask price. To buy the bond of your choice, you can call a broker and put in a bid. Say something like, "I want to buy X bond," and bid a figure based on those you saw in the *Journal*.

ZERO-COUPON BONDS: TRICKY BUSINESS

A regular bond has a coupon—the interest it pays each year. *Zero-coupon bonds*, as the name says, have no coupon. You buy them at a discount from the face value and collect the full face value at the end of the term.

The United States savings bonds you bought as a kid (and may still be buying) work that way: you bought one for $18.75 and years later cashed it in for $25. Zero-coupon bonds come in many types: U.S. government, corporate, and municipal.

Zero-coupon bonds have two important traits:

- *High volatility.* If you hold a zero-coupon bond till maturity and the issuing company is still there with the money, you'll receive the face value of the bond. But if you sell the bond before the term, it may be worth considerably less than you paid. It could also be worth more. With zeros, the interest is reinvested at a locked-in rate: the rate that was set when the bond was issued. With coupon bonds, the proceeds are reinvested at variable rates. Because you've locked in the rate with zeros, they're especially sensative to changes in interest rates.
- *Imputed income.* Although zero-coupon bonds pay no annual interest, you have to pay income taxes as though they did. This is called imputed income.

If you go for corporate zeros, you absolutely must buy only the highest-quality companies. Because you're paid only at the end rather than every year, the company had better be there down the road. Moreover, because you don't receive current income but have to pay taxes as if you did, I believe that zeros should be used only in tax-advantaged accounts. By that I mean accounts where you don't have to pay taxes until you withdraw the money years later. The best-known example is an individual retirement arrangement (IRA). If you're looking at a taxable situation, consider municipal zeros.

You can buy zero-coupon bonds individually from a broker or through mutual funds.

ARE BOND MUTUAL FUNDS FOR YOU?

When I spoke about the need to shop the street for the best bond prices, were you taken aback? Did you think, Whoa, I don't want to do that, or I don't have time for that? If so—or if you have only $1,000 to $5,000 to invest in bonds—you're a candidate for a bond mutual fund.

Because of the way bonds are traded, it doesn't make sense to invest less than $5,000 in an individual bond. If you buy one bond at the average brokerage firm, you'll pay a minimum commission of about $75. So it doesn't pay to buy one bond. Save your money until you've reached $5,000. If you have less money, buy a bond mutual fund. Realize, though, that many bond funds differentiate themselves by offering "bells and whistles," gimmicks such as options and foreign debt obligations. Most people wouldn't buy individual bonds that way.

From a purely financial standpoint, it's preferable to buy individual bonds rather than bond mutual funds—corporate bond funds or tax-free municipal bond funds. Here's why.

If you buy a 10 percent bond—assuming it's a highly rated bond such as a U.S. government issue—you know you'll get your money back when it matures. You also know you'll get a set amount of interest. Let's say you buy a ten percent bond and, suddenly, rates drop. I, meanwhile, buy a similar bond, but the yield has fallen to 8 percent.

So I say to you, "Let's get together and form a mutual fund."

"Are you crazy?" you ask. "I'm getting 10 percent. You're getting 8."

That can happen with an open-end mutual bond fund. Why dilute what you buy? Buy the individual bond.

In more detail, what happens with bond funds is this. As rates come down, and as new people buy into the fund, they dilute the yield, as I just showed. If interest rates go up and bond prices go down and people begin liquidating their funds, they force the money managers' hands. To pay the investors who are liquidating their holdings, the managers may have to part with some bonds at prices lower than they'd like.

Because of the reasons I just gave, and the fact that bond funds never guarantee to pay back your original investment, I don't like bond mutual funds. I think you're better off buying your own bond, even if you have only $5,000 to invest in it. If it were my money, I would buy the bond directly. I would shop the street. But I have a lot of experience and know what to do. Many investors don't have the luxury or savvy of calling around the street. They don't want to research bonds at the library, and they don't want to call from one broker to another. If you're like them but do want bonds in your portfolio, go with a no-load mutual fund that invests in bonds.

Not all U.S. government bond funds advertise the same yield. Yet, given that the bonds they own do have the same yield, how is that possible? Gimmicks. The funds buy bonds at a premium, so the funds have a higher yield than funds owning bonds that sell at par. You can't invest just by past performance and current yield. You have to know how the fund is achieving that yield.

MONEY MARKET FUNDS: OKAY FOR CASH RESERVES

Money market funds are another type of bond fund. These funds attempt to maintain a constant share value, usually one dollar, by investing in high-grade commercial paper and government obligations for very short terms. Tax-free money market funds invest only in tax-free bonds. If your income is high enough to warrant tax-free investments, they can be a good place to park your money until you move it to another form of investment.

DON'T TRADE BONDS

Perusing the *Wall Street Journal*, you discover that a bond you bought a year ago has increased in value 10 percent. You're tempted to sell and take a profit. Should you?

I've never been convinced that trading bonds pays off better than buying and holding to maturity. Leave bond trading to professionals. It's not for individuals.

Investors buy bonds because they're looking for a certain yield and they're looking to get their principal back when the bond matures. Bonds are a way to get above-average income and balance a portfolio so you don't assume all the risk that you do when you invest in stock. If you want to play the market, you might as well be in stocks. So I say, *Don't trade bonds.*

ADVANTAGES OF U.S. TREASURIES

Earlier in the chapter, I gave an introduction to United States Treasury obligations. Here are some advantages that U.S. Treasuries have over every other investment:

- *They're safe.* A corporation may go bankrupt and leave bondholders in the lurch. The U.S. government will always be there.
- *They're double tax-free.* Although you have to pay federal income tax on the interest paid by U.S. Treasuries, they're not subject to state or local income taxes. Depending on where you live, that could be a major saving. In Pennsylvania, the state income tax load is fairly low—less than 3 percent. In New Hampshire, it's zero. But in other states, such as New York and Connecticut, it's enormous.
- *They offer better call protection.* As I've said, most corporate bonds can be called (prepaid at a specified time)—usually five years from the date of issue. Bonds are called because interest rates drop. People who bought high-coupon corporate bonds in the 1980s— paying 9 or 10 percent—that had five-year call protection are now

seeing those bonds called. They thought they would get a 9 percent yield for thirty years. But after the bond is called, they must accept much lower yields if they choose to reinvest in bonds. That's why you may be better off buying a government bond.

Although the vast majority of U.S. Treasury bonds are noncallable, about two dozen issues can be called. The last time the Treasury sold a callable bond was 1984, and government bonds that are callable are callable in the last five years of their maturity. So a thirty-year bond would have twenty-five-year call protection. Find out which U.S. bonds are callable. Check the bond section of the newspaper under maturity date, and you will find two dates. The first represents when the bond can be called; the second is the maturity date. To be sure, call the nearest Federal Reserve Bank.

- *You can buy from the federal government directly*. U.S Treasury bonds and bills differ from corporate bonds in that you can buy them directly from the Federal Reserve. (You don't have that option for state or municipal bonds.) The government holds auctions of bonds at its twelve Federal Reserve Banks. Visit the nearest one, and put in a bid yourself. There's a procedure to follow. Call the Federal Reserve, and they'll tell you how to do it.

The process I just mentioned applies only to new U.S. bonds. It's not for existing bonds. Those are sold on the secondary markets, which are listed in the newspaper under U.S. government bonds. The federal government is always issuing new bonds. As long as the government continues to have $300 billion-a-year deficits (or, for that matter, lesser deficits), it will issue new bonds.

SAVINGS BONDS

I discuss United States savings bonds in chapter 19.

HOW TO BUY BONDS: A SUMMARY

To sum up, when buying bonds:

- Lock in long-term only when interest rates are high.
- Hold bonds till maturity. Leave bond trading to professionals.
- Don't speculate with bonds. Buy only investment-grade bonds: triple-B or higher. Junk bonds are called junk for good reason. You

buy bonds for predictability and security. If you want higher risk, trade stocks.

- Do your homework. Make sure the bonds you buy have call protection: either buy a bond that can't be called—these are listed in the *Standard & Poor's Bond Guide* at the local library—or buy U.S. Treasuries. You don't want unpleasant surprises down the road. A bond is called only when the call is to the issuer's advantage.
- When buying tax-free or unlisted bonds, shop around. Prices can vary considerably from broker to broker.
- If all this sounds too complicated but you want bonds to balance your portfolio, buy a bond mutual fund. Even buying a bond fund can be complicated. Do your homework to make sure the bond fund is managed in a way that's okay with you.

19

SAVINGS ACCOUNTS, CDs, AND OTHER LOW-RISK CHOICES

In our grandparents' generation, people had few choices about where to invest their money. They had stocks and bonds and, for those who shied away from risk, that stately, stone, pillared building on Main Street: The Bank. If you had no confidence in the stock market, the bond market, or the bank, you kept your money at home.

Out of habit, ignorance, or some other reason, many who shun risky investments still keep most of their money in the bank. Bank savings accounts, certificates of deposit, and money market accounts—what the financial industry calls *cash*—are the traditional home for savings. People are familiar with them, and they entail less risk than stocks or bonds. Being low risk, they bring low returns—especially during recessions and periods of low inflation. But they're usually preferable to ensconcing a stash of bills under your mattress.

MONEY IN THE BANK

Although the twenty-first century is almost here, most banks still have passbooks, and they still have passbook interest rates as abysmal as the rates they offered in the 1920s. My father has three bank CDs, whose total worth is about $130,000. Two of the CDs yield 2.36 percent a year, and the other yields about 2.9 percent. He also has a checking account balance of $20,000. It pays 1 point something percent interest.

The other day I asked him why he had so much money in his checking account. "I need it," he said. "I'm going to be making changes around the house. I'm going to need ten thousand dollars."

Granted, interest rates are at twenty-year lows, but my father's money could certainly be earning better than 2 or 3 percent. He should have his checking account money elsewhere. By keeping his money in the low-yield checking account, my father is losing about $800 a year in interest. That's the difference between what $20,000 would earn at 5 percent interest and the 1 percent he is earning. "How do you like paying eight hundred dollars a year for your checking account?" I asked.

"I get free checking," he said.

"No, you don't."

"I get a free safe deposit box too."

"That safe deposit box," I said, "is costing you eight hundred dollars a year. Go out and rent one for thirty-five."

My dad is from the old school. If he had to choose between a sweater costing $10.95 and another costing $15.95, he might buy the $10.95 because it was cheaper—even if he liked the other better, and even though he could easily afford it. Yet he's willing to spend $800 a year for a "free" checking account.

He thinks of banks as solid. He forgets that many people have lost money by having more than $100,000 in banks that went out of business. (The federal government insures bank accounts only up to $100,000.) My dad doesn't trust a lot of things, but he trusts banks. I don't argue with him. That's the way he is, and he's proud of it.

Banks, then, hold a significant place in his investment pantheon. Where do they fit into yours? Do you have most of your money in a savings or checking account? If so, why? To write checks? Habit? Negligence? Ignorance? In the next section, I present some alternatives.

GET THAT MONEY OUT OF THERE

My checking account balance generally runs about two or three hundred dollars. The only reason it's that high is convenience—I write about five checks a month with my checking account and use a different type of account for checks above $250. I could reduce my checking account balance to $100, but then I'd have to keep transferring money to cover my checks. A balance of $200 or $300, I find, limits the transfers to convenient intervals. I would never keep more than a few hundred dollars in a checking account, and unless you enjoy donating money to the bank rather than to yourself, I suggest that you don't either.

If you're averse to risk, write many checks for more than $250, and like the ease of not transferring money to cover them, consider these possibilities. Both offer higher yields than a conventional bank account:

- Money market account with check-writing privileges
- Tax-free municipal bond mutual fund with check-writing privileges

A *money market fund* invests multimillion-dollar sums in income-producing instruments with short maturities—fifty to seventy days on average. The rates it pays investors—people like you—are a little higher than what a bank account pays.

Money market funds invest in three types of obligations: U.S. government debt, offering the highest safety; state and municipal bonds, which are free of federal income taxes; and high-grade commercial paper.

Money market funds are not insured, but because they have highly diversified portfolios that turn over every two months or so and may have high-grade commercial paper or U.S. government obligations, they've proved to be safe investments. I know of none that have failed to make payments. Sometimes, some pieces in a money market fund may default. But one or two companies in a fund's portfolio constitute only a fraction of the fund's assets. And the funds are diversified enough that investors don't know defaults happen, and their investments are barely affected.

You shouldn't look at a money market account as anything other than a parking place. It's a spot to hold your money briefly. For example:

In 1993, the Dow Jones Industrial Average was at its all-time high, having passed 3,500 for the first time. Because the driving force pushing the high marks is people taking money out of lower-yielding investments and shifting into stocks—rather than strong underlying improvements in the economy or the companies issuing the stocks—I have reservations that stocks can sustain these highs. So I don't want to be fully invested in stocks. I want some cash reserve.

In the balanced accounts I manage—*balanced* meaning that a certain allocation goes into fixed-income instruments (such as bonds) and a certain allocation goes into stocks, I also have a certain allocation to cash items. The percentage in cash varies depending on how well valued I view the stock market to be. But I park some money in cash—that is, in a money market account—to shield some money from falls in the stock market and to have cash available if the market drops and stocks become priced more attractively.

When you keep stocks with a brokerage firm, dividends paid on the stock go into the brokerage's money market fund. Investors like being able to write checks against the account, and they like the flexibility of having cash on hand.

That advantage of money market accounts over CDs has become ingrained in our society: money market accounts yield about as much as CDs, but your money is liquid. If you have a CD and need to withdraw money before it matures, you're hit with a severe penalty. A money market fund gives you free checking and lets your dividends accumulate until you choose another place for the money.

Because CD yields are so low these days, some people are investing in longer-term CDs. I'd rather have a short-term bond. Again, what if you need the money before the CD matures? You incur penalties if you liquidate CDs before their term.

The maturities of tax-free bond funds vary. The longer the maturity, the greater the volatility. Short-term *tax-free bond funds* now pay about the same rate as bank accounts, sometimes less. But that's before taxes. Once you factor in taxes, you're ahead with tax-frees—if you're in an income tax bracket higher than 15 percent. Check the yields. On the other hand, long-term tax-free bonds are usually priced so that the point at which it pays to take their lower yields is just below the top tax bracket. Sometimes the difference in yields between taxable and tax-free money market funds is so narrow that it makes sense to invest in a tax-free money market fund even if you're in the lowest tax bracket.

Don't look only at bond fund yields. Look at what's in the portfolio. Stock funds and long-term bond funds are long-term investments, not checking-account alternatives. If you need money in the short term, don't put it in stock funds or long-term bond funds.

Many money market funds have provisions for automatic transfers into your bank checking account. Look over a few months' check stubs to get an average, and figure out how much you need to cover your monthly bills. Then arrange with the money market fund to transfer the money automatically. You'll have the convenience of not having to make the transfers yourself, and in the long run you're likely to earn far more than if you kept the money in the bank.

TWO OTHER ALTERNATIVES:
CMOs AND SHORT-TERM BONDS

Again, the question is, when might you need the money? If you won't need it for at least two years, two alternatives to keeping money in a checking account are CMOs and short-term bonds.

To find the proper place for my dad's bank account money, we have to consider his situation. At age seventy-five, he's retired and derives all his income from investments and from Social Security—part of which is taxed. Taking a tack appropriate for someone whose income is unearned, we'll invest his money in short-term paper. We can get at least 4 percent with little risk. We can buy CMOs, which I've discussed earlier. CMOs can have high commissions—which hurt small investors. For CMOs to make sense, you have to buy them in large enough quantities that the commissions are not excessive. If CMOs strike you as too complex, you can buy short-term bonds, those that mature in four, five, or seven years. (At present interest rates, about 5 percent, I wouldn't buy bonds with terms longer than seven years.) Bonds have liquidity—unlike CDs, on which you pay a stiff penalty if you redeem them before maturity. I'd rather have a high-quality short-term bond with a 5 percent yield than a bank CD paying less than 3 percent. Wouldn't you?

U.S. SAVINGS BONDS

Many U.S. savings bonds are zero-coupon, which I discuss in chapter 18. But because they're not traded on any market, and because people use them for savings, I'm including them in this chapter.

The bonds you may have bought years ago were called E bonds. They're no longer sold, although you can still earn interest on the ones you own. In addition, you can convert them to EE bonds, the most common type of savings bonds sold today.

EE bonds are sold in denominations of $50 to $100,000. They mature in eighteen years, although the maturity can be shortened if interest rates rise. After an EE bond matures, you can convert it to an HH bond. Unlike EE bonds, HH bonds are not zero-coupon bonds; you don't buy them at a discount. The government pays interest on them every six months.

Savings bonds have several advantages over most other savings instruments:

- They have higher yields than passbook accounts.
- The interest they pay (the increase in value, over time, from

discount to par) accumulates tax-deferred. You pay no federal income tax on the interest until the bonds mature.

- You can buy savings bonds painlessly, for instance by purchasing them automatically through the payroll savings plan where you work, or at your local bank.
- They're exempt from state and local income taxes.
- There's a floor on the interest they pay but no ceiling.
- Backed by the full faith and credit of the United States government, savings bonds are about as safe an investment as you can make. And unlike bank accounts, they have no $100,000 insurance limit.

A couple of these points warrant discussion.

The exemption from state and local taxes may mean nothing to you if you live in Delaware or some other state with no income tax. But other states, such as New York and Connecticut, have high income taxes. I live in New Jersey, which has a top tax rate of 7 percent. That's a hefty amount, and not having to pay it on selected investments is a serious plus.

Because the bonds accumulate interest tax-deferred, they have some similarities to IRAs. If you're one of the millions of Americans who are ineligible for a tax-deductible IRA, you can take advantage of this tax-deferred feature. It's especially valuable if you will retire between the time you buy the bonds and the time you cash them in. It makes savings bonds preferable to nondeductible IRAs, which have serious drawbacks (see chapter 23).

Savings bonds are a wonderful tool for instilling good investment habits in children. Years ago, for special occasions (such as confirmations and bar mitzvahs), parents would buy a child a share of stock. Today, commission rates make that pointless. But savings bonds still make sense for the purpose. You pay no commissions, and you're giving a child a $50 item that cost you only $25.

A FINAL WORD ABOUT CASH

With rates under 2.5 percent—which after taxes and inflation is a negative return—why bother with bank accounts or CDs at all? Why not put everything in stocks or bonds?

Well, stocks and bonds have risks. Much of the money coming out of CDs is going into the stock market or long-term bonds, because people are attracted to higher yields. That can be a mistake. You could put $1,000 into a CD, and a year from now it would be worth $1,030. Sounds pathetic, doesn't it? But see how it compares with the performance of a utility stock that pays a dividend of 5 percent.

I'm selling off many of my utility stocks even though I'm a long-term investor. Many people have been attracted to the high dividends of utility stocks, pushing prices way up. By the standard measures of a stock's worth—price to earnings, price to book value, and price to dividend— utility stocks are at lofty levels. Many have risen by 30 or 40 percent in the past fifteen months, largely because people have been turning away from investments whose yields are so low. If fears of inflation return and other investments begin paying higher yields, utility stocks could lose all their recent increase, and then some. I don't know that that's going to happen, but I do know that interest rates are the lowest we've seen in decades. If interest rates rise, you could put $1,000 in a utility stock today and find a year from now that it's worth only $800. At times like that, cash isn't trash.

20

THE UPS AND DOWNS
OF GLOBAL INVESTING

Satellites and computer networks have made financial markets global. Listen to the radio or watch TV, and you instantly learn how the dollar fared against the pound in London. You know immediately how the Japanese stock market, called the Nikkei, performed today.

THE ALLURE OF GLOBAL INVESTING:
AROUND THE WORLD IN EIGHTY WAYS

Some financial experts advise global investments as a way to diversify and to make money when the U.S. economy is in its doldrums. Some favor global mutual funds, which invest in companies outside the United States.

"Stock markets and solid companies exist all over the world," global investors point out. "Don't depend just on the United States." Growth here has slowed markedly, they argue, whereas other parts of the world are expanding rapidly. While U.S. markets may be languishing, others may be thriving. One of my clients owns stock in two Costa Rican companies and a telephone company in Argentina.

A well-known mutual fund group specializing in global investing is the Templeton Funds. John Templeton, who sold the funds in 1992 (the company retains his name), used many of the investment techniques that I use. He was a pioneer in global investing. It made him rich.

Templeton said investors expose themselves to undue risks and miss out on golden opportunities if they confine themselves to American companies. In a way, he's right. But while his point is attractive, be careful. Global investing has two serious drawbacks:

1. Finding out about foreign companies takes enormous effort and money. What does my client know about the Costa Rican economy? What does she know about the Argentine telephone system? How much do the experts know? It's bad enough wondering whether the Argentine telephone company has good management; you also have to hope that the government doesn't nationalize it.

2. When you invest globally, you incur not only the stock market risk but also a currency risk. You buy into huge uncertainty about exchange rates. How will the Argentine peso perform against the dollar? Any gains a foreign company might have can be more than wiped out by currency fluctuations.

Thirty years ago, the Canadian dollar was worth more than the American. In early 1993, it was worth 78 cents. In mid-1992, the British pound was worth two American dollars. In May 1993, it was worth about $1.50. Conversely, in 1985 you got 250 Japanese yen to the dollar. In early 1993, the dollar was down to 107 yen.

"Sure," you can counter, "currency fluctuation can be a black hole. But I read where some gold-mining company in South Africa doubled in value in six months."

Let's assume your information is correct. Did you find out about it *before* the company did so well? How are you going to get information on companies thousands of miles away?

In many countries, people don't speak English. And even if they do, their accounting standards may be quite different. Take Great Britain. When I read a British annual report, I see terms and expressions totally alien to me. And I know what I'm looking for.

Another concern: What happens if conditions in the country where your foreign firm is located turn sour? Are you going to dart out of South Africa and into Germany? You run into a similar problem when you try to dart into and out of hot stocks in the United States. But abroad it's even more complicated because you're a captive of factors beyond your control and perhaps your understanding.

Yet I haven't convinced you. You hear promising tidbits about foreign investing and you think the heyday of Yankee ingenuity is past. How, you ask, can you participate in international growth?

TWO POSSIBLE ANSWERS FOR GLOBAL INVESTING

If you truly believe in spreading your assets by investing globally, I see two sensible ways to do it:

1. Buy a well-established mutual fund that employs people to travel and research foreign companies.

Stay with a fund that's been in that business for a long time and has the resources and experience needed to uncover treasures abroad. As I've said, researchers have to do their homework. They have to "kick the tires" and meet with management. With every company that I invest my money or my clients' money in, I or one of our analysts have met with management. For foreign companies, I don't have the resources to do that. Some mutual funds do. They have employees whose only job is to research companies in the Pacific Rim or Latin America, or wherever.

Yet many global funds haven't performed well recently, because no matter how well the companies they invested in were doing, the exchange rates went against them. Mutual funds, even shrewd ones, can't be shielded from currency fluctuations. It's difficult enough picking stocks close to home. Why add another element to an already jumbled stew?

2. Buy stock in American companies that have major presences overseas.

You can own familiar names and not have to worry the way you would if you bought foreign companies. For example, Sara Lee is a major company abroad. Forty percent of its pretax earnings come from outside the United States. Or take Coca Cola. Eighty percent of Coca Cola's earnings come from outside the United States. Furthermore, many such companies use sophisticated methods to hedge currency fluctuations.

Some global investments will perform handsomely. But you must know what you're doing, or have reliable sources of information. If you want to send some or most of your investment dollars overseas, good luck. I'll keep my money here. With so many acres of diamonds in our own backyard, why seek riches abroad?

PART V

PITFALLS

21

THE HEADACHE OF TAXES

Uncle Sam wants you. More precisely, he wants your money. Worse than any mooching brother-in-law or cousin, Uncle Sam is your most extravagant relative. He virtually guarantees that a healthy portion of your income will help feed his prodigious appetite for dollars. Understanding how the tax laws affect you is a critical part of your financial planning; that's what this chapter is about. The information is general, based on my experience. For specific tax advice, consult an accountant or a tax attorney.

TAXES AND INVESTING

Although taxes should not be a primary consideration in investment decisions, investments have tax consequences. For example, you pay no federal income taxes on the growth of a stock's value while you hold the stock. But when you sell the stock at a profit, you may have to pay a tax on the gain. Because you pay no income tax until you sell, holding stocks over the long term is a way to let your portfolio grow tax-deferred. You get some of the same advantages that an individual retirement arrangement (IRA) offers. Taxes can take a large bite out of investment income, but the tax-free compounding effect lets your money grow at a greater rate than if it were taxed.

Some investors let tax consequences affect their decisions to hold or sell a stock. That's a mistake.

IF IT AIN'T BROKE, BREAK IT

When I think about taxes, my mind turns to the Tax Simplification Act of 1989. Or was it the Tax Reform Act of 1986? Or the Tax Abomination Act of 1977? Once or twice a decade, the federal government recognizes how horrid the tax situation has become. So the government sets out to fix it— and you know what happens then. If something ain't broke, the government breaks it. If it is broke, the government makes it broker.

The federal government taxes saving and encourages borrowing. It's the exact opposite of what the government should be doing. Years ago, your first couple of hundred dollars in dividends was exempt from federal taxes. If that provision were restored, people would be encouraged to invest in equities. The economy, the government, the public would all benefit.

DO IT YOURSELF? ARE YOU KIDDING?

The tax laws have become so wretchedly complex that even knowledgeable people throw up their hands in disgust and hire professionals. Take me. I live in New Jersey and work in Philadelphia. In 1993, I filed returns for Pennsylvania state tax, Philadelphia city tax, Philadelphia business privilege tax, New Jersey state tax, and federal income tax. That's five taxes. On top of that, I have to file quarterly estimated taxes for Philadelphia, New Jersey, Pennsylvania, and federal. I fill out a form almost every month.

Yesterday I got a piece of mail from Haddonfield, the township where I live. At first I thought it was a nice brochure about the school system. Then I read it. They're going to raise my real estate tax because the school budget in the coming year will rise 7.6 percent. That's a lot, and the tax is already high.

In the 1980s, the United States had an administration devoted to lowering the federal tax rates. The top rate dropped from 90 percent to 33. But as the federal tax rates fell, the government gave away less money to the states and municipalities. So those governments raised taxes. All told, Americans have been paying more and more in taxes year by year.

Then you face the Social Security tax. Not long ago, the maximum income on which you were taxed for Social Security was $35,000. In 1993 it was $57,600. Soon it will be close to $70,000. On top of that are taxes for Medicare, where the maximum contribution doesn't kick in until you make $135,000 a year (as of 1993). Also, at high incomes, you start losing the ability to take itemized deductions on Schedule A.

The government makes your life difficult even if you make little money. If you have more than $400 interest income in a year, you're required to fill out estimated tax forms. You have to pay estimated taxes quarterly. But many people have unpredictable incomes, and many don't like to fill out quarterly forms. The government has cracked down hard on people who have to file estimated payments. It charges penalties if they pay too little. My father's income, because he's retired, comes entirely from interest and dividends. Interest rates change. He can't be sure how much interest he'll receive each year. To make sure he isn't slapped with penalties, he overestimates his income. Each quarter, he pays the government more than he needs to. Uncle Sam gets an interest-free loan.

COMPLICATIONS

I like numbers and I did my own taxes for thirty years. I enjoyed doing them (don't hold that against me). But those days, I fear, are gone. Last year was the first time I hired a professional. The return he prepared was more than an inch thick. I thumbed through it and thought, There's no way I could do this myself anymore.

What prompted me to bring in a professional was my litigation against Janney Montgomery Scott and Donald Trump and the tremendous legal expenses I incurred. I didn't know how to handle them on my tax return. In addition, because I have a business, I also have to worry about company taxes. The rules are tricky. Roffman Miller Associates is a Subchapter S corporation. Among other things, it pays my health insurance benefits. Subchapter S corporations don't pay income taxes—they disburse all the money—so I have to pay a tax on my health care benefits. Last year, those benefits came to more than $2,700. They go right on my income tax form as income.

Roffman Miller has a bookkeeper who handles our check writing and all our taxes. My partner, Peter Miller, deals with her. One week he was on vacation and she brought me forms to sign. I was dumbfounded. I couldn't believe how many forms for income taxes and payroll taxes and withholding and this and that the company has to file.

Those burdens are one reason small businesses haven't been starting up or expanding. Small-business owners have shown reluctance to take on new employees. The tax onus and paperwork are immense. New regulations, covering firms with fifty or more employees, call for leave policies, benefits, and other provisions that many companies find unaffordable. So they don't hire. Their decision translates into fewer jobs for the economy and less money for the government.

One friend told me, "I'm not going to work as hard. We're not going to go out and hire people. We don't want to get bigger anymore. The government's taking too much away."

The tax laws have many provisions I never knew about. Last year, for example, I had to pay the alternative minimum tax. I didn't know that on this year's return I can take a credit for what I paid as alternative minimum tax last year. The process is absurdly complicated.

Can or should you do your own taxes? Do you like doing them? Do you have time on your hands? If you answer yes to the following questions, you may be able to use the EZ or 1040A form and do your own taxes with relatively little difficulty:

- Is your annual income under $30,000?
- Do you rent an apartment or have a house with no mortgage?
- Are your medical expenses relatively low?
- Is your interest and dividend income under $400?

If you answered no to any of the questions, you will almost certainly benefit from having a professional prepare your return.

The average person isn't up to it. If you build the discipline I recommended early in the book, if you can save 15 to 20 percent of your income when you're starting your career, you'll eventually have investments and capital gains. When you reach that point, you will probably need professional help with your taxes.

RECORD KEEPING IS VITAL

Whether you prepare your tax return yourself or hire a professional, record keeping is critical. For investments, I suggest keeping four folders:

1. The first is for *buys*. Every time you buy a stock, bond, mutual fund, or other investment, put the transaction statement in the buy folder.
2. The second is for sales. When you *sell*, put the transaction statement in the sales folder.
3. Keep a separate folder for all your *monthly statements*. Every broker will send you a monthly statement if you keep securities with the broker or if you have activity in your account.

4. Keep a folder with all records of *improvements* you make *to your house*. The improvements you make increase the cost basis of your house—and reduce your capital-gains-tax liability—when you sell it. I have a file for every major purchase or house improvement: painting, paperhanging, carpentry, and so on. I keep a separate folder for the grounds—landscaping, tree planting, and the like. They'll simplify my calculation of the cost basis of the house when I sell it.

You can encounter tax problems with stocks or mutual funds. The problem arises on sales of shares of common stock or mutual funds in which you reinvest the dividends. Because you're buying shares over time at different prices, you never know your exact cost basis or profit. It's crucial to keep all your transaction statements so that you have records of all purchases and reinvestments.

I urge all my clients—and I urge you—to *keep thorough, accurate records. Keep them in a safe place. Save the folders indefinitely*. As the years elapse, you tend to forget transactions and house improvements. As a long-term investor, you will need to ferret out information many years down the road. I've owned some stocks for thirty years. They've had numerous splits, capitalization changes, and spin-offs. I've had so many transactions in one stock that I have duplicate sets of records: one set at home and one in the office—in case of fire or other disaster. I keep the same information on computer. Computer software—financial programs such as Quicken, Managing Your Money, Money Counts, and Microsoft Money—make record keeping much easier. Retrieving information, sorting it, manipulating it—in ways impossible or infeasible by hand—become easy on a computer.

PREPARE FOR HIGHER TAXES

When the subject is taxes, few things are certain. One thing I'm sure will happen is higher federal taxes. With the Clinton administration's intent to make a dent in the federal deficit and to reform health care, higher taxes are inevitable. You'd better prepare for the future by assuming that taxes will be higher. If anything, you'd better overprepare.

22

INSURANCE: LIFE, HEALTH, DISABILITY, HOME, AUTO

Rosa, seventy-one, was driving under the Market Street Elevated in West Philadelphia when a car sideswiped hers. The damage, some scraped paint and frazzled nerves, was seemingly minor. She exchanged the required documentation with the other driver, and each drove off. A few days later, she got a call from the man. He claimed he'd been seriously injured and threatened a lawsuit. Always dutiful, Rosa called her automobile insurance agent to report the accident. The agent informed her that she had no insurance—because of some slipup, the company had never received her payment. All liability was strictly hers.

Visions of losing everything she owned, especially her house—where she had lived for more than twenty-five years—sickened her. She agonized over how she could have made such a slipup and put herself in such a perilous position. Only when months had passed and she never again heard from the other driver did she calm down. Only then did the fear of losing her home evaporate.

You spend years building up your possessions, your savings, your surroundings, your career, your house. All can vanish in an instant.

Although you can't always prevent accidents and calamities, you can prevent them from ruining your life. That's the purpose of insurance.

Rosa recognized the value of insurance, yet she still faced the horrifying prospect of losing everything. Insurance, as her story demonstrates, has its own snares. In this chapter, I guide you past them and show you how to secure the *protection you must have*. I concentrate on five types of insurance: life, health, disability, home, and auto. Besides the *what*s, I give some pointers on how and where to buy it.

LIFE INSURANCE: WHY BUY ANYTHING BUT TERM?

The purpose of life insurance is to create an instant estate. That is, to leave to those who depend on you a pile of money that can replace the money lost because you're gone. Nothing can replace you, but money can replace some of your earning power. What type of insurance to buy? To me, the answer is simple. How much to have? That's tough. Whom to buy from? Stay tuned.

First you'll need to understand the different types of life insurance. Here are some definitions, along with comments from insurance agent Tony Fischer of Karr Barth Associates, in Bala Cynwyd, Pennsylvania.

Term insurance is a straight death benefit. You pay money to the insurance company in the form of premiums, and the insurance company pays money to your beneficiary if you die during the term of the policy. Common terms are one year, five years, and ten years. The premium tends to rise as you get older. If you don't renew after the term expires—and then *you* expire—the insurance company owes nothing.

Whole life insurance devotes part of your premium to a death benefit and part to investments. The policy builds up a *cash value* based on those investments. When the proceeds from the investments are high, whole life insurance can theoretically generate enough income to pay the premiums in later years. It's this provision of whole life insurance that agents make sound so appealing.

"When a person buys whole life insurance," says Fischer, "what they're buying is a lot of guarantees. They're buying a guaranteed premium—it will always be level. They're buying guaranteed mortality costs, meaning the pure death costs inside the policy. The insurance company does not have the right to increase those costs. They're also buying a guaranteed cash value, which means that if you pay the premium over a period of time, there are guarantees that X dollars will be there."

Universal life is term insurance with a cash accumulation fund on the side. Unlike whole life, a universal life policy has few guarantees. "The premium's not guaranteed, the mortality costs are not guaranteed, and there is no guaranteed interest rate per se," says Fischer. "There's a minimum guaranteed rate, which is usually four or four and a half percent, and a current guaranteed rate, which is in existence for one year."

Variable universal life is similar to universal life. The difference is that instead of one account in which to invest your money, you have several choices. It's like a family of mutual funds. Choices often include a growth account, an income account, and a balanced account.

"Variable universal life policies are in vogue today," Fischer says. "People have read adverse publicity about life insurance companies in financial trouble. If you have a universal life insurance policy—not variable—with an insurance company whose assets are seized, the assets in the general account of the company are subject to the claims of the company's creditors before the policyholders. If you have a variable universal policy, the money in the separate accounts is not subject to the claims of the creditors. You don't have the risk of losing your money because the company is being seized."

My advice is to concentrate on *term insurance*. It's the least expensive form and, to me, the life insurance of choice.

Life insurance products other than term offer high commissions to the insurance salesman and high profits to the insurance company. You're buying investment products when you should be buying protection. Before making your decision, compare figures from one or more honest agents. You may be convinced that term insurance is for you, or you may prefer one of the alternatives to term. I've stressed the benefits of acquiring the discipline to invest. If you lack that discipline, if you know you won't invest the premium savings you get from buying term, one of the alternative life insurance products could be a better choice for you.

HOW MUCH LIFE INSURANCE SHOULD YOU HAVE?

How much life insurance is a tough question. Agents cite rules of thumb often based on your income. If you earn $50,000 a year, they might recommend $125,000 of coverage. As a perk, many employers offer employees twice their salary in term insurance. These days, life insurance coverage almost has to be at least $100,000. Less than that is not much of an estate.

The issue is, how much will your survivors need if your income suddenly ends because of your death? You and your family know that situation best, and you should discuss it with several agents. Don't rely only on a rule of thumb or take an arbitrary figure I might give.

Also, think of the future. If you just started working, your present income may be low. You might have graduated from engineering school recently and begun a job at $30,000 a year. Five years from now, you might be making $50,000. You shouldn't base your life insurance needs solely on what your earning power is today.

If you have children, you must make sure that they will be taken care of until they're on their own. That means you want to provide for their college education. Who knows what it will cost to educate someone fifteen years from now? We do know that four years of college can cost more than $100,000 now.

NOT EVERYONE NEEDS LIFE INSURANCE

Insurance companies will have you believe that not having insurance is a sacrilege. Life insurance, they say, is like apple pie and motherhood. But maybe you don't need it. Maybe you have your own money and don't need an additional instant estate. Maybe you have no dependents.

If you're single or divorced and your children are grown, why have life insurance? To pay for your funeral? A funeral today costs at least $5,000. I know, because my mother died recently. The cemetery plot cost $2,100. The stone was $750. Add in the coffin and other funeral expenses, and the total bill is $5,000 minimum. Even given those costs, if you're in your seventies or older, should you spend good money—money you might need now—to pay for your funeral? Only you can decide.

Let's say you're young and nowhere near worrying about funerals. Let's say you just graduated from college. You used to be your parents' dependent, but no longer. You're single, and you have no dependents yourself. Because term insurance rates tend to rise as you get older, insurance companies will tell you that if you sign up now, your premiums will be lower than if you sign up five years from now. But does it make sense to lay out that money for premiums when no one will suffer an economic loss if you die? There isn't much of a difference between premiums for a twenty-two-year-old and those for a twenty-nine-year-old. The rates don't rise significantly till you're in your forties. But policies differ. Get the figures. Dope them out. See how much you spend and how much you save. Then decide whether it makes sense to start buying life insurance right away.

HEALTH INSURANCE: YOU'VE GOT TO HAVE IT

The cost of being sick in America today can be disastrous. A day in the hospital can cost more than a thousand dollars. A transplant operation can cost hundreds of thousands.

You're reading this book and, I hope, saving and building an investment portfolio. How can you let yourself lose it all to a catastrophic illness? You must have health insurance—for everyone in your family. It's vital. Yet about 37 million people in this country don't have health insurance.

The Clinton administration wants every American to have health care coverage. It's a fine goal, but when people see what the bill might be—$150 billion or more—it gives them pause. Government policies can change, and as I write, it's unclear who will pay the bill. However the government acts, I underscore that health insurance is critical. Make sure you have it and have enough of it.

The best place to get health insurance is where you work. Traditionally, health insurance has been part of the fringe benefits companies offer. But employers are putting more and more of the responsibility on their employees. Otherwise, health care costs would run away even faster than they are now. When somebody else is picking up the whole tab, people tend to go in for a procedure and say, "What do I care how much it costs? It's not my money. Somebody else is paying for it." Given current tendencies, that attitude will soon be history.

The trend toward managed care means that more and more people will be covered by health maintenance organizations (HMOs). If you have limited resources, consider an HMO plan. HMOs tell you up front what doctor visits and hospital procedures will cost you. They give you few surprises. Many HMOs are comprehensive. Despite that, the premiums on HMOs may be the same or even less than on a standard Blue Shield policy.

I had an HMO policy when I worked at Janney. It would not sell to individuals—only to groups of five or more. Here at Roffman Miller, we joined the chamber of commerce. We get group insurance that way. You could join your local chamber of commerce to obtain a group rate.

Some HMOs now provide coverage for individuals, and both state and federal legislation is pressing HMOs to move in that direction. The premiums are higher for individuals than they are for groups. Check with the member relations departments of HMOs in your area for information.

DISABILITY INSURANCE: VITAL BUT OVERLOOKED

If you were paralyzed by an accident or unable to work because of a chronic illness, could you get by? How would you pay your rent or mortgage? How would you pay your bills? Where would your income come from?

One answer to those questions is disability income insurance. Disability insurance pays a monthly check in case of a disability that temporarily or permanently prevents you from working. The case I've made for health insurance applies also to disability insurance. For many people, disability insurance is more crucial than life insurance. Agent Tony Fischer says: "Middle-aged people have a three to four times greater chance of becoming disabled than of dying. Disability insurance should be even more important to people than life insurance." Although many people understand the need for health insurance and life insurance, far fewer understand the need for disability insurance, so fewer have it. It's costly. Most people who have it are employees whose companies offer it as a benefit.

Like most forms of insurance, disability has many options for coverage, with varying premiums. Here are some of the most important considerations:

- *Waiting period.* Policies almost always have a waiting period before coverage begins: typically thirty, sixty, or ninety days after you become disabled.
- *Term.* How long the policy remains in effect is another variable. Some cover you for a year; some, five years; others, the rest of your life.
- *Own occupation.* If you're a lawyer, an accident or injury might prevent you from working in your field but not in some other field. Some policies pay benefits only if you're unable to work at any occupation; others pay if you're unable to work at your own occupation. Consider this carefully. Do you want to be forced to work in some low-paying job that doesn't suit you?
- *Monthly payment.* The monthly paycheck varies according to how much you want to spend on premiums. The most you can receive is usually 50 to 60 percent of your gross pay. Policies are designed that way—to encourage you to resume work if you're able. If they paid more, you'd be tempted to stay out of work.
- *Premium.* As with other forms of insurance, premiums vary depending on your age and coverage. Here's an example from Tony Fischer: "I prepared a workup for a thirty-five-year-old man this morning. Lifetime benefits, ninety-day elimination period. The monthly benefit was fifteen hundred dollars. The policy had a cost-of-living adjustment, which compounded between four and six percent annually, depending on the Consumer Price Index. The policy also had a residual benefit for long-term partial disability. The cost was approximately seventy-five dollars a month. Figure nine hundred dollars a year."

The older you are when you obtain disability insurance, the more it will cost you. And if you wait too long, you may find that no company will sell it to you. "The older you get," says Fischer, "the more prone you are to diabetes, the more prone to heart attack, the more prone to being a little slower behind the controls of an automobile. You're not walking as quick as you used to.

"What you should look for," Fischer suggests, "are the definitions inside the policy. People who become disabled usually fall into two categories. With most disabilities that require receiving a benefit, the person is disabled for one or two years. In the second category, people will require a lifetime benefit.

"In my opinion—it's only my opinion, and this is the way I sell it— either buy a short-term policy with three to five years of coverage, or buy lifetime benefits. For young professional people starting out, if they don't buy lifetime benefits, I think they should have their heads examined.

"What I would suggest is to compare at least three different policies. A reputable agent, even a company agent, should have no problem bringing in other companies. I do it all the time."

HOMEOWNER'S INSURANCE

Unlike disability insurance, homeowner's is widely used. If your house is mortgaged, it's likely that your mortgage company requires you to have homeowner's insurance. Each month you may have to pay the mortgage company money to be put in escrow for homeowner's insurance.

One contributor to the widespread use of homeowner's insurance is the cost. It's relatively inexpensive. For a $100,000 house with $70,000 of possessions, the yearly premium may be as low as $300 or $350. I just got an insurance policy for my house. The premium is about $800 yearly. But there can be big differences in premiums. Another company gave me a proposal that would have cost $1,600 a year.

A variation that a few companies offer is *perpetual homeowner's insurance*. You pay a large one-time premium, such as $10,000 or $20,000 depending on coverage, and get homeowner's insurance in perpetuity. At the end (when you sell your house, for example), you get your premium back. How do they do that? They invest the premium. The proceeds more than pay for your insurance coverage and still make them a profit.

I don't favor the idea. To me, it's not buying insurance for the sake of insurance. It's a savings program. It's like whole life insurance for a house. I'd rather make my own investments.

For instance, if I'm paying $800 a year for homeowner's insurance, that's $19,200 less than the $20,000 lump sum I might pay for perpetual insurance. Even if I take the $19,200 and put it in as conservative an investment as a U.S. government bond paying 7½ percent, I'll make 1,344 a year. I'll have the $800 I need for the insurance premium and 544 left over.

AUTOMOBILE INSURANCE: IF YOU HAVE A CAR, YOU NEED INSURANCE

Every time you drive your car, you run the risk of wiping yourself out. You can be killed or seriously injured in an accident, of course, or do severe damage to your car. But I'm not talking only about that. Think of the damage you could do to someone else. And beyond that tragedy, think how much money you could be sued for.

Liability insurance, for both your house and your car, is an absolute must. You could end the life of a brain surgeon and be sued for millions. A legal settlement could require you to support the surgeon's children financially. When it comes to liability insurance in a society that's litigious, you must protect yourself.

If you have substantial net worth, you should have a million dollars or so of liability insurance on your house and the same on your car. On top of what you're already paying in premiums, the additional coverage is relatively inexpensive.

To me, insurance is to protect you from catastrophic losses. It's not to cover every little thing. When I was growing up, my father had a car. When somebody broke off the radio antenna—which happened even back then— he would file a claim. I don't want to report minor damage to my car. Pedestrians may walk by and scratch your car; other drivers may dent it. If you report the small losses, the insurance company raises your premium and you end up paying more than you received for the claim.

In my father's day, people had auto insurance policies with $50 deductible. Today, I have $500 deductible. Why? Five hundred dollars is next to nothing when you consider the cost of collision repairs today. A high deductible saves you money in premiums each year. If you don't have an accident, it pays for itself in two or three years. If you're in a serious accident, you can suffer thousands of dollars in damage. That's what insurance is for—that and protection against lawsuits. It's not to pay for the $50 or $250 repair. People's attitudes today are changing rapidly as they see that if they make claims, their insurance premiums go up.

YOU'D BETTER SHOP AROUND

Whom should you see for insurance? Since deregulation, the brokerage industry has tried to be all things to all people. So besides handling transactions on stocks and bonds, it now sells insurance. I think you're better served buying insurance from an insurance specialist.

"Most important," says agent Tony Fischer, "I think you should deal with an agent that you can trust. Quite honestly, there are a lot around who are not very trustworthy or very honest. If you're dealing with a good company, you're not going to get hurt. The most important thing is to deal with a reliable agent who gives a damn about the people he's talking to.'

How do you find an agent you can trust? Get recommendations. Shop around. Companies have considerable differences in coverage, costs, and service. If you're married, you may find that a company that offers good life insurance rates for you has less desirable rates for your wife, or vice versa.

Call three or four insurance brokers. If you deal with a company agent, make sure it's someone like Fischer, someone who has *your* best interests at heart, not the company's. Consider an independent broker. That's someone who deals with various companies and can give a broad array of quotations.

Insurance is a complicated, confusing topic. For more information on life insurance, a book that Fischer recommends is *Life Insurance*, eleventh edition revised, 1988. Written by Kenneth Black Jr. and Harold Skipper Jr., it's published by Prentice Hall.

23

THE END: RETIREMENT, PENSIONS, TRUSTS

Throughout this book, I've spoken about the importance of saving and investing. One reason—I've touched on it often—is to provide for yourself and family when you're no longer working, when you're retired. Another is to leave something to your children or other loved ones after you're gone.

You've worked hard for your money. You've spent years accumulating a nest egg and an estate. Now, how do you keep some of it for your "golden" years? How do you pass it on to your children without having much of it siphoned off? When you face preparing for retirement, when the time comes to choose among myriad pension options and survivor benefits, when you have to think about divvying up your estate, you'll realize this is a critical but difficult topic.

DON'T COUNT ON SOCIAL SECURITY

You're a young person, forty years old. Think back to when you were in high school, twenty-five years ago. Think how fast the years passed. Now

think of twenty-five years in the future. They'll pass even faster. Befor
you know, you'll be facing retirement. When should you start planning fo
it? Now.

It makes good sense to put money away for retirement. Even the govern
ment sees a need for it. So retirement accounts were created, and th
government exempted them from certain taxes. The idea was that if you le
people shelter money from taxes, you can encourage them to save fo
retirement. I encourage you to start saving now.

In theory, most working Americans will receive money from Socia
Security when they retire. Funded by a tax, Social Security is like
savings plan you're forced to contribute to. Unfortunately, you may neve
get all your contributions back. Twenty, thirty, forty years from now, the
Social Security climate will be vastly different.

When the United States had three people working and paying Socia
Security tax for every one person collecting Social Security, the Socia
Security trust fund was in fine shape. When three people collect for every
one who pays, where will the money come from? In addition, the
retirement age in the twenty-first century may rise to seventy.

So if you're between twenty and sixty, you should have few expectations
about your Social Security retirement benefits. Social Security will not
supply enough money to live on, so you have to provide for yourself. Spend
less. Save more. Invest more. Here are some thoughts.

It's never too early to start planning and saving. If you have a job, your
employer may have a pension plan. A company is not required to have a
pension plan just because it employs people. But if it does offer a pension
plan—many companies do—it must meet the many requirements of
federal and state laws. Companies are no longer as quick to offer pensions
as they used to be, especially with more and more employees holding part-
time jobs. Small business is where most job growth in the United States is,
but taking on new full-time employees is expensive. Employers who hire
part-time employees don't have to pay health insurance premiums or
vacation time or unemployment compensation insurance or pension
contributions. These fringe benefits generally run 20 to 30 percent of an
employee's salary.

The hot items in pensions today are *401K* plans. Here your company
may or may not contribute anything toward your pension, and the plan puts
the onus of choosing how much to contribute and where to invest it on you,
the employee.

A 401K encourages employees to save, and it's gotten companies away
from promising to take care of employees to the grave.

Some 401K plans restrict where you can put the money. My former employer, Janney Montgomery Scott, has an arrangement with the Delaware family of funds. Employees can put their profit-sharing and savings plan contributions in several of the family's funds, including a growth stock fund, short-term or long-term government bonds, or money market fund. The fund family has just expanded from five choices to eight. Twice a year—it used to be quarterly—employees can switch their money from one fund in the family to another.

At one time, when I was at Janney, they didn't have that arrangement. The firm managed all the pension money itself. I always contributed the maximum permitted.

IRAs FOR SELF-EMPLOYED PEOPLE AND THOSE WHOSE COMPANIES OFFER NO PENSION

For many people, the prime retirement program is the individual retirement arrangement (IRA). An IRA lets a working person who is eligible contribute up to $2,000 a year. If one member of a married couple is eligible and the other earns no compensation (or less than $250 a year), the couple may contribute up to $2,250 a year in an IRA.

IRAs have two features that make them especially appealing for retirement investment: (1) The earnings on money invested in an IRA are tax-deferred, and (2) if you qualify, your IRA contribution is deductible from your federal adjusted gross income (AGI).

You're eligible to have a tax-deductible IRA if you're self-employed or your company offers no pension plan—unless your spouse works for a company that sponsors a pension plan. In that case, your eligibility for a tax-deductibile IRA depends on your adjusted gross income. The deductibility phases out as the AGI approaches a threshold of $35,000 for single taxpayers and $50,000 for married taxpayers.

You pay no taxes on an IRA's earnings until you begin withdrawing money. You may begin withdrawing when you reach age $59^{1}/_{2}$. If you withdraw before that age, you pay taxes on the amount withdrawn, along with a steep penalty. You must begin withdrawing from your IRA no later than April 1 of the year after the year you turn $70^{1}/_{2}$.

Many types of investments are permitted in IRAs, including stocks, bonds, mutual funds, CDs, and savings accounts. Because the earnings accrue tax deferred, IRAs take full advantage of the magic of compound interest. For example, an income-producing mutual fund invested in an IRA grows more rapidly than the same investment outside an IRA. You may have more than one IRA, and you may change the type of investments you put in an IRA.

You needn't set up an IRA in the year you take your first deduction for it. You can set up an IRA until April 15 of the next year. Also, you can make deductible contributions to the IRA until that date. For example, you can set up an IRA for 1994 from January 1, 1994, until April 15, 1995, and make your 1994 contribution any time during 1994 and until April 15, 1995.

If you are ineligible for a tax-deductible IRA, you are permitted to have a nondeductible one. I strongly recommend against doing that. The paperwork entailed with nondeductible IRAs—tangled record-keeping and filing a required form with the Internal Revenue Service every year forever—is a nightmare that I believe makes their use prohibitive.

SEPs AND KEOGHS LET YOU CONTRIBUTE MORE

Other retirement investments let you put more money away than an IRA does. A simplified employee pension (SEP) is like an IRA, and it can apply to whole companies.

Keogh plans, another way to shelter retirement money, have been replaced by pension and profit-sharing plans. Keoghs let you put away even more money than a SEP.

IRAs, SEPs, and Keogh plans can be complicated. I advise you to use them to your advantage. If possible, use alternatives that let you put away more money than you can in an IRA. For detailed information and answers to your questions, see a reliable accountant.

PENSION MONEY LOWERS YOUR GROSS INCOME
AND GROWS TAX DEFERRED

Although federal law limits how much you can contribute in pension money each year, pension money has several advantages over other savings and investments. These advantages make it especially attractive:

- *You don't pay taxes on the money you contribute.* The money you contribute to your pension isn't reported as income. It comes right off the top.
- *Earnings accumulate tax-deferred.* The money your pension earns is tax-deferred. You pay no taxes on the earnings until you start withdrawing money.
- *Your employer may match your contribution.* Many employers help their employees by contributing to employee pensions. If you work

for an enlightened firm, it may match a certain percentage of your contribution. The employer may not match one dollar for every one you put in, but it may contribute one dollar for every two you put in. The employer's contribution does not count as income to you.

The first two features I mentioned—tax deductibility and deferral—make pensions the best tax shelter left to Americans. Not only is a pension a form of forced savings, but it's a much better tax shelter than anything else I can think of. Moreover, you have the miracle of compound interest. Donald Trump once called his Taj Mahal casino-hotel the eighth wonder of the world. In my lexicon, the eighth wonder is compound interest.

The employer match is another enticing feature. If your employer matches your contribution one for one, your investment immediately doubles. That's a 100 percent return immediately. Where else can you get that return? Even if your employer matches one for two, you have an immediate 50 percent return. That's still gigantic, a return you're unlikely to duplicate anywhere else.

The upshot of these features is that you can scarcely afford not to take advantage of them. I love retirement saving. It's the most powerful way to save money long term. Everybody should use it. But what if you're just beginning your career and earning very little? Most people don't have the luxury of contributing the maximum allowed. That's why the people who take the maximum are generally the highest paid. I know it's hard to look to the future when the present is arduous. But consider this. If you devote 20 percent of your gross income to your pension, it's not a 20 percent cut in pay. It's 20 percent off your gross. The cut from your take-home pay is less than 20 percent. Also, the reduction in your gross pay could lower your tax bracket. So *contribute as much to your pension as you can.*

TAX-DEFERRED ANNUITIES

Tax-deferred annuities are issued only through insurance companies but are available from banks, stockbrokers, financial planners, and insurance agents. They are products you buy with a lump sum of money. The money is invested for later withdrawal, generally at retirement or after age fifty-nine and a half. Although the contribution to an annuity is not tax deductible, the earnings are not taxed until you withdraw the money. You can withdraw the money as a lump sum or monthly, quarterly, semiannually, or annually.

Note the following:

- The quality of the insurance company issuing the annuity is critical. Stay with companies rated A or better by the leading rating agencies.
- Beware of the enticement of high interest rates in the early years of the annuity. Sometimes, high rates are come-ons that soon drop; you then receive a much lower return.
- Annuities other than fixed annuities are complicated. When considering one of those types, speak with a trusted financial adviser.

Is there a place for annuities in your retirement portfolio? Yes. It depends on your age. You can be too old for annuities, or too young. When you're five or six years away from age fifty-nine and a half (when you can begin withdrawing retirement money without penalty), that's an ideal time to purchase an annuity. If you withdraw the money before that age, you incur a penalty and have to pay taxes on the money withdrawn. So the best time to buy an annuity is when you're in your fifties. Buy an annuity too young, and you tie up money too long, I think. If you buy an annuity at age twenty-four, you'll penalize yourself if you take the money out before retirement age. Only purchase an annuity if you can afford to tie up the money until that age.

Of course, you could put money in an IRA when you're twenty-four and run the same risk. The significant difference is that in most cases, the IRA or pension money has the benefit of tax deductibility. The annuity does not. The annuity shelters the income from the money you contribute, but not the contribution itself.

Let's say you're fifty-three years old. Why put money into an annuity rather than an IRA or SEP? As I said earlier, the amount of money you can contribute to an IRA or SEP is limited. You don't have that limit with an annuity. You could put a million dollars or more into an annuity. The annuity lets you shelter more money than those other programs. But years before you ever think of buying an annuity, you should be putting money into an IRA or a pension plan.

TAX-FREES VERSUS ANNUITIES

Tax-free investments such as municipal bonds are another alternative for retirement money. So which is better?

My partner, Peter Miller, says that an annuity is likely to bring a higher return than tax-frees. But there's a catch: you have no guarantee of what the tax rate will be when you withdraw your annuity money. The government can change the rules on you in midstream. If there's a 75 percent tax bracket when you withdraw your annuity money and you're in that bracket, you'll surrender to the government most of the money you withdraw. With tax-frees, it doesn't matter how high the tax rate goes; you pay no taxes on them. Choosing tax-frees rather than an annuity is a hedge against the government's raising the tax brackets. Regardless of the tax rate, tax-frees are tax-free—except to calculate taxes due on Social Security benefits and, in some cases, the federal alternative minimum tax.

HOW TO INVEST RETIREMENT MONEY

An IRA is not an investment. It's a way to invest. The type of investment available in IRAs varies. You have to decide where to put it.

Throughout this book, I've suggested many ways to invest your money. Investing retirement money is similar. The main differences are these:

- Because you ordinarily can't withdraw the money for years without a penalty, you can take an especially long-term view.
- Because contributions and earnings grow tax-deferred, it's pointless to have tax-free investments in retirement accounts. In fact, you'll make less money than if you used taxable investments for your retirement account.

When interest rates are as high as 9 percent, when you can get guaranteed government bonds paying 9 percent, why take a risk with stocks? If you look at the performance of common stock over decades, the average return is between 9 and 10 percent a year. But owning stocks still brings you much risk, particularly in the short term.

Still, because of their potential for high returns—especially over the long term—I believe that stocks should be in most portfolios, including retirement accounts. In tax-advantaged accounts such as retirement accounts, I'd rather use income stocks. These are stocks that pay above-average dividends. Growth stocks tend to pay lower dividends than income stocks. They bring more of their return from increases in the stocks' value than from dividends. By using income stocks in a retirement account, you get more money right now in the form of dividends, and those dividends are compounding without being taxed now. Their growth is tax-deferred.

I would rather put growth stocks in taxable accounts. You're not taxed on the increase in a stock's value until you sell it. So the tax-deferred feature of a retirement account does not confer an advantage when you hold stock for decades. Conversely, ordinary accounts have an advantage over retirement accounts when it comes to losses from selling stock: losses from the sale of stock are deductible in an ordinary account but not in a retirement account.

CMOs are ideally suited for tax-advantaged accounts such as retirement accounts. CMOs are often called when interest rates drop. Every time that happens to a CMO you own, you have extensive paperwork on your income tax forms. Retirement accounts spare you all that paperwork.

COLLECTING YOUR RETIREMENT MONEY

Although you *may* begin withdrawing money from a pension plan or IRA when you're fifty-nine and a half, you *must* begin withdrawing it no later than April 1 of the year after the year you turn seventy and a half. How much you withdraw depends on your age, how much you have in your account, and how much you need to live on.

Your age is important for two reasons:

1. You don't want to draw down all your money years before you die. You want to spread out your withdrawals so that the money lasts about as long as you do. But how do you know how long that will be? As Peter Miller says, "If you knew when you were going to die, all this would be much easier."
2. The Internal Revenue Service has formulas that you must use in determining the minimum amount of money to withdraw each year. Based on actuarial tables, the formulas work something like this: You're seventy-four years old and have $350,000 in your retirement account. Your life expectancy is thirteen years. You must withdraw at least $26,923 each year. For further information, including the necessary tables, consult IRS Publication 590, *Individual Retirement Arrangements*.

How much you need to live on is also crucial. In the year or two before retiring, you should pay particularly close attention to your income and expenses. Realize that some expenses will change considerably once you retire. Heating and air conditioning your house, for example, may cost much more now that you're spending more time there. Automobile expenses may drop because you're no longer commuting two hundred miles to work each week. And so on.

Remember, too, that the pertinent figure on your current income is your net pay—how much you take home after taxes—not the gross. Your taxes may drop after you retire because you're making less money and are in a lower tax bracket. So the key question is how much you'll need in your pocket, not the sum on your weekly paycheck.

SURVIVOR OPTIONS

When you die, your pension money doesn't necessarily die with you. Proceeds may go to your survivor. Usually, your spouse (if you're married) is the beneficiary of a retirement account. For you to have another beneficiary, your spouse must sign a paper waiving the right.

Shortly before retiring (if you have a pension other than your own IRA or SEP), you will be asked to choose survivor options. For example, you can set things up so that your survivor receives a lump-sum payment of pension money on your death. Or you can arrange your pension payments such that if you die, your survivor will get 100 percent of the monthly check you will get. Some plans give you an option that pays two thirds or half your payment.

Each option has a trade-off. The monthly check you receive as a pensioner varies depending on the survivor option you choose.

The sheer number of choices can be overwhelming. The complexity of the subject makes it even more so. And you have to choose between alternative futures that no one can predict. So how do you figure it all out? Speak with someone who knows the subject inside out. Find someone who can truly explain the issues and choices in a way that you understand. Most pension administrators have someone on staff whose sole job is to explain these things.

Once you understand your options and their ramifications, make your own decision. Certainly discuss it with loved ones who will be affected. I believe that the decision process boils down to you. Don't let a detached professional make the ultimate decision for you. Use your own gut.

PURPOSES OF TRUSTS

A trust fund is a fund dedicated to a certain purpose and no other. You can set up a trust fund that pays a child $2,000 a month beginning at age twenty-one. You can set up a fund for your child's college education. You can set up a trust fund that buys open land in an area you love.

The average citizen usually uses trusts for three purposes:

1. To give money to a child or children with certain stipulations. You use a trust because you don't trust your children's judgment on how to use the money.

2. To shelter money from estate taxes. Money in a trust can pass from one generation to another without being subject to the federal estate tax. Under the law as of June 1993, the first $600,000 in a person's estate is exempt from federal estate taxes. Money above that threshold is not taxed if it passes to a spouse—husband and wife don't get hit hard with taxes if they have their money set up right. But if it passes to children, grandchildren, or others, it's subject to the estate tax. The top bracket for that tax is a whopping 60 percent.

One way to avoid taxes is to give money to children as you go. Under the law, each parent can give each child $10,000 a year tax-free. (Gifts above that amount are taxed to the giver.) A married couple with three children can give away $60,000 a year with no taxes due on the gifts.

3. To avoid probate. Probate establishes the validity of a will. It can be time-consuming and expensive. Money you want to go to your heirs can be tied up for years. When all is resolved, your heirs could get substantially less than the amount you left them originally.

A trust is usually held by a trust company or a bank's trust department. It is controlled by an individual or group called a trustee. When you establish a trust, you decide who will hold it and who will be the trustee.

The money in the trust is shielded from other assets of the outfit that holds the fund. Even if the company's assets are seized, trust fund money is not subject to takeover by creditors.

Trust, as Peter Miller says, means you don't trust. "You have to remember," Peter says, "that when you set up a trust for your kids and give somebody else decision-making power over the money, you're saying, 'I don't trust my kids. I trust someone else more.' Maybe you think they're young people who don't have the necessary experience. Maybe you think they're just not trustworthy.

"I have a friend whose father set up a trust for him. The trust gave him so much every five years. He didn't get the bulk of it till he was forty-five. And he was broke by fifty. His father was absolutely right. My view is, people don't change. If you don't trust the person you want to leave your money to, you might as well not trust them ever.

"One problem with trusts in recent years," Peter says, "is that many banks have become trustees and done a poor job of managing the trust. The beneficiaries can't control the money, and the argument is that maybe the parents should have given the money directly to them. The beneficiaries, the argument goes, might have done just as lousy a job."

DON'T BE IN SUCH A HURRY TO GIVE MONEY TO CHILDREN

Aiming to avoid inheritance taxes and probate, many parents rush to give money to their children. Don't be in too much of a rush. Don't give money to your children simply because you think you should or must. People used to give money to their children because the earnings from that money were taxed at the child's bracket, which was usually lower than the parents'. Often the child paid no taxes at all. Then Congress passed the "kiddie tax." Now the first $600 a child under fourteen earns is tax-free. Taxes on the next $600 are at the child's rate. Income above $1,200 a year is taxed to the child—at the same rate as the parents. No matter who holds the money, the tax on it is the same. After age fourteen, all income is taxed at the child's rate.

You gain little by putting money in your children's names before they're fourteen. It makes little difference in the tax bite, and by holding the money yourself, you retain control of it. Grandparents often give money to grandchildren, because they don't want the parents to spend the money. They want it to go directly to the grandchildren. They're saying they don't trust the parents.

What if you want to provide for your children's education? Under the Uniform Gifts to Minors Act, you establish a standard trust fund. You set yourself up as the custodian and put the money in the child's name. You control the money until the child reaches twenty-one. All along it's the child's money, but you have control of it till the child is twenty-one.

The downside is that at that point, the child can do anything with it—regardless of your wishes. In these gifts to minors, you have no ultimate say in what the money is used for. It's for anything the child wants. Peter Miller says: "A friend of mine gave his son money for education. The kid got the money, quit college, bought a motorcycle, and went to California. He told his parents to go to hell."

Here's another story, also courtesy of Peter Miller:

"I believe that you should never give your money away too soon. Consider keeping it until you're dead. Rule one is that if you give your money away, the kids won't come visit you.

"I'm not saying to spend all the money yourself. I'm saying, don't give it away so fast. I've seen parents give all their money away and be left holding the bag. There's no guarantee that the kids will take care of you.

"If you give your kids money, you never know what they might do. You can have problems with the people they marry. A man I knew set up a trust fund for his kids. He died, and according to the trust, the wife got the income but not the principal. The principal went to the kids. But the son died, and the wife of the son, the daughter-in-law, got the money. The parents never liked her. They have a bad relationship. And the money is outside the family. The wife has no control over the money, which had been hers.

"So the husband, who was trying to avoid taxes, took a lot of power and money away from his wife. If he were alive today, I think he would want his wife controlling the money more than the daughter-in-law."

Keep in mind that unforeseen events can defeat all your plans. The kids can change. They can grow up and join a cult. You can put away money for their education, and they use it for something else.

WITH A LIVING TRUST, YOU RETAIN MORE CONTROL

One type of trust, the living trust, supposedly lets you control your money until you die. You set it up for whomever you want, and you can still take the income out of it. If you need to get to it, you can. You can make the investment decisions; you can change who gets the money. That has its advantages. Circumstances change as the years pass.

Now, too, we've found that trusts can be broken. That happened in the Philadelphia area with the trust left by the physician and inventor Albert C. Barnes. The owner of a magnificent art collection, Barnes set up a foundation to teach art and preserve his paintings. Until a lawsuit in the late 1950s, the collection was closed to the public and had other severe restrictions, even though the foundation received tax benefits.

Later, the Barnes trustees wanted to change other provisions of the trust. In essence, they argued that the trust was more important than the will of the person who set it up. For the good of the trust, they argued, they should violate the will. The court agreed.

SOME QUESTIONS TO PONDER ABOUT TRUSTS

When you think about setting up a trust, think it all the way through. Be cautious. Look at all the consequences. Consider the negatives: The trust can be broken after your death. Situations change. The government can change the rules on you. And with every trust, you give up some control. Be sure you want to give up all control or some control while you're still alive.

Peter Miller says: "My question to people is, How much do you care what goes on after you die? You're dead. Don't worry about it. Worry more about living than dying. The problem in investing is not dying; then it's over. The problem is living. People who inherit money are lucky. They shouldn't be complaining.

"How important are taxes to you after your death? A lot of people hate taxes—even if they're dead, they don't want to pay taxes. If you don't mind paying taxes after your death, don't bother with a trust. If not for the tax consequences, the only decision about whether to set up a trust is how much you trust the person you want to give money to.

"A trust means you don't trust. If you do trust a person, just give him the money. You can always give money to your children. Just don't give it to them too soon. Don't give up control prematurely. If your kids need a house and you want to help fund it, it's much better if the kids ask you for the money and you write them a check.

"The main question is, How much do you trust somebody's judgment? How much do you trust yourself to handle your money? If you trust your kids better than yourself, maybe you should give them money sooner."

In the space available here, I've barely begun to touch on the subjects of this chapter. As you can see, they're tricky and complex. For full and up-to-date information, consult a highly recommended tax accountant, attorney, or other specialist.

PART VI

ANSWERS

24

SOURCES OF INFORMATION

Your Cousin Harry shares a tip on a stock purportedly known to a select few. You read a newspaper article about a hot new company and decide it might be the next Xerox. Your mailman brings a glossy circular from a Wall Street pundit predicting financial collapse within eighteen months.

The financial information available today is almost endless. There are business newspapers and the business sections of many daily papers. There are the money magazines, such as *Forbes*, *Fortune*, *Barron's*, and *Kiplinger's Personal Finance*. There are radio and television programs. And hundreds and hundreds of others sources.

How reliable are they? What should you read? What should you pay attention to? What should you ignore?

READ THE *WALL STREET JOURNAL*

The day doesn't have enough hours to let you read all you should or could. I start by reading the *Wall Street Journal* daily. For my money, the *Journal* is the first place to turn for financial information. It's loaded with news of the world, and it often shows how that news relates to investments.

219

If you read the *Journal* regularly, you'll learn that there are no easy answers. You have to interpret the news. Decisions are never easy. The *Journal* shows you both sides of a story. Read it long enough, and you begin absorbing different opinions. Almost every day, it profiles a money manager. You see that one manager believes this and another believes that.

For many years, I've been interviewed by reporters from newspapers, magazines, radio, and television. *Wall Street Journal* reporters stand out. They're specialists. At many newspapers, one person writes financial stories of all types—banks, airlines, pizza bakers, tool manufacturers. Many financial writers are generalists and can't cover stories with the same thoroughness and authority as the *Journal*'s reporters.

The *Journal* keeps you abreast of what's happening, but it rarely forecasts. When a stock falls apart or skyrockets, the *Journal* tells you about it the next day; it doesn't predict before the fact. The *Journal* comes out the next day and explains all the reasons the stock has moved so much. Despite the immense base of information the *Journal* obviously has on companies, it won't publish that information ahead of time. My partner Peter Miller often asks, "Why didn't the *Journal* tell me this yesterday?" If we could get the *Journal* a day early, we'd all be billionaires.

MAGAZINES AND NEWSLETTERS

If you send for a prospectus or information from a brokerage house, you're likely to be bombarded with:

- Offers from magazines and newsletters
- Brochures touting advice from gurus and mutual fund experts, such as the guy who predicted the 1987 crash to within one tenth of a point
- Publications on how to make sure the federal government doesn't confiscate your life savings

I read several financial magazines: *Business Week*, *Financial World*, *Forbes*, and *Fortune*. Every year, *Forbes*'s February 15 issue has its Honor Roll of best-performing mutual funds. All these magazines have something to offer. I read them for information, not investment advice. I just want facts. I want to make up my own mind.

Hundreds of newsletters are published monthly—or with some other frequency. But how do you know which to believe? For years, I read *Dow*

Theory by Richard Russell. He's an interesting guy. He put in many quips about life, but he rarely told you what to buy or sell. It was amazing how little information he gave you, but he wrote well. He lived in San Diego and told you what a wonderful town it was.

Marty Zweig advertises that his newsletter, *The Zweig Forecast*, is the best as far as performance goes. Zweig manages billions of dollars in people's investments. He uses numerous indicators of whether to be in stocks, and which to be in. He observes the Federal Reserve. He looks at this statistic and that one. He often sells a stock with no regard for the condition or management of the company. It's the exact opposite of what I do. But Zweig has an impressive track record.

In the mid-1980s, Zweig began a mutual fund. Peter Miller participated in the underwriting. Miller says: "I got stacks of leads—subscribers to his newsletter, who were potential investors in the fund. I'd call them and say, 'For as little as a couple thousand dollars, you can have Marty Zweig invest for you, instead of reading his newsletter.'

"Most of them bought the fund, because they said, 'Damned if I can do what he says he does.' As far as I could tell, nobody who subscribed to the newsletter read it. People found it impossible to follow."

Even if you understood Zweig's advice, you couldn't do what he does. You couldn't buy as many stocks as he writes about. You couldn't trade as actively as he does without being killed by commissions. Zweig trades in such volume that his commissions are pennies per share. You'll pay up to a dollar a share. So your performance can never match his. If you were a broker, however, and had clients taking advice from Zweig, you could make a fortune.

The newsletter I like best is the *Dick Davis Digest*. Davis uses many sources—money managers, analysts, other market newsletters. He culls the thoughts of highly talented people and gives you good synopses of them. He prints highlights.

BOOKS

Financial advice is a common topic for books. Shelves in bookstores, office supply stores, and libraries have dozens of books on managing your money—books on stocks, taxes, retirement, insurance, and more. Some have helpful information. Remember, though: No matter who or what you read, the final decision should be yours. Make sure you understand what you're investing in. If not, get more information, or invest in something you do understand.

VALUE LINE

For financial statistics, you get the most bang for your buck from the *Value Line Investment Survey*. Published weekly, *Value Line* follows hundreds of stocks. Every three months, it has a full-page update and rates each of the seventeen hundred stocks it covers. *Value Line* presents information concisely and is brimming with financial statistics on each stock, including:

- Recent price
- Estimated price-to-earnings ratio
- Pension liability
- Quarterly sales
- Working capital
- Monthly price ranges over the past fifteen years
- Projected price appreciation

Along with statistics, *Value Line* ranks stocks for timeliness and safety. It also gives advice. I think you should use it only for the information. I wouldn't take the financial advice. In May 1993, Peter Miller looked up a stock in a January issue of *Value Line*. The stock cost $44 and had a timeliness of 1, *Value Line*'s highest rating. When Peter checked the stock's price in mid-May, it had risen a point from the previous day—to $30. So *Value Line*'s evaluations can miss rather badly. But again, the publication is useful for information.

A yearly subscription to *Value Line*, which fills a binder about three inches thick, costs $525. As an individual investor, you may consider that too expensive. You can find *Value Line* at many libraries.

CALL THE COMPANY

Once you've settled on companies to invest in, get in touch with them. One valuable piece of information that *Value Line* gives you is company phone numbers and investment contacts. You can call the company, ask to speak with the investor relations officer, and request some of the most important financial literature:

- Annual reports from the past three years
- The last four quarterly reports
- A 10Q and a 10K, two publications filed with the Securities and Exchange Commission

Every time I investigate a company, I ask for that literature. Then I sit down and read it. If you're thinking of buying stock in a company, it's essential to read the material the company itself puts out. If you don't like what the company prints—which puts the best side forward—you might as well forget about buying it. You're unlikely to find negatives in company publications. In fact, it's difficult to find negatives anywhere. As I said before, the *Wall Street Journal* prints negative information, but only after the fact.

BE WARY OF TIPS FROM AMATEURS

If relatives, friends, or colleagues know you're interested in money management, they're bound to give you occasional hot tips. Be wary. Where do they get their information? How much do they know?

Peter Miller tells this story: "I had a client who was an ex-stockbroker. He had been a broker before he went back to running the family business. So the guy was sophisticated in the market. He called me up and asked me to buy a stock when it was ten dollars a share. I did and it went to two dollars a share. I said to him, 'Where the hell did you get the advice to buy this in the first place?' He said, 'From my barber.'

"When the guy asked me to buy the stock, I assumed he knew what he was doing—being a former stockbroker. But before I bought the stock for him, I should have asked, 'Where'd you get your information?' If he had told me his barber, I would have said, 'Wait a minute!'

"Now maybe the barber cuts the hair of the company's CEO. Maybe the barber knows something most people don't. But you have to ask questions.

"When I got into the brokerage business in 1980, oil and gas were booming. I went to a meeting at one company. A guy comes in and starts rolling up charts: geological charts and well-drilling sites. A couple of brokers are asking technical questions. I couldn't believe it. I ask myself, How the hell am I going to know all this stuff? I don't know what they're talking about.

"Starting out as a broker, I would call people to sell them stock, and they would ask me questions. I thought I had to know about every stock. Eventually I realized I didn't. As I got older, I learned that you don't have to know everything. You don't have to be a chicken to know a rotten egg.

"I learned to say, 'I don't know about that, and I don't want to know about it. Here's what I know about; here's what I'm trying to tell you about. Yes or no?' A guy would ask questions about some obscure stock, and I would answer, 'That's one of the 10,000 stocks I don't follow.'"

FINANCIAL TELEVISION: SOUND BITES, BUT WHAT MORE?

Financial advice also appears electronically. You can watch CNBC on cable. All day long during the week, it broadcasts financial news. Scattered amid all that news are advertisements. Some are hard to separate from the news stories. Even if CNBC had no ads, you should recognize that there's a difference between information and knowledge, between being bombarded with facts and knowing what to make of them.

DOING YOUR HOMEWORK

Reading is important. I think you should read—more than you should watch television or listen to the radio news. I think you make a mistake listening to financial news in sound bites. If you read the *Wall Street Journal* every day and listen to the financial news bites, you'll realize where the electronic media get much of their financial information.

Still, says Peter Miller, "you can read so much that you get to the point where you drive yourself crazy. You have to believe yourself. I know a lot of people who read. If they read something they agree with, it's great. And if they read something they disagree with, it's wrong. Don't let them change your mind."

Every stock is a buy or a sell or an I-don't-know. Most people don't know. On the occasions when you do know, don't second guess yourself. Don't go against what you know. If you think a company is sound, trust your judgment. You needn't find an expert to agree with you or disagree with you before acting.

If you can make a decision, go with it. If you can't make a decision, keep asking questions and read till you feel you have the information you need to make a decision. If you still can't make a decision, move on. Or hire somebody to manage your money. Of course, that requires a decision too.

What this all boils down to is that investing is virtually a full-time job. It requires homework. Do yours. Go back over this book. Check other sources. Then make up your mind, and invest.

25

ANSWERS TO TOUGH QUESTIONS

Recently, I was giving a seminar to a group of inexperienced investors. I was explaining the difference between growth stocks and income stocks. A dear old lady in the front row kept waving her hand. Finally, I had to stop and ask her what she wanted. She stood up and said, "Mr. Roffman, I don't want to know which stock is which. I just want to know which stocks are going up."

It's easy to tell people to buy stocks. But what to buy? By now I think you know that there are no easy answers. You must do your homework. Let me give you my four watchwords of investing:

- *Management*: Companies with superior management are the cornerstone of my investment philosophy. I look for companies with histories of consistent, proven, high-quality leadership.
- *Long term*: Company management must focus on the long-term growth of shareholder equity. I seek to identify managers who concentrate on sound, long-term strategies rather than expedient quarterly targets.

As an individual investor, you should have a long-term focus too. Don't waver. Don't constantly monitor the stock prices of your companies. Stick with them as long as the fundamentals remain unchanged.

- *Balance*: Conservative balance sheets are essential for all equity and fixed-income investments. High debt levels can lead to loss of control and changes in corporate objectives. Don't invest in companies that are overloaded with debt.
- *Simplicity:* I focus my research on companies and industries that I know and that my clients and I can readily understand.

This last chapter is a storehouse for issues that I have yet to discuss or that don't fit in easily elsewhere. Here I present a few of the tough questions that investors often ask me. Along with my responses, I aim to give you the means to answer them yourself—in keeping with my purpose throughout the book.

I expect the economy to lapse into a serious decline. Do you recommend selling short?

Selling short gives you a chance to profit when you think a stock's price will fall substantially. You have your broker borrow the stock from someone who already owns it. The broker sells the stock and holds the proceeds from the sale as collateral. Eventually, you must replace the borrowed shares and hope to do so at a lower price. The difference, less commissions and any interim dividends you might owe, is your profit.

The risk in selling short comes when the price rises rather than falls. Then you'll be forced to pay the difference. If many other investors have also sold the stock short, you could be competing with them when you repurchase the stock. That could drive the price higher still.

Whereas the most you can lose when you buy a stock is the price you paid, there is theoretically no limit to how much you can lose when you sell short. After Resorts International opened in Atlantic City in 1978, the stock was selling at $5 a share. It soon rose to more than $100. A well-known investor thought the rise was unfounded and sold the stock short. The price kept rising. It went from $100 to $150. He sold more short. It went from $150 to $200, and he sold more short. Finally he was forced to buy the shares back because the broker demanded more collateral to cover the loan—money he could not raise in the short time required.

If you buy a $10 stock and the company goes bankrupt, you'll lose $10. But a $10 stock could rise to hundreds of dollars a share, and Resorts did. Eventually Resorts dropped below the price our investor paid for it. He would have been right in his expectation about the stock, but he didn't have the holding power. He had to cover. He lost $26 million.

I prefer to bet *on* companies rather than against them. Substantial wealth can be made that way. Unless you are a professional, I never recommend selling short.

Dollars make me nervous. I like gold. What do you think of buying Krugerrands or the metal itself?

For three thousand years, gold has been an effective, and visually beautiful, hedge against inflation. But gold has been in a ten-year decline. Gold shot up from $35 an ounce to $800 in the early 1980s. Since then, it has dropped below $330. Why the fall? Because gold should never have cost $800 an ounce. It was a time of inflation such as people hadn't seen in generations. They went berserk and pumped the price to ridiculous levels. When interest rates began coming down, and when inflation—and the fear of inflation—subsided, so did the cost of gold. The high prices soon came back to earth. But...

You can't say that because gold has performed miserably in the last ten years or so, it's finished. You have to look at three thousand years of history. I don't think inflation is dead. When inflationary fears or pressures are on the rise, I think it's okay to have some limited exposure to gold. Make it no more than 5 percent of your total portfolio.

Krugerrands became popular in the early eighties, when people wanted to own gold. Krugerrands were a way of owning gold without owning bullion. You didn't need to own the metal itself. Some people relish the touch and feel of the metal. Like people who stuff money under a mattress, they feel comfortable with tangible objects. The problem is, if you have bullion, you need to have it assayed. And bullion earns no interest.

A way of investing that's better than bullion ownership is buying stock in a good company that mines gold. If the price of gold goes up, so will the stock. Some gold companies pay dividends. You're earning money as you invest. That's the way to play gold. Not by owning the metal.

I've started buying a gold stock for some of my clients' portfolios. A well-managed company called American Barrick Resources, it's a domestic producer of gold. Why do I like it? One, it has enormous reserves. Two, it produces about 1.8 million ounces a year, but it's been able to reduce its cost of producing gold every year for the past five years.

How much faith do you have in the Federal Reserve and its monetary policy?

As I've said, I don't believe that we've licked inflation in this country. It's sleeping. The Federal Reserve can affect short-term rates through monetary policy: controlling the money supply and the cost of funds it lends to banks and other customers. The Fed has been doing that for years. But long-term rates, over which the Fed has little control, have been holding stubbornly at much higher levels.

You have a double whammy. When the government reduces short-term rates, and investors can get only 3 percent on a CD rather than 8 percent, they tend to seek longer-term investments, which have higher yields. As more investors seek long-term vehicles, they tend to keep the price propped high.

In 1992–93, the Fed reduced short-term interest rates to stimulate economic growth. Reducing short-term rates was the Fed's principal tool in that effort; it reduced rates something like six times in a year.

To influence the economy in the past, the federal government used a big quiver. The quiver had many arrows in it, many tools to affect public policies, encourage job creation, explore new horizons. When the government lowers interest rates, it does so to stimulate the economy. To cool off an overheated economy, the Fed can pursue a tighter monetary policy, which makes interest rates rise. The Fed's actions mostly affect short-term rates. Long-term are more influenced by expectations of inflation. Short-term rates fell by more than half beginning in 1992, but long-term rates did not come down nearly as much.

I have a mortgage at 10 percent. Friends who just bought houses tell me they got mortgages at 7½ percent. Is it time to refinance?

Some rules of thumb say it's worthwhile to refinance when the difference in interest rates is 2 percentage points or more. The true answer is not so monolithic. It depends on several factors. The primary factor is how long you plan to stay in the house. Others are:

- How many points will you have to pay to refinance?
- When do you reach the crossover—the place where the savings equal the costs of refinancing?

  Do the arithmetic. Look at your amortization schedule. For a $100,000 thirty-year mortgage at 10 percent, the monthly payment is $877.57. At 7 percent, the monthly payment is $665.30. Assuming 3 points for the mortgage origination fee and $1,500 in title insurance and other closing costs, you'll pay a total of $4,500 to refinance. By saving $212.27 a month in interest, you will need just over twenty-one months to recoup that total. The twenty-one months is the crossover point. After that point, refinancing gives you a net gain.

Not all mortgages cost 3 points. Usually, they scale down from 3 points to 0. A 0-point mortgage almost always has a higher interest rate than a 3-point. Again, check the amortization schedule and calculate the crossover point.

The key is the probability that you will still be in the house after the crossover point. If you think you will, refinance. If you think you'll sell before then, it probably doesn't pay to refinance.

Someone used the term DRIP. What's that?

DRIP stands for *dividend reinvestment program*. Many companies offer such programs, which let you reinvest dividends directly through the company. The dividends buy you shares (or fractions of shares) of new stock. You needn't use a broker.

The plans circumvent the broker, although that isn't the main purpose. The main purpose is to induce people to invest in a company, hold the stock, and buy more. It makes for loyal investors.

I encourage investors to take advantage of DRIPs. They can save you considerable sums of money that you'd otherwise spend on commissions. They're an effective way of circumventing a broker when you don't need to use one.

In the 1980s, I made the mistake of investing in a limited partnership. I can't sell it without taking a beating. What should I do?

Not much, unfortunately. You are going to take a beating. Brokers often persuade the unknowing to buy terrible investments. Like junk bonds, limited partnerships brought great returns to brokers in the 1970s and 1980s but misery to most investors.

Limited partnerships arose in the late 1970s. The government created them to stimulate certain areas of the economy. The government let you take—in tax credits—three or four times the dollars you put into the investment. Brokers sold the partnerships as tax shelters.

Let's say you invested $50,000 in low-income housing. Let's say the government gave you a four-to-one break, so you got to write off $200,000. And let's say you were in the 50 percent bracket (which still existed in the late seventies). You couldn't lose. You put in $50,000 and got $100,000 in tax deductions. Many limited partnerships made no economic sense in themselves, but made sense to investors as tax shelters.

Investors didn't read the thick prospectuses. They just bought. What sold limited partnerships was greed. The investor got a tax write-off. The broker got 8 percent commission. If he'd sold $100,000 worth of *bonds*, he'd have made $1,000 gross commission, but if he sold $100,000 worth of *partnerships*, he got $8,000 commission. Clients go to brokers for guidance. Many brokers guided them to the highest yield to the broker.

What killed limited partnerships was a change in the tax laws. Congress and the IRS decided that many had no economic justification and disallowed the tax credits. For many limited partnerships, the tax write-offs were thrown out. The little market that ever existed for them disappeared.

A cousin of mine bought seven limited partnerships. He paid $25,000 for each of them. I asked him what he thought they were worth today. He wasn't sure, but he thought each was worth $25,000.

"I'd be surprised if you could sell them for twenty-five cents on the dollar," I said. He sat there incredulous. "Why don't you call your broker and ask him how much he could get you?" I asked. Of the seven, the best was worth thirty cents on the dollar. The *best*.

Limited partnerships are a striking example of Wall Street excess. As I always say, learn from your mistakes and move on.

When I was young, interest rates seemed to stay the same for years. So did prices. I remember a first-class stamp costing three cents in 1935 and three cents in 1958. Why is the economic climate so much more volatile today?

It would take pages to answer that fully, but here's a short take. Thanks to satellites, computers, and high-speed communication and travel, time and space have become compressed. What used to take days or weeks now often takes just minutes.

One group this change has hit hard is the investment community. Wall Street has become frightfully oriented toward the short term. That has forced corporations to do the same. Many chief executives are so concerned about next quarter's earnings that they defer basic research. Basic research—essential to develop revolutionary new products that help the company and the country compete—can take as long as ten years to pay off, if ever. And many executives and managers firmly believe that if they don't perform now, they won't be around in ten months, let alone ten years.

Investors, financial publications, and the media also promote the short-term view. Investors scrutinize quarterly reports. They clamor for instant information. Via on-line services such as Prodigy, they can get nearly up-to-the-minute price quotations on thousands of stocks.

The *Wall Street Journal*, a newspaper I respect highly, has a mutual fund section with performance ratings over a mere thirteen weeks. Those figures are useless at best and misleading or harmful at worst. Again, they help pressure corporate America into excessive concern about profits for today and the hell with tomorrow. Because of this approach, the stock market in the short term has become as unpredictable as next season's hurricanes.

The U.S. government falls for this line of thinking too. In the 1980s, the government quadrupled the national debt—raising it from $1 trillion to $4 trillion. It took two hundred years to accumulate that first trillion in debt, but less than ten to build the next three trillion. A classic case of short-term thinking. We all pay for it down the road, and so will our children and their children.

My money manager is attracting many new clients. I'm concerned that he won't be able to attract enough capable employees to keep his standards high. I'm also worried that he won't be around forever. What are your thoughts?

For the first part of the question—getting good employees—I can assure you, many good people are out there. The economy has been stagnant for so long that some capable people I know have been unable to find decent jobs for two or three years. We can get good people.

Yesterday I went to a meeting. The speaker was the chairman of a new bank, with $26 billion in assets. He said that of the twenty-five largest banks in the world, not one is a United States bank. Not one. The reason America has none in the top twenty-five is that this country has too many banks. Over the next five to ten years, there will be considerable consolidation. If that happens, banks will let an awful lot of good employees go.

The brokerage industry went through a round like that in the late 1980s, after the crash of '87. Another round is coming. In 1993, times were good in the brokerage business. Trading volumes were high, markets were lively, new products were being sold. But a bear market is coming. Whether it comes in 1994 or 1995 or 1996, I can't say. But it's coming. Another wave of consolidation will occur. When thousands of people lose their jobs, that's a recession. When you lose your job, it's a depression. Hardly a day goes by that we don't get resumés from talented people looking for work.

As for the second part of the question, let me say this:

One thing about life is that you can't stop the clock. It's tempting to say, "I don't have any problems. Everything's fine. Let's keep things as they are." Life doesn't work that way. Circumstances change, and you can't control them. *You* change. You get older. Your health worsens. Your children grow up.

To worry that your money manager may not be around in twenty years, you can worry about everything that way. While ideally we would like to buy a stock that we can hold for two decades, the truth is that we'll have to watch that stock and reevaluate it over a long period of time.

Who can predict the future? At the 1876 World's Fair in Philadelphia, they introduced the telephone. Articles appeared in the papers asking, "What good is it? Why would anybody ever use it?"

At around the same time—I think it was during Ulysses S. Grant's administration—the head of the Patent Office said they should shut down the office because everything that's going to be invented has been invented.

Life goes on. It evolves. You do the best you can. The past you can't do anything about, and the future you can't control. What you can deal with is today. Each day you have to make decisions based on what's available to you.

Can you sum up your investment philosophy in a few words?

I believe that patience—a long-term view—is essential. And I believe in old-fashioned principles that the average person can understand. I shun the complex new products that Wall Street frequently invents. Respect for fundamentals translates into discipline—discipline not only in investing but in everything. A bond, for example, should have assets behind it. You shouldn't buy a bond based on expectations. Stocks, yes. Bonds, no.

Years ago, Will Rogers said people should worry about the return *of* their money rather than the return *on* it. When I talk with clients, I use the line frequently. People appreciate it. It sounds great now, but everyone forgot about it in the eighties.

Investing is serious business. If you have $100,000 or more to invest, I believe you'll benefit from hiring a professional money manager. If you have only $5,000 or $10,000, you won't be able to hire a money manager for yourself. But you can get professional management by buying a mutual fund. For that amount of money, a mutual fund makes much more sense than individual stocks. If you're under forty-five or so, look for a growth fund. If you're older than that, look for an income fund.

f you had only one piece of investment advice to give, what would it be?

can't compact it that easily. How about two? Invest for the long term, and understand what you're doing. About the worst thing you can do as an investor is quarter-to-quarter comparisons—of stocks, mutual funds, or money managers. You have to give a stock or a fund or a money manager a full cycle in the economy. That's one bull market and one bear market, three or four years at least.

If you're unhappy with an investment, a mutual fund, or a money manager, ask yourself, What am I unhappy about? Decide what's happening and what's making you unhappy. If you're uncomfortable because you're not getting the service you'd like, speak up. If you're unhappy because other funds or managers are outperforming yours, look out.

Smart investing is much more than saying that my neighbor is earning 8 percent while I'm getting only 4. If you want to duplicate the market—or at least come close to duplicating it—buy an index fund. Professional money managers don't just invest your money. They're also there to help you, to give you guidance, to find out what you want, to give and take, to answer questions.

Investing is not a competition. It's not you against your neighbor or other investors. Investing is an individual practice. Don't worry about how an investment measures up to Wall Street expectations. Look at how it does for you. You can always find people producing greater results, but how much greater risk are they taking? Are you the type of person to take that greater risk? Just because everyone else is doing something, that's not necessarily a reason for you to follow. Remember I mentioned that the best-performing mutual funds of 1991 focused on the biotechnology industry? It's excessively risky to focus on one area. If you had bought biotech stocks at the end of 1991 because they had risen 76 percent since July, you would have seen them *fall* almost 23 percent in the next six months.

Do you know ahead of time which industrial sector, stock, mutual fund, or money manager will do the best in the coming quarter? No one does. The results you see published are retrospective. Today we can say that fund X or manager Y performed the best in the last quarter. We can't say with any certainty who will do best next quarter. We won't know that until the results are in. You can't use hindsight to predict the future.

I've used the same broker for years. Should I maintain the relationship?

It depends on the broker. Unscrupulous brokers who churn your account don't deserve your business, and you deserve better. If your broker loses you big money over several years but makes lots of money for himself, or constantly prods you to buy and sell, hand that broker a pink slip. Conscientious brokers who look out for you the way independent money managers do—that's a different story. If you have a broker like that, maintain the relationship. Follow the principles I put forth in this book— take charge of your financial future—and you'll be well on your way to reaching your monetary and personal goals.

For questions, comments, or to relate a story of your own to Marvin Roffman for his next book, please feel free to call him at (800) 995-1030.

INDEX